MW01049168

HOLT SCIENCE & TECHNOLOGY

Astronomy

HOLT, RINEHART AND WINSTON

A Harcourt Education Company

Orlando • **Austin** • New York • San Diego • Toronto • London

Acknowledgments

Contributing Authors

Mary Kay Hemenway, Ph.D.
Research Associate and Senior Lecturer
Department of Astronomy
The University of Texas at Austin
Austin, Texas

Karen J. Meech, Ph.D.
Astronomer
Institute for Astronomy
University of Hawaii
Honolulu, Hawaii

Inclusion Specialist

Karen Clay
Inclusion Specialist Consultant
Boston, Massachusetts

Safety Reviewer

Jack Gerlovich, Ph.D.
Associate Professor
School of Education
Drake University
Des Moines, Iowa

Academic Reviewers

Dan Bruton, Ph.D.
Associate Professor
Department of Physics and Astronomy
Stephen F. Austin State University
Nacogdoches, Texas

Wesley N. Colley, Ph.D.
Lecturer
Department of Astronomy
University of Virginia
Charlottesville, Virginia

Mary Kay Hemenway, Ph.D.
Research Associate and Senior Lecturer
Astronomy Department
The University of Texas
Austin, Texas

Sten Odenwald, Ph.D.
Astronomer
NASA Goddard Space Flight Center and Raytheon ITSS
Greenbelt, Maryland

Teacher Reviewers

Diedre S. Adams
Physical Science Instructor
Science Department
West Vigo Middle School
West Terre Haute, Indiana

Laura Buchanan
Science Teacher and Department Chairperson
Corkran Middle School
Glen Burnie, Maryland

Randy Dye, M.S.
Middle School Science Department Head
Earth Science
Wood Middle School
Waynesville School District #6, Missouri

Meredith Hanson
Science Teacher
Westside Middle School
Rocky Face, Georgia

Laura Kitselman
Science Teacher and Coordinator
Loudoun Country Day School
Leesburg, Virginia

Printed in the United States of America

ISBN 0-03-025549-X

5 6 7 048 08 07 06 05

J Astronomy

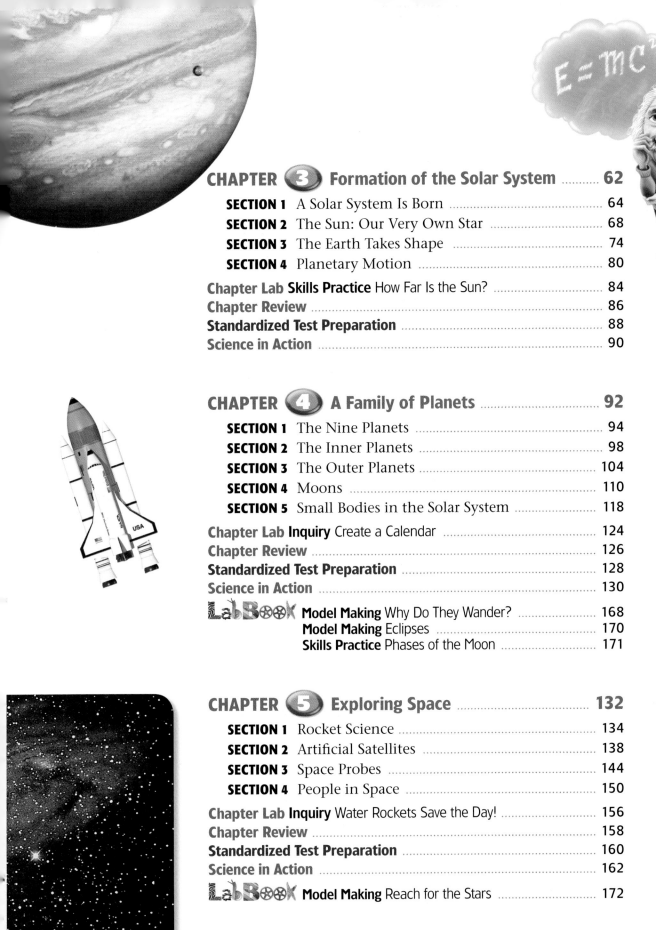

Contents   **v**

Labs and Activities

How to Use Your Textbook

Your Roadmap for Success with Holt Science and Technology

Reading Warm-Up

A Reading Warm-Up at the beginning of every section provides you with the section's objectives and key terms. The objectives tell you what you'll need to know after you finish reading the section.

Key terms are listed for each section. Learn the definitions of these terms because you will most likely be tested on them. Each key term is highlighted in the text and is defined at point of use and in the margin. You can also use the glossary to locate definitions quickly.

STUDY TIP Reread the objectives and the definitions to the key terms when studying for a test to be sure you know the material.

Get Organized

A Reading Strategy at the beginning of every section provides tips to help you organize and remember the information covered in the section. Keep a science notebook so that you are ready to take notes when your teacher reviews the material in class. Keep your assignments in this notebook so that you can review them when studying for the chapter test.

SECTION 3

The Earth Takes Shape

In many ways, Earth seems to be a perfect place for life.

We live on the third planet from the sun. The Earth, shown in **Figure 1,** is mostly made of rock, and nearly three-fourths of its surface is covered with water. It is surrounded by a protective atmosphere of mostly nitrogen and oxygen and smaller amounts of other gases. But Earth has not always been such an oasis in the solar system.

Formation of the Solid Earth

The Earth formed as planetesimals in the solar system collided and combined. From what scientists can tell, the Earth formed within the first 10 million years of the collapse of the solar nebula!

The Effects of Gravity

When a young planet is still small, it can have an irregular shape, somewhat like a potato. But as the planet gains more matter, the force of gravity increases. When a rocky planet, such as Earth, reaches a diameter of about 350 km, the force of gravity becomes greater than the strength of the rock. As the Earth grew to this size, the rock at its center was crushed by gravity and the planet started to become round.

The Effects of Heat

As the Earth was changing shape, it was also heating up. Planetesimals continued to collide with the Earth, and the energy of their motion heated the planet. Radioactive material, which was present in the Earth as it formed, also heated the young planet. After Earth reached a certain size, the temperature rose faster than the interior could cool, and the rocky material inside began to melt. Today, the Earth is still cooling from the energy that was generated when it formed. Volcanoes, earthquakes, and hot springs are effects of this energy trapped inside the Earth. As you will learn later, the effects of heat and gravity also helped form the Earth's layers when the Earth was very young.

Reading Check What factors heated the Earth during its early formation? *(See the Appendix for answers to Reading Checks.)*

READING WARM-UP

Objectives
- Describe the formation of the solid Earth.
- Describe the structure of the Earth.
- Explain the development of Earth's atmosphere and the influence of early life on the atmosphere.
- Describe how the Earth's oceans and continents formed.

Terms to Learn
crust
mantle
core

READING STRATEGY

Discussion Read this section silently. Write down questions that you have about this section. Discuss your questions in a small group.

Figure 1 *When Earth is seen from space, one of its unique features—the presence of water—is apparent.*

624 Chapter 20 Formation of the Solar System

Be Resourceful — Use the Web

SCILINKS®

Internet Connect boxes in your textbook take you to resources that you can use for science projects, reports, and research papers. Go to scilinks.org, and type in the SciLinks code to get information on a topic.

go.hrw.com

Visit go.hrw.com Find worksheets, **Current Science®** magazine articles online, and other materials that go with your textbook at **go.hrw.com.** Click on the textbook icon and the table of contents to see all of the resources for each chapter.

How the Earth's Layers Formed

Have you ever watched the oil separate from vinegar in a bottle of salad dressing? The vinegar sinks because it is denser than oil. The Earth's layers formed in much the same way. As rocks melted, denser elements, such as nickel and iron, sank to the center of the Earth and formed the core. Less dense elements floated to the surface and became the crust. This process is shown in **Figure 2**.

The **crust** is the thin, outermost layer of the Earth. It is 5 to 100 km thick. Crustal rock is made of elements that have low densities, such as oxygen, silicon, and aluminum. The **mantle** is the layer of Earth beneath the crust. It extends 2,900 km below the surface. Mantle rock is made of elements such as magnesium and iron and is denser than crustal rock. The **core** is the central part of the Earth below the mantle. It contains the densest elements (nickel and iron) and extends to the center of the Earth—almost 6,400 km below the surface.

crust the thin and solid outermost layer of the Earth above the mantle

mantle the layer of rock between the Earth's crust and core

core the central part of the Earth below the mantle

Figure 2 The Formation of Earth's Layers

❶ All elements in the early Earth are randomly mixed.

❷ Rocks melt, and denser elements sink toward the center. Less dense elements rise and form layers.

❸ According to composition, the Earth is divided into three layers: the crust, the mantle, and the core.

The Growth of Continents

After a while, some of the rocks were light enough to pile up on the surface. These rocks were the beginning of the earliest continents. The continents gradually thickened and slowly rose above the surface of the ocean. These scattered young continents did not stay in the same place, however. The slow transfer of thermal energy in the mantle pushed them around. Approximately 2.5 billion years ago, continents really started to grow. And by 1.5 billion years ago, the upper mantle had cooled and had become denser and heavier. At this time, it was easier for the cooler parts of the mantle to sink. These conditions made it easier for the continents to move in the same way that they do today.

INTERNET ACTIVITY
For another activity related to this chapter, go to **go.hrw.com** and type in the keyword **HZ5SSOLW.**

SECTION Review

Summary
- The effects of gravity and heat created the shape and structure of Earth.
- The Earth is divided into three main layers based on composition: the crust, mantle, and core.
- The presence of life dramatically changed Earth's atmosphere by adding free oxygen.
- Earth's oceans formed shortly after the Earth did, when it had cooled off enough for rain to fall. Continents formed when lighter materials gathered on the surface and rose above sea level.

Using Key Terms
1. Use each of the following terms in a separate sentence: *crust, mantle,* and *core.*

Understanding Key Ideas
2. Earth's first atmosphere was mostly made of
   a. nitrogen and oxygen.
   b. chlorine, nitrogen, and sulfur.
   c. carbon dioxide and water vapor.
   d. water vapor and oxygen.
3. Describe the structure of the Earth.
4. Why did the Earth separate into distinct layers?
5. Describe the development of Earth's atmosphere. How did life affect Earth's atmosphere?
6. Explain how Earth's oceans and continents formed.

Critical Thinking
7. **Applying Concepts** How did the effects of gravity help shape the Earth?
8. **Making Inferences** How would the removal of forests affect the Earth's atmosphere?

Interpreting Graphics
Use the illustration below to answer the questions that follow.

9. Which of the layers is composed mostly of the elements magnesium and iron?
10. Which of the layers is composed mostly of the elements iron and nickel?

SciLINKS
Developed and maintained by the National Science Teachers Association
For a variety of links related to this chapter, go to www.scilinks.org
Topic: The Layers of the Earth; The Oceans
SciLinks code: HSM0862; HSM1069

629

Use the Illustrations and Photos

Art shows complex ideas and processes. Learn to analyze the art so that you better understand the material you read in the text.

Tables and graphs display important information in an organized way to help you see relationships.

A picture is worth a thousand words. Look at the photographs to see relevant examples of science concepts that you are reading about.

Answer the Section Reviews

Section Reviews test your knowledge of the main points of the section. Critical Thinking items challenge you to think about the material in greater depth and to find connections that you infer from the text.

STUDY TIP When you can't answer a question, reread the section. The answer is usually there.

Do Your Homework

Your teacher may assign worksheets to help you understand and remember the material in the chapter.

STUDY TIP Don't try to answer the questions without reading the text and reviewing your class notes. A little preparation up front will make your homework assignments a lot easier. Answering the items in the Chapter Review will help prepare you for the chapter test.

Visit Holt Online Learning
If your teacher gives you a special password to log onto the Holt Online Learning site, you'll find your complete textbook on the Web. In addition, you'll find some great learning tools and practice quizzes. You'll be able to see how well you know the material from your textbook.

Visit CNN Student News
You'll find up-to-date events in science at **cnnstudentnews.com.**

SAFETY FIRST!

Exploring, inventing, and investigating are essential to the study of science. However, these activities can also be dangerous. To make sure that your experiments and explorations are safe, you must be aware of a variety of safety guidelines. You have probably heard of the saying, "It is better to be safe than sorry." This is particularly true in a science classroom where experiments and explorations are being performed. Being uninformed and careless can result in serious injuries. Don't take chances with your own safety or with anyone else's.

The following pages describe important guidelines for staying safe in the science classroom. Your teacher may also have safety guidelines and tips that are specific to your classroom and laboratory. Take the time to be safe.

Safety Rules!

Start Out Right

Always get your teacher's permission before attempting any laboratory exploration. Read the procedures carefully, and pay particular attention to safety information and caution statements. If you are unsure about what a safety symbol means, look it up or ask your teacher. You cannot be too careful when it comes to safety. If an accident does occur, inform your teacher immediately regardless of how minor you think the accident is.

If you are instructed to note the odor of a substance, wave the fumes toward your nose with your hand. Never put your nose close to the source.

Safety Symbols

All of the experiments and investigations in this book and their related worksheets include important safety symbols to alert you to particular safety concerns. Become familiar with these symbols so that when you see them, you will know what they mean and what to do. It is important that you read this entire safety section to learn about specific dangers in the laboratory.

Eye protection

Clothing protection

Hand safety

Heating safety

Electric safety

Chemical safety

Animal safety

Sharp object

Plant safety

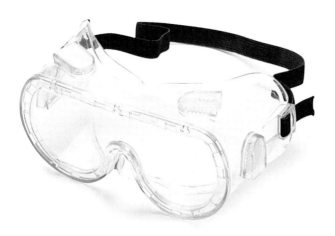

Eye Safety

Wear safety goggles when working around chemicals, acids, bases, or any type of flame or heating device. Wear safety goggles any time there is even the slightest chance that harm could come to your eyes. If any substance gets into your eyes, notify your teacher immediately and flush your eyes with running water for at least 15 minutes. Treat any unknown chemical as if it were a dangerous chemical. Never look directly into the sun. Doing so could cause permanent blindness.

Avoid wearing contact lenses in a laboratory situation. Even if you are wearing safety goggles, chemicals can get between the contact lenses and your eyes. If your doctor requires that you wear contact lenses instead of glasses, wear eye-cup safety goggles in the lab.

Safety Equipment

Know the locations of the nearest fire alarms and any other safety equipment, such as fire blankets and eyewash fountains, as identified by your teacher, and know the procedures for using the equipment.

Neatness

Keep your work area free of all unnecessary books and papers. Tie back long hair, and secure loose sleeves or other loose articles of clothing, such as ties and bows. Remove dangling jewelry. Don't wear open-toed shoes or sandals in the laboratory. Never eat, drink, or apply cosmetics in a laboratory setting. Food, drink, and cosmetics can easily become contaminated with dangerous materials.

Certain hair products (such as aerosol hair spray) are flammable and should not be worn while working near an open flame. Avoid wearing hair spray or hair gel on lab days.

Sharp/Pointed Objects

Use knives and other sharp instruments with extreme care. Never cut objects while holding them in your hands. Place objects on a suitable work surface for cutting.

Be extra careful when using any glassware. When adding a heavy object to a graduated cylinder, tilt the cylinder so that the object slides slowly to the bottom.

Heat

Wear safety goggles when using a heating device or a flame. Whenever possible, use an electric hot plate as a heat source instead of using an open flame. When heating materials in a test tube, always angle the test tube away from yourself and others. To avoid burns, wear heat-resistant gloves whenever instructed to do so.

Electricity

Be careful with electrical cords. When using a microscope with a lamp, do not place the cord where it could trip someone. Do not let cords hang over a table edge in a way that could cause equipment to fall if the cord is accidentally pulled. Do not use equipment with damaged cords. Be sure that your hands are dry and that the electrical equipment is in the "off" position before plugging it in. Turn off and unplug electrical equipment when you are finished.

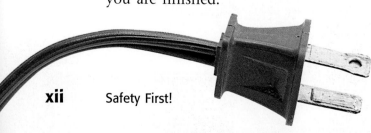

Chemicals

Wear safety goggles when handling any potentially dangerous chemicals, acids, or bases. If a chemical is unknown, handle it as you would a dangerous chemical. Wear an apron and protective gloves when you work with acids or bases or whenever you are told to do so. If a spill gets on your skin or clothing, rinse it off immediately with water for at least 5 minutes while calling to your teacher.

Never mix chemicals unless your teacher tells you to do so. Never taste, touch, or smell chemicals unless you are specifically directed to do so. Before working with a flammable liquid or gas, check for the presence of any source of flame, spark, or heat.

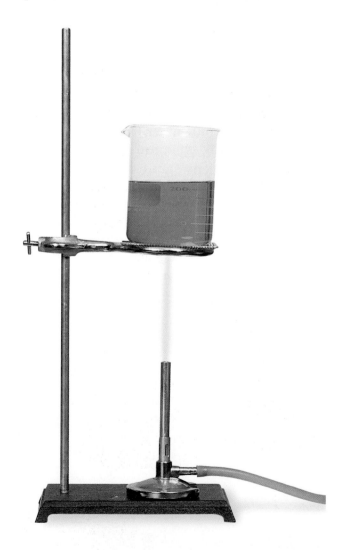

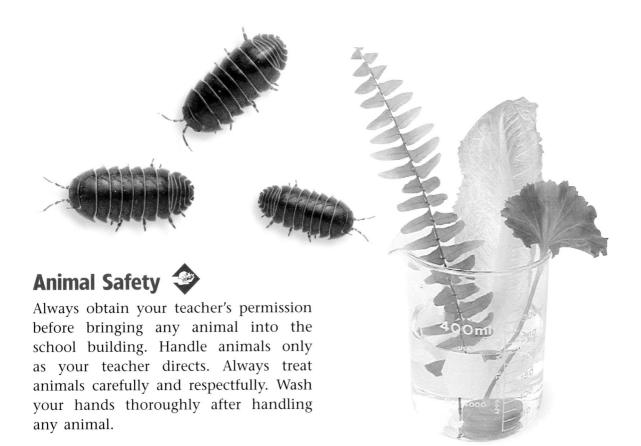

Animal Safety

Always obtain your teacher's permission before bringing any animal into the school building. Handle animals only as your teacher directs. Always treat animals carefully and respectfully. Wash your hands thoroughly after handling any animal.

Plant Safety

Do not eat any part of a plant or plant seed used in the laboratory. Wash your hands thoroughly after handling any part of a plant. When in nature, do not pick any wild plants unless your teacher instructs you to do so.

Glassware

Examine all glassware before use. Be sure that glassware is clean and free of chips and cracks. Report damaged glassware to your teacher. Glass containers used for heating should be made of heat-resistant glass.

1

Studying Space

About the PHOTO

This time-exposure photograph was taken at an observatory located high in the mountains of Chile. As the night passed, the photograph recorded the stars as they circled the southern celestial pole. Just as Earth's rotation causes the sun to appear to move across the sky during the day, Earth's rotation also causes the stars to appear to move across the night sky.

PRE-READING ACTIVITY

FOLDNOTES **Three-Panel Flip Chart**
Before you read the chapter, create the FoldNote entitled "Three-Panel Flip Chart" described in the **Study Skills** section of the Appendix. Label the flaps of the three-panel flip chart with "Astronomy," "Telescopes," and "Mapping the stars." As you read the chapter, write information you learn about each category under the appropriate flap.

STARTUP ACTIVITY

Making an Astrolabe

In this activity, you will make an astronomical device called an *astrolabe* (AS troh LAYB). Ancient astronomers used astrolabes to measure the location of stars in the sky. You will use the astrolabe to measure the angle, or altitude, of an object.

Procedure

1. Tie one end of a **piece of thread** that is 15 cm long to the center of the straight edge of a **protractor.** Attach a **paper clip** to the other end of the string.

2. Tape a **soda straw** lengthwise along the straight edge of the protractor. Your astrolabe is complete!

3. Go outside, and hold the astrolabe in front of you.

4. Look through the straw at a distant object, such as a treetop. The curve of the astrolabe should point toward the ground.

5. Hold the astrolabe still, and carefully pinch the string between your thumb and the protractor. Count the number of degrees between the string and the 90° marker on the protractor. This angle is the altitude of the object.

Analysis

1. What is the altitude of the object? How would the altitude change if you moved closer to the object?

2. Explain how you would use an astrolabe to find the altitude of a star. What are the advantages and disadvantages of this method of measurement?

Astronomy: The Original Science

Imagine that it is 5,000 years ago. Clocks and modern calendars have not been invented. How would you tell the time or know what day it is? One way to tell the time is to study the movement of stars, planets, and the moon.

People in ancient cultures used the seasonal cycles of the stars, planets, and the moon to mark the passage of time. For example, by observing these yearly cycles, early farmers learned the best times of year to plant and harvest various crops. Studying the movement of objects in the sky was so important to ancient people that they built observatories, such as the one shown in **Figure 1.** Over time, the study of the night sky became the science of astronomy. **Astronomy** is the study of the universe. Although ancient cultures did not fully understand how the planets, moons, and stars move in relation to each other, their observations led to the first calendars.

Our Modern Calendar

The years, months, and days of our modern calendar are based on the observation of bodies in our solar system. A **year** is the time required for the Earth to orbit once around the sun. A **month** is roughly the amount of time required for the moon to orbit once around the Earth. (The word *month* comes from the word *moon.*) A **day** is the time required for the Earth to rotate once on its axis.

astronomy the study of the universe

year the time required for the Earth to orbit once around the sun

Figure 1 *This building is located at Chichén Itzá in the Yucatán, Mexico. It is thought to be an ancient Mayan observatory.*

Who's Who of Early Astronomy

Astronomical observations have given us much more than the modern calendar that we use. The careful work of early astronomers helped people understand their place in the universe. The earliest astronomers had only oral histories to learn from. Almost everything they knew about the universe came from what they could discover with their eyes and minds. Not surprisingly, most early astronomers thought that the universe consisted of the sun, the moon, and the planets. They thought that the stars were at the edge of the universe. Claudius Ptolemy (KLAW dee uhs TAHL uh mee) and Nicolaus Copernicus (NIK uh LAY uhs koh PUHR ni kuhs) were two early scientists who influenced the way that people thought about the structure of the universe.

month a division of the year that is based on the orbit of the moon around the Earth

day the time required for Earth to rotate once on its axis

Ptolemy: An Earth-Centered Universe

In 140 CE, Ptolemy, a Greek astronomer, wrote a book that combined all of the ancient knowledge of astronomy that he could find. He expanded ancient theories with careful mathematical calculations in what was called the *Ptolemaic theory.* Ptolemy thought that the Earth was at the center of the universe and that the other planets and the sun revolved around the Earth. Although the Ptolemaic theory, shown in **Figure 2,** was incorrect, it predicted the motions of the planets better than any other theory at the time did. For over 1,500 years in Europe, the Ptolemaic theory was the most popular theory for the structure of the universe.

Figure 2 *According to the Ptolemaic theory, the Earth is at the center of the universe.*

Copernicus: A Sun-Centered Universe

In 1543, a Polish astronomer named Copernicus published a new theory that would eventually revolutionize astronomy. According to his theory, which is shown in **Figure 3,** the sun is at the center of the universe, and all of the planets—including the Earth—orbit the sun. Although Copernicus correctly thought that the planets orbit the sun, his theory did not replace the Ptolemaic theory immediately. When Copernicus's theory was accepted, major changes in science and society called the *Copernican revolution* took place.

✓ Reading Check What was Copernicus's theory? *(See the Appendix for answers to Reading Checks.)*

Figure 3 *According to Copernicus's theory, the sun is at the center of the universe.*

Tycho Brahe: A Wealth of Data

In the late-1500s, Danish astronomer Tycho Brahe (TIE koh BRAW uh) used several large tools, including the one shown in **Figure 4,** to make the most detailed astronomical observations that had been recorded so far. Brahe favored a theory of an Earth-centered universe that was different from the Ptolemaic theory. Brahe thought that the sun and the moon revolved around the Earth and that the other planets revolved around the sun. While his theory was not correct, Brahe recorded very precise observations of the planets and stars that helped future astronomers.

Johannes Kepler: Laws of Planetary Motion

After Brahe died, his assistant, Johannes Kepler, continued Brahe's work. Kepler did not agree with Brahe's theory, but he recognized how valuable Brahe's data were. In 1609, after analyzing the data, Kepler announced that all of the planets revolve around the sun in elliptical orbits and that the sun is not in the exact center of the orbits. Kepler also stated three laws of planetary motion. These laws are still used today.

Figure 4 *Brahe (upper right) used a mural quadrant, which is a large quarter-circle on a wall, to measure the positions of stars and planets.*

Galileo: Turning a Telescope to the Sky

In 1609, Galileo Galilei became one of the first people to use a telescope to observe objects in space. Galileo discovered craters and mountains on the Earth's moon, four of Jupiter's moons, sunspots on the sun, and the phases of Venus. These discoveries showed that the planets are not "wandering stars" but are physical bodies like the Earth.

Isaac Newton: The Laws of Gravity

In 1687, a scientist named Sir Isaac Newton showed that all objects in the universe attract each other through gravitational force. The force of gravity depends on the mass of the objects and the distance between them. Newton's law of gravity explained why all of the planets orbit the most massive object in the solar system—the sun. Thus, Newton helped explain the observations of the scientists who came before him.

✓ **Reading Check** How did the work of Isaac Newton help explain the observations of earlier scientists?

Modern Astronomy

The invention of the telescope and the description of gravity were two milestones in the development of modern astronomy. In the 200 years following Newton's discoveries, scientists made many discoveries about our solar system. But they did not learn that our galaxy has cosmic neighbors until the 1920s.

Edwin Hubble: Beyond the Edge of the Milky Way

Before the 1920s, many astronomers thought that our galaxy, the Milky Way, included every object in space. In 1924, Edwin Hubble proved that other galaxies existed beyond the edge of the Milky Way. His data confirmed the beliefs of some astronomers that the universe is much larger than our galaxy. Today, larger and better telescopes on the Earth and in space, new models of the universe, and spacecraft help astronomers study space. Computers, shown in **Figure 5,** help process data and control the movement of telescopes. These tools have helped answer many questions about the universe. Yet new technology has presented questions that were unthinkable even 10 years ago.

Figure 5 *Computers are used to control telescopes and process large amounts of data.*

SECTION Review

Summary

- Astronomy, the study of the universe, is one of the oldest sciences.
- The units of the modern calendar—days, months, and years—are based on observations of objects in space.
- Ptolemaic theory states that the Earth is at the center of the universe.
- Copernican theory states that the sun is at the center of the universe.
- Modern astronomy has shown that there are billions of galaxies.

Using Key Terms

1. Use each of the following terms in a separate sentence: *year, day, month,* and *astronomy.*

Understanding Key Ideas

2. What happens in 1 year?
   a. The moon completes one orbit around the Earth.
   b. The sun travels once around the Earth.
   c. The Earth revolves once on its axis.
   d. The Earth completes one orbit around the sun.

3. What is the difference between the Ptolemaic and Copernican theories? Who was more accurate: Ptolemy or Copernicus?

4. What contributions did Brahe and Kepler make to astronomy?

5. What contributions did Galileo, Newton, and Hubble make to astronomy?

Math Skills

6. How many times did Earth orbit the sun between 140 CE, when Ptolemy introduced his theories, and 1543, when Copernicus introduced his theories?

Critical Thinking

7. **Analyzing Relationships** What advantage did Galileo have over earlier astronomers?

8. **Making Inferences** Why is astronomy such an old science?

Telescopes

What color are Saturn's rings? What does the surface of the moon look like? To answer these questions, you could use a device called a telescope.

For professional astronomers and amateur stargazers, the telescope is the standard tool for observing the sky. A **telescope** is an instrument that gathers electromagnetic radiation from objects in space and concentrates it for better observation.

Optical Telescopes

Optical telescopes, which are the most common type of telescope, are used to study visible light from objects in the universe. Without using an optical telescope, you can see at most about 3,000 stars in the night sky. Using an optical telescope, however, you can see millions of stars and other objects.

An optical telescope collects visible light and focuses it to a focal point for closer observation. A *focal point* is the point where the rays of light that pass through a lens or that reflect from a mirror converge. The simplest optical telescope has two lenses. One lens, called the *objective lens,* collects light and forms an image at the back of the telescope. The bigger the objective lens is, the more light the telescope can gather. The second lens is located in the eyepiece of the telescope. This lens magnifies the image produced by the objective lens. **Figure 1** shows how much more of the moon you can see by using an optical telescope.

✓ **Reading Check** What are the functions of the two lenses in an optical telescope? (*See the Appendix for answers to Reading Checks.*)

Figure 1 *By using telescopes, people can study objects such as the moon in greater detail.*

Figure 2 Refracting and Reflecting Telescopes

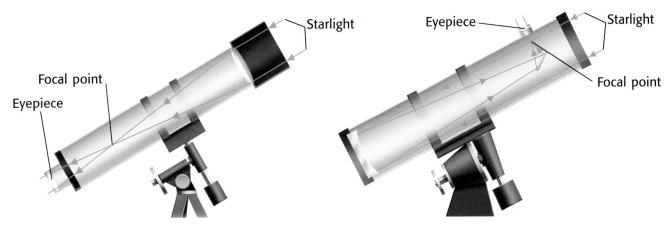

Refracting telescopes use lenses to gather and focus light.

Reflecting telescopes use mirrors to gather and focus light.

Refracting Telescopes

Telescopes that use lenses to gather and focus light are called **refracting telescopes.** As shown in **Figure 2,** a refracting telescope has an objective lens that bends light that passes through it and focuses the light to be magnified by an eyepiece. Refracting telescopes have two disadvantages. First, lenses focus different colors of light at slightly different distances, so images cannot be perfectly focused. Second, the size of a refracting telescope is also limited by the size of the objective lens. If the lens is too large, the glass sags under its own weight and images are distorted. These limitations are two reasons that most professional astronomers use reflecting telescopes.

Reflecting Telescopes

A telescope that uses a curved mirror to gather and focus light is called a **reflecting telescope.** Light enters the telescope and is reflected from a large, curved mirror to a flat mirror. As shown in **Figure 2,** the flat mirror focuses the image and reflects the light to be magnified by the eyepiece.

One advantage of reflecting telescopes is that the mirrors can be very large. Large mirrors allow reflecting telescopes to gather more light than refracting telescopes do. Another advantage is that curved mirrors are polished on their curved side, which prevents light from entering the glass. Thus, any flaws in the glass do not affect the light. A third advantage is that mirrors can focus all colors of light to the same focal point. Therefore, reflecting telescopes allow all colors of light from an object to be seen in focus at the same time.

telescope an instrument that collects electromagnetic radiation from the sky and concentrates it for better observation

refracting telescope a telescope that uses a set of lenses to gather and focus light from distant objects

reflecting telescope a telescope that uses a curved mirror to gather and focus light from distant objects

Very Large Reflecting Telescopes

In some very large reflecting telescopes, several mirrors work together to collect light and focus it in the same area. The Keck Telescopes in Hawaii, shown in **Figure 3,** are twin telescopes that each have 36 hexagonal mirrors that work together. Linking several mirrors allows more light to be collected and focused in one spot.

Figure 3 *The Keck Telescopes are in Hawaii. The 36 hexagonal mirrors in each telescope (shown in the inset) combine to form a light-reflecting surface that is 10 m across.*

Optical Telescopes and the Atmosphere

The light gathered by telescopes on the Earth is affected by the atmosphere. The Earth's atmosphere causes starlight to shimmer and blur due to the motion of the air above the telescope. Also, light pollution from large cities can make the sky look bright. As a result, an observer's ability to view faint objects is limited. Astronomers often place telescopes in dry areas to avoid moisture in the air. Mountaintops are also good locations for telescopes because the air is thinner at higher elevations. In addition, mountaintops generally have less air pollution and light pollution than other areas do.

✓ Reading Check How does the atmosphere affect the images produced by optical telescopes?

Optical Telescopes in Space

To avoid interference by the atmosphere, scientists have put telescopes in space. Although the mirror in the *Hubble Space Telescope,* shown in **Figure 4,** is only 2.4 m across, this optical telescope can detect very faint objects in space.

Figure 4 *The* Hubble Space Telescope *has produced very clear images of objects in deep space.*

The Electromagnetic Spectrum

For thousands of years, humans have used their eyes to observe stars and planets. But scientists eventually discovered that visible light, the light that we can see, is not the only form of radiation. In 1852, James Clerk Maxwell proved that visible light is a part of the electromagnetic spectrum. The **electromagnetic spectrum** is made up of all of the wavelengths of electromagnetic radiation.

Detecting Electromagnetic Radiation

Each color of light is a different wavelength of electromagnetic radiation. Humans can see radiation from red light, which has a long wavelength, to blue light, which has a shorter wavelength. But visible light is only a small part of the electromagnetic spectrum, as shown in **Figure 5.** The rest of the electromagnetic spectrum—radio waves, microwaves, infrared light, ultraviolet light, X rays, and gamma rays—is invisible. The Earth's atmosphere blocks most invisible radiation from objects in space. In this way, the atmosphere functions as a protective shield around the Earth. Radiation that can pass through the atmosphere includes some radio waves, microwaves, infrared light, visible light, and some ultraviolet light.

electromagnetic spectrum all of the frequencies or wavelengths of electromagnetic radiation

Figure 5 *Visible light is only a small band of the electromagnetic spectrum. Radio waves have the longest wavelengths, and gamma rays have the shortest wavelengths.*

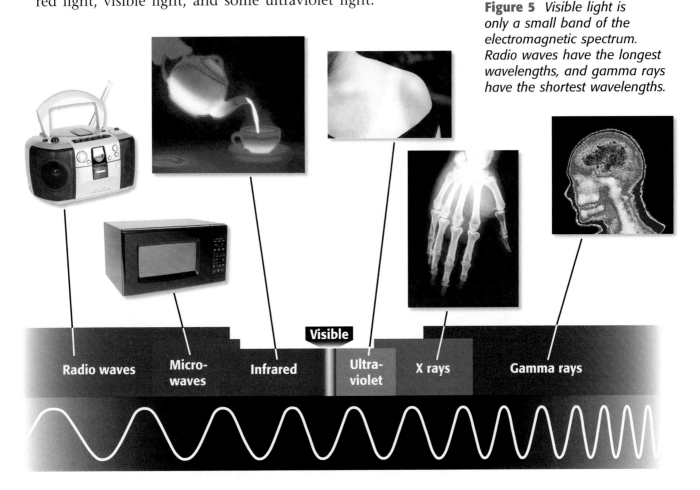

Radio waves | Micro-waves | Infrared | Visible | Ultra-violet | X rays | Gamma rays

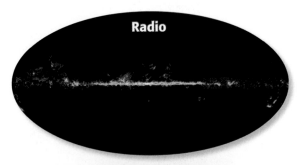

Radio

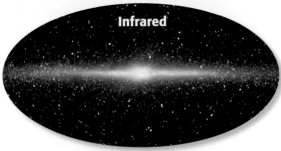

Infrared

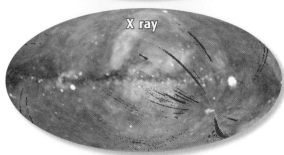

X ray

Gamma ray

Figure 6 *Each image shows the Milky Way as it would appear if we could see other wavelengths of electromagnetic radiation.*

Nonoptical Telescopes

To study invisible radiation, scientists use non-optical telescopes. Nonoptical telescopes detect radiation that cannot be seen by the human eye. Astronomers study the entire electromagnetic spectrum because each type of radiation reveals different clues about an object. As **Figure 6** shows, our galaxy looks very different when it is observed at various wavelengths. A different type of telescope was used to produce each image. The "cloud" that goes across the image is the Milky Way galaxy.

Radio Telescopes

Radio telescopes detect radio waves. Radio telescopes have to be much larger than optical telescopes because radio wavelengths are about 1 million times longer than optical wavelengths. Most radio radiation reaches the ground and can be detected both during the day and night. The surface of radio telescopes does not have to be as flawless as the lenses and mirrors of optical telescopes. In fact, the surface of a radio telescope does not have to be solid.

Linking Radio Telescopes

Astronomers can get more detailed images of the universe by linking radio telescopes together. When radio telescopes are linked together, they work like a single giant telescope. For example, the Very Large Array (VLA) consists of 27 radio telescopes that are spread over 30 km. Working together, the telescopes function as a single telescope that is 30 km across!

CONNECTION TO
Physics

Detecting Infrared Radiation In this activity, you will replicate Sir William Herschel's discovery of invisible infrared radiation. First, paint the bulbs of three thermometers black. Place a sheet of white paper inside a tall cardboard box. Tape the thermometers parallel to each other, and place them inside the box. Cut a small notch in the top of the box, and position a small glass prism so that a spectrum is projected inside the box. Arrange the thermometers so that one is just outside the red end of the spectrum, with no direct light on it. After 10 min, record the temperatures. Which thermometer recorded the highest temperature? Explain why.

Nonoptical Telescopes in Space

Because most electromagnetic waves are blocked by the Earth's atmosphere, scientists have placed ultraviolet telescopes, infrared telescopes, gamma-ray telescopes, and X-ray telescopes in space. The *Chandra X-Ray Observatory*, a space-based telescope that detects X rays, is illustrated in **Figure 7.** X-ray telescopes in space can be much more sensitive than optical telescopes. For example, NASA has tested an X-ray telescope that can detect an object that is the size of a frisbee on the surface of the sun. If an optical telescope had a similar power, it could detect a hair on the head of an astronaut on the moon!

✔ **Reading Check** Why are X-ray telescopes placed in space?

Figure 7 *The* Chandra X-Ray Observatory *can detect black holes and some of the most distant objects in the universe.*

SECTION Review

Summary

- Refracting telescopes use lenses to gather and focus light.
- Reflecting telescopes use mirrors to gather and focus light.
- Astronomers study all wavelengths of the electromagnetic spectrum, including radio waves, microwaves, infrared light, visible light, ultraviolet light, X rays, and gamma rays.
- The atmosphere blocks most forms of electromagnetic radiation from reaching the Earth. To overcome this limitation, astronomers place telescopes in space.

Using Key Terms

For each pair of terms, explain how the meanings of the terms differ.

1. *refracting telescope* and *reflecting telescope*

2. *telescope* and *electromagnetic spectrum*

Understanding Key Ideas

3. How does the atmosphere affect astronomical observations?
   a. It focuses visible light.
   b. It blocks most electromagnetic radiation.
   c. It blocks all radio waves.
   d. It does not affect astronomical observations.

4. Describe how reflecting and refracting telescopes work.

5. What limits the size of a refracting telescope? Explain.

6. What advantages do reflecting telescopes have over refracting telescopes?

7. List the types of radiation in the electromagnetic spectrum, from the longest wavelength to the shortest wavelength. Then, describe how astronomers study each type of radiation.

Math Skills

8. A telescope's light-gathering power is proportional to the area of its objective lens or mirror. If the diameter of a lens is 1 m, what is the area of the lens? (Hint: *area* = $3.1416 \times radius^2$)

Critical Thinking

9. **Applying Concepts** Describe three reasons why Hawaii is a good location for a telescope.

10. **Making Inferences** Why doesn't the surface of a radio telescope have to be as flawless as the surface of a mirror in an optical telescope?

11. **Making Inferences** What limitation of a refracting telescope could be overcome by placing the telescope in space?

SCI LINKS.

NSTA
Developed and maintained by the National Science Teachers Association

For a variety of links related to this chapter, go to www.scilinks.org

Topic: Telescopes
SciLinks code: HSM1500

Mapping the Stars

Have you ever seen Orion the Hunter or the Big Dipper in the night sky? Ancient cultures linked stars together to form patterns that represented characters from myths and objects in their lives.

READING WARM-UP

Objectives

- Explain how constellations are used to organize the night sky.
- Describe how the altitude of a star is measured.
- Explain how the celestial sphere is used to describe the location of objects in the sky.
- Compare size and scale in the universe, and explain how red shift indicates that the universe is expanding.

Terms to Learn

constellation   horizon
zenith   light-year
altitude

READING STRATEGY

Paired Summarizing Read this section silently. In pairs, take turns summarizing the material. Stop to discuss ideas that seem confusing.

Today, we can see the same star patterns that people in ancient cultures saw. Modern astronomers still use many of the names given to stars centuries ago. But astronomers can now describe a star's location precisely. Advances in astronomy have led to a better understanding of how far away stars are and how big the universe is.

Patterns in the Sky

When people in ancient cultures connected stars in patterns, they named sections of the sky based on the patterns. These patterns are called *constellations*. **Constellations** are sections of the sky that contain recognizable star patterns. Understanding the location and movement of constellations helped people navigate and keep track of time.

Different civilizations had different names for the same constellations. For example, where the Greeks saw a hunter (Orion) in the northern sky, the Japanese saw a drum, as shown in **Figure 1.** Today, different cultures still interpret the sky in different ways, but astronomers have agreed on the names and locations of the constellations.

Figure 1 *The ancient Greeks saw Orion as a hunter, but the Japanese saw the same set of stars as a drum.*

Figure 2 *This sky map shows some of the constellations in the Northern Hemisphere at midnight in the spring. Ursa Major (the Great Bear) is a region of the sky that includes all of the stars that make up that constellation.*

constellation a region of the sky that contains a recognizable star pattern and that is used to describe the location of objects in space

Constellations Help Organize the Sky

When you think of constellations, you probably think of the stick figures made by connecting bright stars with imaginary lines. To an astronomer, however, a constellation is something more. As you can see in **Figure 2,** a constellation is a region of the sky. Each constellation shares a border with neighboring constellations. For example, in the same way that the state of Texas is a region of the United States, Ursa Major is a region of the sky. Every star or galaxy is located within 1 of 88 constellations.

Seasonal Changes

The sky map in **Figure 2** shows what the midnight sky in the Northern Hemisphere looks like in the spring. But as the Earth revolves around the sun, the apparent locations of the constellations change from season to season. In addition, different constellations are visible in the Southern Hemisphere. Thus, a child in Chile can see different constellations than you can. Therefore, this map is not accurate for the other three seasons or for the Southern Hemisphere. Sky maps for summer, fall, and winter in the Northern Hemisphere appear in the Appendix of this book.

Reading Check Why are different constellations visible in the Northern and Southern Hemispheres? (*See the Appendix for answers to Reading Checks.*)

Using a Sky Map

1. Hold your **textbook** over your head with the cover facing upward. Turn the book so that the direction at the bottom of the sky map is the same as the direction you are facing.

2. Notice the locations of the constellations in relation to each other.

3. If you look up at the sky at night in the spring, you should see the stars positioned as they are on your map.

4. Why are *E* and *W* on sky maps the reverse of how they appear on land maps?

Figure 3 *Using an astrolabe, you can determine the altitude of a star by measuring the angle between the horizon and a star. The altitude of any object depends on where you are and when you look.*

Zenith

Altitude

Horizon

Finding Stars in the Night Sky

Have you ever tried to show someone a star by pointing to it? Did the person miss what you were seeing? If you use an instrument called an *astrolabe,* shown in **Figure 3,** you can describe the location of a star or planet. To use an astrolabe correctly, you need to understand the three points of reference shown in **Figure 4.** This method is useful to describe the location of a star relative to where you are. But if you want to describe a star's location in relation to the Earth, you need to use the celestial sphere, shown in **Figure 5.**

zenith the point in the sky directly above an observer on Earth

altitude the angle between an object in the sky and the horizon

horizon the line where the sky and the Earth appear to meet

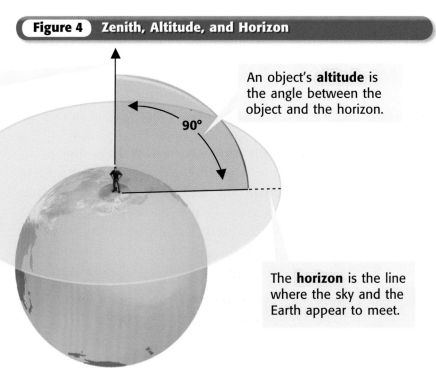

Figure 4 Zenith, Altitude, and Horizon

The **zenith** is an imaginary point in the sky directly above an observer on Earth. The zenith always has an altitude of 90°.

An object's **altitude** is the angle between the object and the horizon.

90°

The **horizon** is the line where the sky and the Earth appear to meet.

Figure 5   **The Celestial Sphere**

To talk to each other about the location of a star, astronomers must have a common method of describing a star's location. The method that astronomers have invented is based on a reference system known as the *celestial sphere*. The celestial sphere is an imaginary sphere that surrounds the Earth. Just as we use latitude and longitude to plot positions on Earth, astronomers use right ascension and declination to plot positions in the sky. *Right ascension* is a measure of how far east an object is from the *vernal equinox*, the location of the sun on the first day of spring. *Declination* is a measure of how far north or south an object is from the celestial equator.

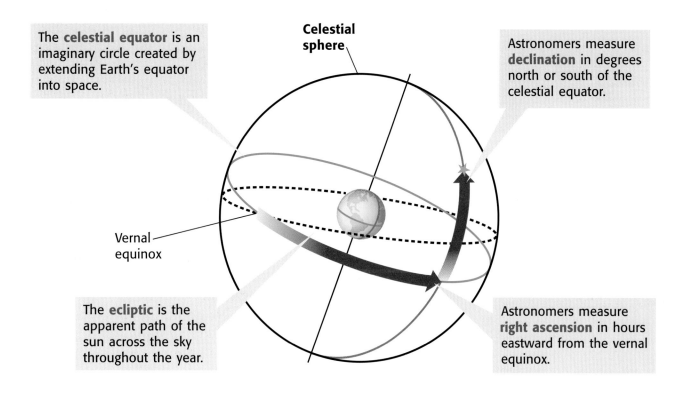

The **celestial equator** is an imaginary circle created by extending Earth's equator into space.

Celestial sphere

Astronomers measure **declination** in degrees north or south of the celestial equator.

Vernal equinox

The **ecliptic** is the apparent path of the sun across the sky throughout the year.

Astronomers measure **right ascension** in hours eastward from the vernal equinox.

The Path of Stars Across the Sky

Just as the sun appears to move across the sky during the day, most stars and planets rise and set throughout the night. This apparent motion is caused by the Earth's rotation. As the Earth spins on its axis, stars and planets appear to move. Near the poles, however, stars are circumpolar. *Circumpolar stars* are stars that can be seen at all times of year and all times of night. These stars never set, and they appear to circle the celestial poles. You also see different stars in the sky depending on the time of year. Why? The reason is that as the Earth travels around the sun, different areas of the universe are visible.

Reading Check How is the apparent movement of the sun similar to the apparent movement of most stars during the night?

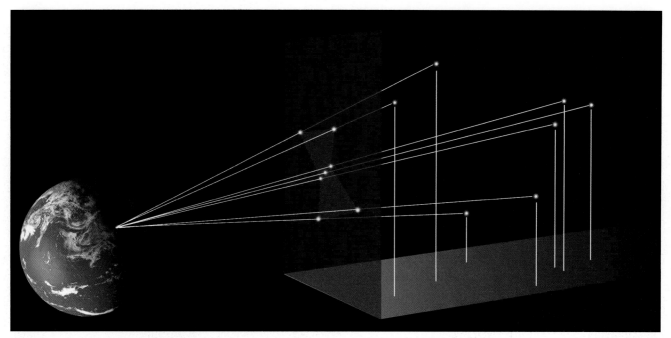

Figure 6 *While the stars in the constellation Orion may appear to be near each other when they are seen from Earth, they are actually very far apart.*

The Size and Scale of the Universe

Imagine looking out the window of a moving car. Nearby trees appear to move more quickly than farther trees do. Objects that are very far away do not appear to move at all. The same principle applies to stars and planets. In the 1500s, Nicolaus Copernicus noticed that the planets appeared to move relative to each other but that the stars did not. Thus, he thought that the stars must be much farther away than the planets.

Measuring Distance in Space

light-year the distance that light travels in one year; about 9.46 trillion kilometers

Today, we know that Copernicus was correct. The stars are much farther away than the planets are. In fact, stars are so distant that a new unit of length—the light-year—was created to measure their distance. A **light-year** is a unit of length equal to the distance that light travels in 1 year. One light-year is equal to about 9.46 trillion kilometers! The farthest objects we can observe are more than 10 billion light-years away. Although the stars may appear to be at similar distances from Earth, their distances vary greatly. For example, **Figure 6** shows how far away the stars that make up part of Orion are.

✓ **Reading Check** How far does light travel in 1 year?

Considering Scale in the Universe

When you think about the universe and all of the objects it contains, it is important to consider scale. For example, stars appear to be very small in the night sky. But we know that most stars are a lot larger than Earth. **Figure 7** will help you understand the scale of objects in the universe.

For another activity related to this chapter, go to **go.hrw.com** and type in the keyword **HZ5OBSW.**

Figure 7 From Home Plate to 10 Million Light-Years Away

1 Let's start with home plate in a baseball stadium. You are looking down from a distance of about 10 m.

2 At 1,000 m (1 km) away, you can see the baseball stadium and the surrounding neighborhood.

3 At 100 km away, you see the city that contains the stadium and the countryside around the city.

4 At 100,000 km away, you can see the Earth and the moon.

5 At 1,500,000,000 km (83 light-minutes) away, you can look back at the sun and the inner planets.

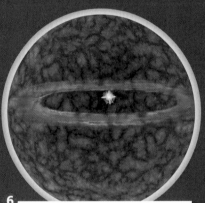

6 At 150 light-days, the solar system, surrounded by a cloud of comets and other icy debris, can be seen.

7 By the time you are 10 light-years away, the sun resembles any other star in space.

8 At 1 million light-years away, our galaxy looks like the Andromeda galaxy, a cloud of stars set in the blackness of space.

9 At 10 million light-years away, you can see a handful of galaxies called the *Local Group*.

Figure 8 *As an object moves away from an observer at a high speed, the light from the object appears redder. As the object moves toward the observer, the light from the object appears bluer.*

The Doppler Effect

Have you ever noticed that when a driver in an approaching car blows the horn, the horn sounds higher pitched as the car approaches and lower pitched after the car passes? This effect is called the *Doppler effect*. As shown in **Figure 8,** the Doppler effect also occurs with light. If a light source, such as a star or galaxy, is moving quickly away from an observer, the light emitted looks redder than it normally does. This effect is called *redshift.* If a star or galaxy is moving quickly toward an observer, its light appears bluer than it normally does. This effect is known as *blueshift.*

An Expanding Universe

After discovering that the universe is made up of many other galaxies like our own, Edwin Hubble analyzed the light from galaxies and stars to study the general direction that objects in the universe are moving. Hubble soon made another startling discovery—the light from all galaxies except our close neighbors is affected by redshift. This means that galaxies are rapidly moving apart from each other. In other words, because all galaxies except our close neighbors are moving apart, the universe must be expanding. **Figure 9** shows evidence of redshift recorded by the *Hubble Space Telescope* in 2002.

Reading Check What logical conclusion could be made if the light from all of the galaxies were affected by blueshift?

Figure 9 *The galaxy that is cut off at the bottom of this image is moving away from us at a much slower speed than the other galaxies are. Distant galaxies are visible as faint disks.*

SECTION
Review

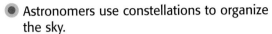

Summary

- Astronomers use constellations to organize the sky.
- Altitude, or the angle between an object and the horizon, can be used to describe the location of an object in the sky.
- The celestial sphere is an imaginary sphere that surrounds the Earth. Using the celestial sphere, astronomers can accurately describe the location of an object without reference to an observer.
- A light-year is the distance that light travels in 1 year.
- The Doppler effect causes the light emitted by objects that are moving away from an observer to appear to shift toward the red end of the spectrum. Objects moving toward an observer are shifted to the blue end of the spectrum.
- Observations of redshift and blueshift indicate that the universe is expanding.

Using Key Terms

The statements below are false. For each statement, replace the underlined term to make a true statement.

1. <u>Zenith</u> is the angle between an object and the horizon.

2. The distance that light travels in 1 year is called a <u>light-meter</u>.

Understanding Key Ideas

3. Stars appear to move across the night sky because of
   a. the rotation of Earth on its axis.
   b. the movement of the Milky Way galaxy.
   c. the movement of stars in the universe.
   d. the revolution of Earth around the sun.

4. How do astronomers use the celestial sphere to plot a star's exact position?

5. How do constellations relate to patterns of stars? How are constellations like states?

6. Why are different sky maps needed for different times of the year?

7. What are redshift and blueshift? Why are these effects useful in the study of the universe?

Critical Thinking

8. **Applying Concepts** Light from the Andromeda galaxy is affected by blueshift. What can you conclude about this galaxy?

9. **Making Comparisons** Explain how Copernicus concluded that stars were farther away than planets. Draw a diagram showing how this principle applies to another example.

Interpreting Graphics

The diagram below shows the altitude of Star A and Star B. Use the diagram below to answer the questions that follow.

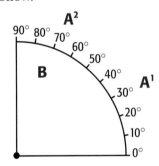

10. What is the approximate altitude of star B?

11. In 4 h, star A moved from A^1 to A^2. How many degrees did the star move each hour?

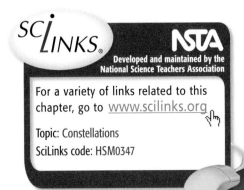

Developed and maintained by the National Science Teachers Association

For a variety of links related to this chapter, go to www.scilinks.org

Topic: Constellations
SciLinks code: HSM0347

Skills Practice Lab

Through the Looking Glass

Have you ever looked toward the horizon or up into the sky and wished that you could see farther? Do you think that a telescope might help you see farther? Astronomers use huge telescopes to study the universe. You can build your own telescope to get a glimpse of how these enormous, technologically advanced telescopes help astronomers see distant objects.

Procedure

1. Use modeling clay to form a base that holds one of the lenses upright on your desktop. When the lights are turned off, your teacher will turn on a lamp at the front of the classroom. Rotate your lens so that the light from the lamp passes through the lens.

2. Hold the paper so that the light passing through the lens lands on the paper. To sharpen the image of the light on the paper, slowly move the paper closer to or farther from the lens. Hold the paper in the position in which the image is sharpest.

3. Using the metric ruler, measure the distance between the lens and the paper. Record this distance.

④ How far is the paper from the lens? This distance, called the *focal length,* is the distance that the paper has to be from the lens for the image to be in focus.

⑤ Repeat steps 1–4 using the other lens.

⑥ Measuring from one end of the long cardboard tube, mark the focal length of the lens that has the longer focal length. Place a mark 2 cm past this line toward the other end of the tube, and label the mark "Cut."

⑦ Measuring from one end of the short cardboard tube, mark the focal length of the lens that has the shorter focal length. Place a mark 2 cm past this line toward the other end of the tube, and label the mark "Cut."

⑧ Shorten the tubes by cutting along the marks labeled "Cut." Wear safety goggles when you make these cuts.

⑨ Tape the lens that has the longer focal length to one end of the longer tube. Tape the other lens to one end of the shorter tube. Slip the empty end of one tube inside the empty end of the other tube. Be sure that there is one lens at each end of this new, longer tube.

⑩ Congratulations! You have just constructed a telescope. To use your telescope, look through the short tube (the eyepiece) and point the long end at various objects in the room. You can focus the telescope by adjusting its length. Are the images right side up or upside down? Observe birds, insects, trees, or other outside objects. Record the images that you see. **Caution:** NEVER look directly at the sun! Looking directly at the sun could cause permanent blindness.

Analyze the Results

① **Analyzing Results** Which type of telescope did you just construct: a refracting telescope or a reflecting telescope? What makes your telescope one type and not the other?

② **Identifying Patterns** What factor determines the focal length of a lens?

Draw Conclusions

③ **Evaluating Results** How would you improve your telescope?

Chapter Review

USING KEY TERMS

1 Use each of the following terms in a separate sentence: *year, month, day, astronomy, electromagnetic spectrum, constellation,* and *altitude.*

For each pair of terms, explain how the meanings of the terms differ.

2 *reflecting telescope* and *refracting telescope*

3 *zenith* and *horizon*

4 *year* and *light-year*

UNDERSTANDING KEY IDEAS

Multiple Choice

5 Which of the following answer choices lists types of electromagnetic radiation from longest wavelength to shortest wavelength?

a. radio waves, ultraviolet light, infrared light

b. infrared light, microwaves, X rays

c. X rays, ultraviolet light, gamma rays

d. microwaves, infrared light, visible light

6 The length of a day is based on the amount of time that

a. Earth takes to orbit the sun one time.

b. Earth takes to rotate once on its axis.

c. the moon takes to orbit Earth one time.

d. the moon takes to rotate once on its axis.

7 Which of the following statements about X rays and radio waves from objects in space is true?

a. Both types of radiation can be observed by using the same telescope.

b. Separate telescopes are needed to observe each type of radiation, but both telescopes can be on Earth.

c. Separate telescopes are needed to observe each type of radiation, but both telescopes must be in space.

d. Separate telescopes are needed to observe each type of radiation, but only one of the telescopes must be in space.

8 According to ___, Earth is at the center of the universe.

a. the Ptolemaic theory

b. Copernicus's theory

c. Galileo's theory

d. None of the above

9 Which scientist was one of the first scientists to successfully use a telescope to observe the night sky?

a. Brahe   c. Hubble

b. Galileo   d. Kepler

10 Astronomers divide the sky into

a. galaxies.   c. zeniths.

b. constellations.   d. phases.

11 ___ determines which stars you see in the sky.

a. Your latitude

b. The time of year

c. The time of night

d. All of the above

12 The altitude of an object in the sky is the object's angular distance

a. above the horizon.

b. from the north celestial pole.

c. from the zenith.

d. from the prime meridian.

13 Right ascension is a measure of how far east an object in the sky is from

a. the observer.

b. the vernal equinox.

c. the moon.

d. Venus.

14 Telescopes that work on Earth's surface include all of the following EXCEPT

a. radio telescopes.

b. refracting telescopes.

c. X-ray telescopes.

d. reflecting telescopes.

Short Answer

15 Explain how right ascension and declination are similar to latitude and longitude.

16 How does a reflecting telescope work?

CRITICAL THINKING

17 **Concept Mapping** Use the following terms to create a concept map: *right ascension, declination, celestial sphere, degrees, hours, celestial equator,* and *vernal equinox.*

18 **Making Inferences** Why was seeing objects in the sky easier for people in ancient cultures than it is for most people today? What tools help modern people study objects in space in greater detail than was possible in the past?

19 **Making Inferences** Because many forms of radiation from space do not penetrate Earth's atmosphere, astronomers' ability to detect this radiation is limited. But how does the protection of the atmosphere benefit humans?

20 **Analyzing Ideas** Explain why the Ptolemaic theory seems logical based on daily observations of the rising and setting of the sun.

INTERPRETING GRAPHICS

Use the sky map below to answer the questions that follow. (Example: The star Aldebaran is located at about 4 h, 30 min right ascension, 16° declination.)

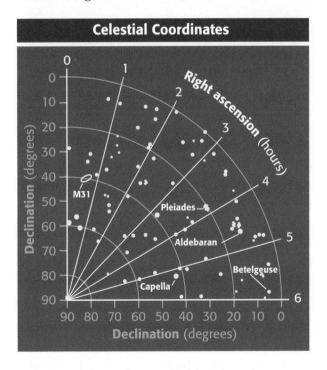

21 What object is located near 5 h, 55 min right ascension, and 7° declination?

22 What are the celestial coordinates for the Andromeda galaxy (M31)? Round off the right ascension to the nearest half-hour.

Standardized Test Preparation

READING

Read each of the passages below. Then, answer the questions that follow each passage.

Passage 1 In the early Roman calendar, a year had exactly 365 days. The calendar worked well until people realized that the seasons were beginning and ending later each year. To fix this problem, Julius Caesar developed the Julian calendar based on a 365.25-day calendar year. He added 90 days to the year 46 BCE and added an extra day every 4 years. A year in which an extra day is added to the calendar is called a *leap year*. In the mid-1500s, astronomers determined that there are actually 365.2422 days in a year, so Pope Gregory XIII developed the Gregorian calendar. He dropped 10 days from the year 1582 and restricted leap years to years that are divisible by 4 but not by 100 (except for years that are divisible by 400). Today, most countries use the Gregorian calendar.

1. According to the passage, which of the following years is a leap year?

 A 46 BCE

 B 1582

 C 1600

 D 1800

2. How long is a year?

 F 365 days

 G 365.224 days

 H 365.2422 days

 I 365.25 days

3. Why did Julius Caesar change the early Roman calendar?

 A to deal with the fact that the seasons were beginning and ending later each year

 B to compete with the Gregorian calendar

 C to add an extra day every year

 D to shorten the length of a year

Passage 2 The earliest known evidence of astronomical observations is a group of stones near Nabta in southern Egypt that is between 6,000 and 7,000 years old. According to archeoastronomers, some of the stones are positioned such that they would have lined up with the sun during the summer solstice 6,000 years ago. The summer solstice occurs on the longest day of the year. At the Nabta site, the noonday sun is at its zenith (directly overhead) for about three weeks before and after the summer solstice. When the sun is at its zenith, upright objects do not cast shadows. For many civilizations in the Tropics, the zenith sun has had ceremonial significance for thousands of years. The same is probably true for the civilizations that used the Nabta site. Artifacts found at the site near Nabta suggest that the site was created by African cattle herders. These people probably used the site for many purposes, including trade, social bonding, and ritual.

1. In the passage, what does *archeoastronomer* mean?

 A an archeologist that studies Egyptian culture

 B an astronomer that studies the zenith sun

 C an archeologist that studies ancient astronomy

 D an astronomer that studies archeologists

2. Why don't upright objects cast a shadow when the sun is at its zenith?

 F because the sun is directly overhead

 G because the summer solstice is occurring

 H because the sun is below the horizon

 I because the sun is at its zenith on the longest day of the year

The diagram below shows a galaxy moving in relation to four observers. The concentric circles illustrate the Doppler effect at each location. Use the diagram below to answer the questions that follow.

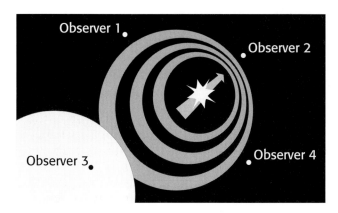

1. Which of the following observers would see the light from the galaxy affected by redshift?

   A observers 1 and 2

   B observer 3

   C observers 3 and 4

   D observers 1 and 4

2. Which of the following observers would see the light from the galaxy affected by blueshift?

   F observer 1

   G observers 2 and 4

   H observers 3 and 4

   I observer 2

3. How would the wavelengths of light detected by observer 4 appear?

   A The wavelengths would appear shorter than they really are.

   B The wavelengths would appear longer than they really are.

   C The wavelengths would appear unchanged.

   D The wavelengths would alternate between blue and red.

Read each question below, and choose the best answer.

1. If light travels 300,000 km/s, how long does light reflected from Mars take to reach Earth when Mars is 65,000,000 km away ?

   A 22 s

   B 217 s

   C 2,170 s

   D 2,200 s

2. Star A is 8 million kilometers from star B. What is this distance expressed in meters?

   F 0.8 m

   G 8,000 m

   H 8×10^6 m

   I 8×10^9 m

3. If each hexagonal mirror in the Keck Telescopes is 1.8 m across, how many mirrors would be needed to create a light-reflecting surface that is 10.8 m across?

   A 3.2

   B 5

   C 6

   D 6.2

4. If the altitude of a star is 37°, what is the angle between the star and the zenith?

   F 143°

   G 90°

   H 53°

   I 37°

5. You are studying an image made by the *Hubble Space Telescope*. If you observe 90 stars in an area that is 1 cm², which of the following estimates is the best estimate for the number of stars in 15 cm²?

   A 700

   B 900

   C 1,200

   D 1,350

Standardized Test Preparation

Science in Action

Science Fiction

"Why I Left Harry's All-Night Hamburgers" by Lawrence Watt-Evans

The main character was 16, and he needed to find a job. So, he began working at Harry's All-Night Hamburgers. His shift was from midnight to 7:30 A.M. so that he could still go to school. Harry's All-Night Hamburgers was pretty quiet most nights, but once in a while some unusual characters came by. For example, one guy came in dressed for Arctic weather even though it was April. Then there were the folks who parked a very strange vehicle in the parking lot for anyone to see. The main character starts questioning the visitors, and what he learns startles and fascinates him. Soon, he's thinking about leaving Harry's. Find out why when you read "Why I Left Harry's All-Night Hamburgers," in the *Holt Anthology of Science Fiction*.

Social Studies ACTiViTY

WRITING SKILL The main character in the story learns that Earth is a pretty strange place. Find out about some of the places mentioned in the story, and create an illustrated travel guide that describes some of the foreign places that interest you.

HOLT ANTHOLOGY OF
Science Fiction

HOLT, RINEHART AND WINSTON

Science, Technology, and Society

Light Pollution

When your parents were your age, they could look up at the night sky and see many more stars than you can now. In a large city, seeing more than 50 stars or planets in the night sky can be difficult. Light pollution is a growing—or you could say "glowing"—problem. If you have ever seen a white glow over the horizon in the night sky, you have seen the effects of light pollution. Most light pollution comes from outdoor lights that are excessively bright or misdirected. Light pollution not only limits the number of stars that the average person can see but also limits what astronomers can detect. Light pollution affects migrating animals, too. Luckily, there are ways to reduce light pollution. The International Dark Sky Association is working to reduce light pollution around the world. Find out how you can reduce light pollution in your community or home.

Math ACTiViTY

A Virginia high school student named Jennifer Barlow started "National Dark Sky Week." If light pollution is reduced for 1 week each year, for what percentage of the year would light pollution be reduced?

People in Science

Neil deGrasse Tyson

Star Writer When Neil deGrasse Tyson was nine years old, he visited a planetarium for the first time. Tyson was so affected by the experience he decided at that moment to dedicate his life to studying the universe. Tyson began studying the stars through a telescope on the roof of his apartment building. This interest led Tyson to attend the Bronx High School of Science, where he studied astronomy and physics. Tyson's passion for astronomy continued when he was a student at Harvard. However, Tyson soon realized that he wanted to share his love of astronomy with the public. So, today Tyson is America's best-known astrophysicist. When something really exciting happens in the universe, such as the discovery of evidence of water on Mars, Tyson is often asked to explain the discovery to the public. He has been interviewed hundreds of times on TV programs and has written several books. Tyson also writes a monthly column in the magazine *Natural History*. But writing and appearing on TV isn't even his day job! Tyson is the director of the Hayden Planetarium in New York—the same planetarium that ignited his interest in astronomy when he was nine years old!

Language Arts ACTIVITY

WRITING SKILL Be a star writer! Visit a planetarium or find a Web site that offers a virtual tour of the universe. Write a magazine-style article about the experience.

To learn more about these Science in Action topics, visit go.hrw.com and type in the keyword **HZ5OBSF**.

Current Science

Check out Current Science® articles related to this chapter by visiting go.hrw.com. Just type in the keyword **HZ5CS18**.

Science in Action **29**

2

Stars, Galaxies, and the Universe

About the PHOTO

This image was taken by the *Hubble Space Telescope* and shows the IC 2163 galaxy (right) swinging past the NGC 2207 galaxy (left). Strong forces from NGC 2207 have caused stars and gas to fling out of IC 2163 into long streamers.

PRE-READING ACTIVITY

FOLDNOTES **Three-Panel Flip Chart**
Before you read the chapter, create the FoldNote entitled "Three-Panel Flip Chart" described in the **Study Skills** section of the Appendix. Label the flaps of the three-panel flip chart with "Stars," "Galaxies," and "The universe." As you read the chapter, write information you learn about each category under the appropriate flap.

Exploring the Movement of Galaxies in the Universe

Not all galaxies are the same. Galaxies can differ by size, shape, and how they move in space. In this activity, you will explore how the galaxies in the photo move in space.

Procedure

1. Fill a **one-quart glass jar** three-fourths of the way with **water.**

2. Take a pinch of **glitter,** and sprinkle it on the surface of the water.

3. Quickly stir the water with a **wooden spoon.** Be sure to stir the water in a circular pattern.

4. After you stop stirring, look at the water from the sides of the jar and from the top of the jar.

Analysis

1. What kind of motion did the water make after you stopped stirring the water?

2. How is the motion similar to the galaxies in the photo?

3. Make up a name that describes the galaxies in the photo.

Stars

Do you remember the children's song "Twinkle, Twinkle Little Star"? In the song, you sing "How I wonder what you are!" Well, what are stars? And what are they made of?

Most stars look like faint dots of light in the night sky. But stars are actually huge, hot, bright balls of gas that are trillions of kilometers away from Earth. How do astronomers learn about stars when the stars are too far away to visit? Astronomers study starlight!

Color of Stars

Look at the flames on the candle and the Bunsen burner shown in **Figure 1.** Which flame is hottest? How can you tell? Although red and yellow may be thought of as "warm" colors and blue may be thought of as a "cool" color, scientists consider red and yellow to be cool colors and blue to be a warm color. For example, the blue flame of the Bunsen burner is much hotter than the yellow flame of the candle.

If you look carefully at the night sky, you might notice the different colors of some stars. Betelgeuse (BET uhl JOOZ), which is red, and Rigel (RIE juhl), which is blue, are the stars that form two corners of the constellation Orion, shown in **Figure 1.** Because these two stars are different colors, we can conclude that they have different temperatures.

✓ Reading Check Which star is hotter, Betelgeuse or Rigel? **Explain your answer.** (*See the Appendix for answers to Reading Checks.*)

Objectives

- Describe how color indicates the temperature of a star.
- Explain how a scientist can identify a of star's composition.
- Describe how scientists classify stars.
- Compare absolute magnitude with apparent magnitude.
- Identify how astronomers measure distances from Earth to stars.
- Describe the difference between the apparent motion and the actual motion of stars.

Terms to Learn

spectrum
apparent magnitude
absolute magnitude
light-year
parallax

Prediction Guide Before reading this section, write the title of each heading in this section. Next, under each heading, write what you think you will learn.

Figure 1 *In the same way that we know the blue flame of the Bunsen burner is hotter than the yellow flame of the candle, astronomers know that Rigel is hotter than Betelgeuse.*

Composition of Stars

A star is made up of different elements in the form of gases. The inner layers of a star are very dense and hot. But the outer layers of a star, or a star's atmosphere, are made up of cool gases. Elements in a star's atmosphere absorb some of the light that radiates from the star. Because different elements absorb different wavelengths of light, astronomers can tell what elements a star is made of from the light they observe from the star.

The Colors of Light

When you look at white light through a glass prism, you see a rainbow of colors called a **spectrum.** The spectrum consists of millions of colors, including red, orange, yellow, green, blue, indigo, and violet. A hot, solid object, such as the glowing wire inside a light bulb, gives off a *continuous spectrum*—a spectrum that shows all the colors. However, the spectrum of a star is different. Astronomers use an instrument called a *spectrograph* to break a star's light into a spectrum. The spectrum gives astronomers information about the composition and temperature of a star. To understand how to read a star's spectrum, think about something more familiar—a neon sign.

Making an ID

Many restaurants use neon signs to attract customers. The gas in a neon sign glows when an electric current flows through the gas. If you were to look at the sign with a spectrograph, you would not see a continuous spectrum. Instead, you would see *emission lines*. Emission lines are lines that are made when certain wavelengths of light, or colors, are given off by hot gases. When an element emits light, only some colors in the spectrum show up, while all the other colors are missing. Each element has a unique set of bright emission lines. Emission lines are like fingerprints for the elements. You can see emission lines for four elements in **Figure 2.**

spectrum the band of color produced when white light passes through a prism

Ne (neon)

H (hydrogen)

He (helium)

Na (sodium)

Figure 2 *Neon gas produces a unique set of emission lines, as do the elements hydrogen, helium, and sodium.*

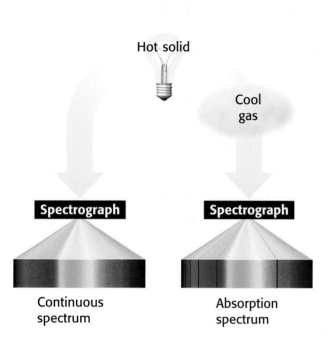

Hot solid

Cool gas

Spectrograph

Spectrograph

Continuous spectrum

Absorption spectrum

Figure 3 *A continuous spectrum (left) shows all colors while an absorption spectrum (right) absorbs some colors. Black lines appear in the spectrum where colors are absorbed.*

CONNECTION TO Biology

Rods, Cones, and Stars

WRITING SKILL Have you ever wondered why it's hard to see the different colors of stars? Our eyes are not sensitive to colors when light levels are low. There are two types of light-sensitive cells in the eye: rods and cones. Research the functions of rods and cones. In your **science journal,** write a paragraph that explains why we can't see colors well in low light.

Trapping the Light—Cosmic Detective Work

Like an element that is charged by an electric current, a star also produces a spectrum. However, while the spectrum of an electrically charged element is made of bright emission lines, a star's spectrum is made of dark emission lines. A star's atmosphere absorbs certain colors of light in the spectrum, which causes black lines to appear.

Identifying Elements Using Dark Lines

Because a star's atmosphere absorbs colors of light instead of emitting them, the spectrum of a star is called an *absorption spectrum*. An absorption spectrum is produced when light from a hot solid or dense gas passes through a cooler gas. Therefore, a star gives off an absorption spectrum because a star's atmosphere is cooler than the inner layers of the star. The black lines of a star's spectrum represent places where less light gets through. **Figure 3** compares a continuous spectrum and an absorption spectrum. What do you notice about the absorption spectrum that is different?

The pattern of lines in a star's absorption spectrum shows some of the elements that are in the star's atmosphere. If a star were made of one element, we could easily identify the element from the star's absorption spectrum. But a star is a mixture of elements and all the different sets of lines for a star's elements appear together in its spectrum. Sorting the patterns is often a puzzle.

✓ **Reading Check** What does a star's absorption spectrum show?

Classifying Stars

In the 1800s, astronomers started to collect and classify the spectra of many stars. At first, letters were assigned to each type of spectra. Stars were classified according to the elements of which they were made. Later, scientists realized that the stars were classified in the wrong order.

Differences in Temperature

Stars are now classified by how hot they are. Temperature differences between stars result in color differences that you can see. For example, the original class O stars are blue—the hottest stars. Look at **Table 1.** Notice that the stars are arranged in order from highest temperature to lowest temperature.

Table 1 Types of Stars

Class	Color	Surface temperature (°C)	Elements detected	Examples of stars
O	blue	above 30,000	helium	10 Lacertae
B	blue-white	10,000–30,000	helium and hydrogen	Rigel, Spica
A	blue-white	7,500–10,000	hydrogen	Vega, Sirius
F	yellow-white	6,000–7,500	hydrogen and heavier elements	Canopus, Procyon
G	yellow	5,000–6,000	calcium and other metals	the sun, Capella
K	orange	3,500–5,000	calcium and molecules	Arcturus, Aldebaran
M	red	less than 3,500	molecules	Betelgeuse, Antares

Differences in Brightness

With only their eyes to aid them, early astronomers created a system to classify stars based on their brightness. They called the brightest stars in the sky *first-magnitude* stars and the dimmest stars *sixth-magnitude* stars. But when they began to use telescopes, astronomers were able to see many stars that had been too dim to see before. Rather than replace the old system of magnitudes, they added to it. Positive numbers represent dimmer stars, and negative numbers represent brighter stars. For example, by using large telescopes, astronomers can see stars as dim as 29th magnitude. And the brightest star in the night sky, Sirius, has a magnitude of -1.4. The Big Dipper, shown in **Figure 4,** contains both bright stars and dim stars.

Figure 4 *The Big Dipper contains both bright stars and dim stars. What is the magnitude of the brightest star in the Big Dipper?*

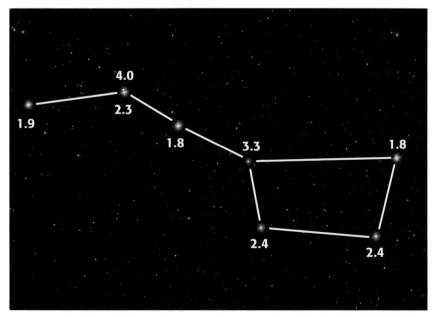

Stargazing

WRITING SKILL Someone looking at the night sky in a city would not see as many stars as someone looking at the sky in the country. With a parent, research why this is true. Try to find a place near your home that would be ideal for stargazing. If you find one, schedule a night to stargaze. Write down what you see in the night sky.

Figure 5 *You can estimate how far away each street light is by looking at its apparent brightness. Does this process work when estimating the distance of stars from Earth?*

apparent magnitude the brightness of a star as seen from the Earth

absolute magnitude the brightness that a star would have at a distance of 32.6 light-years from Earth

Starlight, Star Bright

Magnitude is used to show how bright one object is compared with another object. Every five magnitudes is equal to a factor of 100 times in brightness. The brightest blue stars, for example, have an absolute magnitude of −10. The sun has an absolute magnitude of about +5. How much brighter is a blue star than the sun? Because each five magnitudes is a factor of 100 and the blue star is 15 magnitudes greater than the sun, the blue star must be 100 × 100 × 100, or 1,000,000 (1 million), times brighter than the sun!

How Bright Is That Star?

If you look at a row of street lights, such as those shown in **Figure 5,** do they all look the same? Of course not! The nearest ones look bright, and the farthest ones look dim.

Apparent Magnitude

The brightness of a light or star is called **apparent magnitude.** If you measure the brightness of a street light with a light meter, you will find that the light's brightness depends on the square of the ratio between the light and the light meter. For example, a light that is 10 m away from you will appear 4 (2×2, or 2^2) times brighter than a light that is 20 m away from you. The same light will appear 9 (3×3, or 3^2) times brighter than a light that is 30 m away. But unlike street lights, some stars are brighter than other stars because of their size or energy output, not because of their distance from Earth. So, how can you tell how bright a star is and why?

Reading Check What is apparent magnitude?

Absolute Magnitude

Astronomers use a star's apparent magnitude and its distance from Earth to calculate its absolute magnitude. **Absolute magnitude** is the actual brightness of a star. If all stars were the same distance away, their absolute magnitudes would be the same as their apparent magnitudes. The sun, for example, has an absolute magnitude of +4.8, which is ordinary for a star. But because the sun is so close to Earth, the sun's apparent magnitude is −26.8, which makes it the brightest object in the sky.

Figure 6 Measuring a Star's Parallax

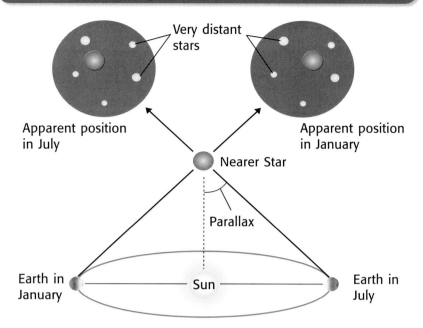

Very distant stars

Apparent position in July

Apparent position in January

Nearer Star

Parallax

Earth in January

Sun

Earth in July

light-year the distance that light travels in one year; about 9.5 trillion kilometers

parallax an apparent shift in the position of an object when viewed from different locations

Distance to the Stars

Because stars are so far away, astronomers use light-years to measure the distances from Earth to the stars. A **light-year** is the distance that light travels in one year. Obviously, it would be easier to give the distance to the North Star as 431 light-years than as 4,080,000,000,000,000 km. But how do astronomers measure a star's distance from Earth?

Stars near the Earth seem to move, while more-distant stars seem to stay in one place as Earth revolves around the sun, as shown in **Figure 6.** A star's apparent shift in position is called **parallax.** Notice that the location of the nearer star in **Figure 6** seems to shift in relation to the pattern of more-distant stars. This shift can be seen only through telescopes. Astronomers use parallax and simple trigonometry (a type of math) to find the actual distance to stars that are close to Earth.

Reading Check What is a light-year?

Motions of Stars

As you know, daytime and nighttime are caused by the Earth's rotation. The Earth's tilt and revolution around the sun cause the seasons. During each season, the Earth faces a different part of the sky at night. Look again at **Figure 6.** In January, the Earth's night side faces a different part of the sky than it faces in July. This is why you see a different set of constellations at different times of the year.

Not All Thumbs!

1. Hold your thumb in front of your face at arm's length.

2. Close one eye, and focus on an **object** some distance behind your thumb.

3. Slowly turn your head side to side a small amount. Notice how your thumb seems to be moving compared with the background you are looking at.

4. Now, move your thumb in close to your face, and move your head the same amount. Does your thumb seem to move more?

Figure 7 *As Earth rotates on its axis, the stars appear to rotate around Polaris.*

For another activity related to this chapter, go to **go.hrw.com** and type in the keyword **HZ5UNVW.**

The Apparent Motion of Stars

Because of Earth's rotation, the sun appears to move across the sky. Likewise, if you look at the night sky long enough, the stars also appear to move. In fact, at night you can observe that the whole sky is rotating above us. Look at **Figure 7.** All the stars you see appear to rotate around Polaris, the North Star, which is almost directly above Earth's North Pole. Because of Earth's rotation, all of the stars in the sky appear to make one complete circle around Polaris every 24 h.

The Actual Motion of Stars

You now know that the apparent motion of the sun and stars in our sky is due to Earth's rotation. But each star is also moving in space. Because stars are so distant, however, their actual motion is hard to see. If you could put thousands of years into one hour, a star's movement would be obvious. **Figure 8** shows how familiar star patterns slowly change their shapes.

✓ Reading Check Why is the actual motion of stars hard to see?

Figure 8 *Over time, the shapes of star patterns, such as the Big Dipper and other groups, change.*

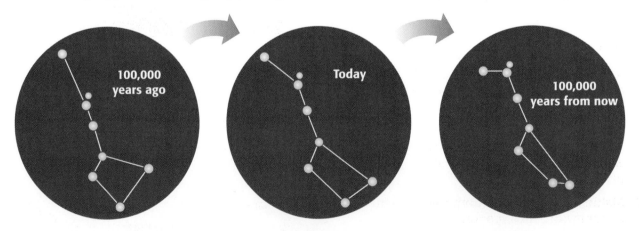

Summary

- The color of a star depends on its temperature. Hot stars are blue. Cool stars are red.
- The spectrum of a star shows the composition of a star.
- Scientists classify stars by temperature and brightness.
- Apparent magnitude is the brightness of a star as seen from Earth.

- Absolute magnitude is the measured brightness of a star at a distance of 32.6 light-years.
- Astronomers use parallax and trigonometry to measure distances from Earth to stars.
- Stars appear to move because of Earth's rotation. However, the actual motion of stars is very hard to see because stars are so distant.

Using Key Terms

1. Use the following terms in the same sentence: *apparent magnitude* and *absolute magnitude*.

2. Use each of the following terms in a separate sentence: *spectrum, light-year,* and *parallax*.

Understanding Key Ideas

3. When you look at white light through a glass prism, you see a rainbow of colors called a
   a. spectograph.
   b. spectrum.
   c. parallax.
   d. light-year.

4. Class F stars are
   a. blue.
   b. yellow.
   c. yellow-white.
   d. red.

5. Describe how scientists classify stars.

6. Explain how color indicates the temperature of a star.

Critical Thinking

7. **Applying Concepts** If a certain star displayed a large parallax, what could you say about the star's distance from Earth?

8. **Making Comparisons** Compare a continuous spectrum with an absorption spectrum. Then, explain how an absorption spectrum can identify a star's composition.

9. **Making Comparisons** Compare apparent motion with actual motion.

Interpreting Graphics

10. Look at the two figures below. How many hours passed between the first image and the second image? Explain your answer.

SCiLINKS.

NSTA
Developed and maintained by the
National Science Teachers Association

For a variety of links related to this chapter, go to www.scilinks.org

Topic: Stars
SciLinks code: HSM1448

The Life Cycle of Stars

Some stars exist for billions of years. But how are they born? And what happens when a star dies?

Because stars exist for billions of years, scientists cannot observe a star throughout its entire life. Therefore, scientists have developed theories about the life cycle of stars by studying them in different stages of development.

READING WARM-UP

Objectives

● Describe different types of stars.
● Describe the quantities that are plotted in the H-R diagram.
● Explain how stars at different stages in their life cycle appear on the H-R diagram.

Terms to Learn

red giant   supernova
white dwarf   neutron star
H-R diagram   pulsar
main sequence   black hole

READING STRATEGY

Paired Summarizing Read this section silently. In pairs, take turns summarizing the material. Stop to discuss ideas that seem confusing.

The Beginning and End of Stars

A star enters the first stage of its life cycle as a ball of gas and dust. Gravity pulls the gas and dust together into a sphere. As the sphere becomes denser, it gets hotter and the hydrogen changes to helium in a process called *nuclear fusion.*

As stars get older, they lose some of their material. Stars usually lose material slowly, but sometimes they can lose material in a big explosion. Either way, when a star dies, much of its material returns to space. In space, some of the material combines with more gas and dust to form new stars.

Different Types of Stars

Stars can be classified by their size, mass, brightness, color, temperature, spectrum, and age. Some types of stars include *main-sequence stars*, *giants*, *supergiants*, and *white dwarf stars*. A star can be classified as one type of star early in its life cycle and then can be classified as another star when it gets older. For example, the star shown in **Figure 1** has reached the final stage in its life cycle. It has run out of fuel, which has caused the central parts of the star to collapse inward.

Figure 1 *This star (center) has entered the last stage of its life cycle.*

Main-Sequence Stars

After a star forms, it enters the second and longest stage of its life cycle known as the main sequence. During this stage, energy is generated in the core of the star as hydrogen atoms fuse into helium atoms. This process releases an enormous amount of energy. The size of a main-sequence star will change very little as long as the star has a continuous supply of hydrogen atoms to fuse into helium atoms.

Giants and Supergiants

After the main-sequence stage, a star can enter the third stage of its life cycle. In this third stage, a star can become a red giant. A **red giant** is a star that expands and cools once it uses all of its hydrogen. Eventually, the loss of hydrogen causes the center of the star to shrink. As the center of the star shrinks, the atmosphere of the star grows very large and cools to form a red giant or a red supergiant, as shown in **Figure 2.** Red giants can be 10 or more times bigger than the sun. Supergiants are at least 100 times bigger than the sun.

✓ Reading Check What is the difference between a red giant star and a red supergiant star? *(See the Appendix for answers to Reading Checks.)*

White Dwarfs

In the final stages of a star's life cycle, a star that has the same mass as the sun or smaller can be classified as a white dwarf. A **white dwarf** is a small hot star that is the leftover center of an older star. A white dwarf has no hydrogen left and can no longer generate energy by fusing hydrogen atoms into helium atoms. White dwarfs can shine for billions of years before they cool completely.

Figure 2 *The red supergiant star Antares is shown above. Antares is located in the constellation of Scorpius.*

red giant a large, reddish star late in its life cycle

white dwarf a small, hot, dim star that is the leftover center of an old star

CONNECTION TO Astronomy

WRITING SKILL **Long Live the Sun** Our sun probably took about 10 million years to become a main-sequence star. It has been shining for about 5 billion years. In another 5 billion years, our sun will burn up most of its hydrogen and expand to become a red giant. When this change happens, the sun's diameter will increase. How will this change affect Earth and our solar system? Use the Internet or library resources to find out what might happen as the sun gets older and how the changes in the sun might affect our solar system. Gather your findings, and write a report on what you find out about the life cycle the sun.

A Tool for Studying Stars

In 1911, a Danish astronomer named Ejnar Hertzsprung (IE nawr HUHRTS sproong) compared the brightness and temperature of stars on a graph. Two years later, American astronomer Henry Norris Russell made some similar graphs. Although these astronomers used different data, they had similar results. The combination of their ideas is now called the Hertzsprung-Russell diagram, or H-R diagram. The **H-R diagram** is a graph that shows the relationship between a star's surface temperature and its absolute magnitude. Over the years, the H-R diagram has become a tool for studying the lives of stars. It shows not only how stars are classified by brightness and temperature but also how stars change over time.

H-R diagram Hertzsprung-Russell diagram, a graph that shows the relationship between a star's surface temperature and absolute magnitude

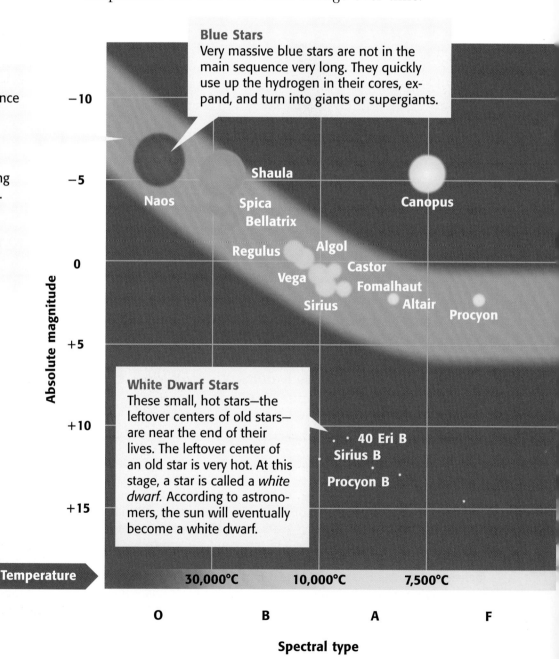

Main-Sequence Stars
Stars in the main sequence form a band that runs along the middle of the H-R diagram. The sun is a main-sequence star. The sun has been shining for about 5 billion years. Scientists think the sun is in midlife and that it will remain on the main sequence for another 5 billion years.

Blue Stars
Very massive blue stars are not in the main sequence very long. They quickly use up the hydrogen in their cores, expand, and turn into giants or supergiants.

White Dwarf Stars
These small, hot stars—the leftover centers of old stars—are near the end of their lives. The leftover center of an old star is very hot. At this stage, a star is called a *white dwarf.* According to astronomers, the sun will eventually become a white dwarf.

Absolute magnitude

−10
−5
0
+5
+10
+15

Shaula
Naos
Spica
Bellatrix
Regulus
Algol
Vega
Castor
Fomalhaut
Sirius
Altair
Procyon
Canopus
40 Eri B
Sirius B
Procyon B

Temperature

30,000°C   10,000°C   7,500°C

O   B   A   F

Spectral type

Reading the H-R Diagram

The modern H-R diagram is shown below. Temperature is given along the bottom of the diagram and absolute magnitude, or brightness, is given along the left side. Hot (blue) stars are located on the left, and cool (red) stars are on the right. Bright stars are at the top, and dim stars are at the bottom. The brightest stars are 1 million times brighter than the sun. The dimmest stars are 1/10,000 as bright as the sun. The diagonal pattern on the H-R diagram where most stars lie, is called the **main sequence.** A star spends most of its lifetime in the main sequence. As main-sequence stars age, they move up and to the right on the H-R diagram to become giants or supergiants and then down and to the left to become white dwarfs.

main sequence the location on the H-R diagram where most stars lie

Giants and Supergiants
When a star runs out of hydrogen in its core, the center of the star shrinks inward and the outer parts expand outward. For a star the size of our sun, the star's atmosphere will grow very large and become cool. When this change happens, the star becomes a *red giant*. If the star is very massive, it becomes a supergiant.

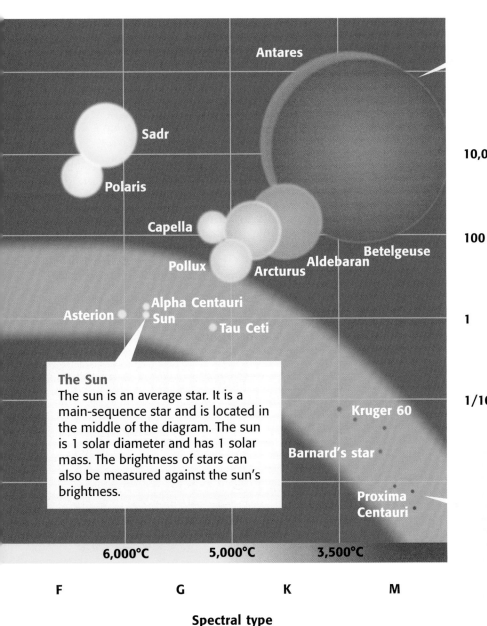

The Sun
The sun is an average star. It is a main-sequence star and is located in the middle of the diagram. The sun is 1 solar diameter and has 1 solar mass. The brightness of stars can also be measured against the sun's brightness.

Red Dwarf Stars
At the lower end of the main sequence are the red dwarf stars, which are low-mass stars. Low-mass stars remain on the main sequence a long time. The stars that have the lowest mass are among the oldest stars in the universe.

When Stars Get Old

Although stars may stay on the main sequence for a long time, they don't stay there forever. Average stars, such as the sun, become red giants and then white dwarfs. However, stars that are more massive than the sun may explode with such intensity that they become a variety of strange objects such as supernovas, neutron stars, pulsars, and black holes.

Supernovas

Massive blue stars use their hydrogen much faster than stars like the sun do. Therefore, blue stars generate more energy than stars like the sun do, which makes blue stars very hot and blue! And compared with other stars, blue stars don't have long lives. At the end of its life, a blue star may explode in a large, bright flash called a *supernova*. A **supernova** is a gigantic explosion in which a massive star collapses. The explosion is so powerful that it can be brighter than an entire galaxy for several days. The ringed structure shown in **Figure 3** is the result of a supernova explosion.

Neutron Stars and Pulsars

After a supernova occurs, the materials in the center of a supernova are squeezed together to form a new star. This new star is about two times the mass of the sun. The particles inside the star's core are forced together to form neutrons. A star that has collapsed under gravity to the point at which all of its particles are neutrons is called a **neutron star.**

If a neutron star is spinning, it is called a **pulsar.** A pulsar sends out a beam of radiation that spins very rapidly. The beam is detected on Earth by radio telescopes as rapid clicks, or pulses.

supernova a gigantic explosion in which a massive star collapses and throws its outer layers into space

neutron star a star that has collapsed under gravity to the point that the electrons and protons have smashed together to form neutrons

pulsar a rapidly spinning neutron star that emits rapid pulses of radio and optical energy

Figure 3 Explosion of a Supernova

Supernova 1987A was the first supernova visible to the unaided eye in 400 years. The first image shows what the original star must have looked like only a few hours before the explosion. Today, the star's remains form a double ring of gas and dust, as shown at right.

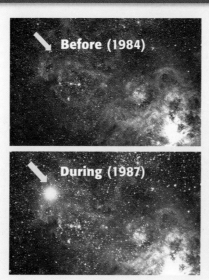

Before (1984)

During (1987)

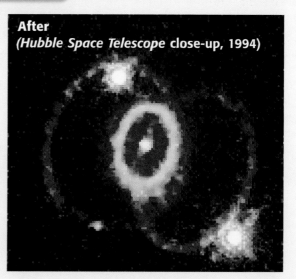

After
(*Hubble Space Telescope* close-up, 1994)

Black Holes

Sometimes the leftovers of a supernova are so massive that they collapse to form a black hole. A **black hole** is an object that is so massive that even light cannot escape its gravity. So, it is called a *black hole*. A black hole doesn't gobble up other stars like some movies show. Because black holes do not give off light, locating them is difficult. If a star is nearby, some gas or dust from the star will spiral into the black hole and give off X rays. These X rays allow astronomers to detect the existence of black holes.

black hole an object so massive and dense that even light cannot escape its gravity

✓ **Reading Check** What is a black hole? How do astronomers detect the presence of black holes?

SECTION Review

Summary

- New stars form from the material of old stars that have gone through their lives.
- Types of stars include main-sequence stars, giants and supergiants, and white dwarf stars.
- The H-R diagram shows the brightness of a star in relation to the temperature of a star. It also shows the life cycle of stars.
- Most stars are main-sequence stars.
- Massive stars become supernovas. Their cores can change into neutron stars or black holes.

Using Key Terms

For each pair of terms, explain how the meanings of the terms differ.

1. *white dwarf* and *red giant*

2. *supernova* and *neutron star*

3. *pulsar* and *black hole*

Understanding Key Ideas

4. The sun is a
   a. white dwarf.
   b. main-sequence star.
   c. red giant.
   d. red dwarf.

5. A star begins as a ball of gas and dust pulled together by
   a. black holes.
   b. electrons and protons.
   c. heavy metals.
   d. gravity.

6. Are blue stars young or old? How can you tell?

7. In main-sequence stars, what is the relationship between brightness and temperature?

8. Arrange the following stages in order of their appearance in the life cycle of a star: white dwarf, red giant, and main-sequence star. Explain your answer.

Math Skills

9. The sun's present radius is 700,000 km. If the sun's radius increased by 150 times, what would its radius be?

Critical Thinking

10. **Applying Concepts** Given that there are more low-mass stars than high-mass stars in the universe, do you think there are more white dwarfs or more black holes in the universe? Explain.

11. **Analyzing Processes** Describe what might happen to a star after it becomes a supernova.

12. **Evaluating Data** How does the H-R diagram explain the life cycle of a star?

SCLINKS®

NSTA
Developed and maintained by the
National Science Teachers Association

For a variety of links related to this chapter, go to www.scilinks.org

Topic: Supernova
SciLinks code: HSM1482

SECTION

3

galaxy a collection of stars, dust, and gas bound together by gravity

Galaxies

Your complete address is part of a much larger system than your street, city, state, country, and even the planet Earth. You also live in the Milky Way galaxy.

Large groups of stars, dust, and gas are called **galaxies.** Galaxies come in a variety of sizes and shapes. The largest galaxies contain more than a trillion stars. Astronomers don't count the stars, of course. They estimate how many sun-sized stars the galaxy might have by studying the size and brightness of the galaxy.

Types of Galaxies

There are many different types of galaxies. Edwin Hubble, the astronomer for whom the *Hubble Space Telescope* is named, began to classify galaxies, mostly by their shapes, in the 1920s. Astronomers still use the galaxy classification that Hubble developed.

Spiral Galaxies

When someone says the word *galaxy,* most people probably think of a spiral galaxy. *Spiral galaxies,* such as the one shown in **Figure 1,** have a bulge at the center and spiral arms. The spiral arms are made up of gas, dust, and new stars that have formed in these denser regions of gas and dust.

✓ **Reading Check** What are two characteristics of spiral galaxies? What makes up the arms of a spiral galaxy? (*See the Appendix for answers to Reading Checks*.)

Figure 1 **Types of Galaxies**

▼ **Spiral Galaxy**
The Andromeda galaxy is a spiral galaxy that looks similar to what our galaxy, the Milky Way, is thought to look like.

The Milky Way

It is hard to tell what type of galaxy we live in because the gas, dust, and stars keep astronomers from having a good view of our galaxy. Observing other galaxies and making measurements inside our galaxy, the Milky Way, has led astronomers to think that our solar system is in a spiral galaxy.

Elliptical Galaxies

About one-third of all galaxies are simply massive blobs of stars. Many look like spheres, and others are more stretched out. Because we don't know how they are oriented, some of these galaxies could be cucumber shaped, with the round end facing our galaxy. These galaxies are called *elliptical galaxies*. Elliptical galaxies usually have very bright centers and very little dust and gas. Elliptical galaxies contain mostly old stars. Because there is so little free-flowing gas in an elliptical galaxy, few new stars form. Some elliptical galaxies, such as M87, shown in **Figure 1,** are huge and are called *giant elliptical galaxies*. Other elliptical galaxies are much smaller and are called *dwarf elliptical galaxies*.

Irregular Galaxies

When Hubble first classified galaxies, he had a group of leftovers. He named the leftovers "irregulars." *Irregular galaxies* are galaxies that don't fit into any other class. As their name suggests, their shape is irregular. Many of these galaxies, such as the Large Magellanic Cloud, shown in **Figure 1,** are close companions of large spiral galaxies. The large spiral galaxies may be distorting the shape of these irregular galaxies.

▼ **Elliptical Galaxy**
Unlike the Milky Way, the galaxy known as M87 has no spiral arms.

▼ **Irregular Galaxy**
The Large Magellanic Cloud, an irregular galaxy, is located within our galactic neighborhood.

Contents of Galaxies

Galaxies are composed of billions of stars and some planetary systems, too. Some of these stars form large features, such as gas clouds and star clusters, as shown in **Figure 2.**

Gas Clouds

The Latin word for "cloud" is *nebula*. In space, **nebulas** (or nebulae) are large clouds of gas and dust. Some types of nebulas glow, while others absorb light and hide stars. Still, other nebulas reflect starlight and produce some amazing images. Some nebulas are regions in which new stars form. **Figure 2** shows part of the Eagle nebula. Spiral galaxies usually contain nebulas, but elliptical galaxies contain very few.

Star Clusters

Globular clusters are groups of older stars. A **globular cluster** is a group of stars that looks like a ball, as shown in **Figure 2.** There may be up to one million stars in a globular cluster. Globular clusters are located in a spherical *halo* that surrounds spiral galaxies such as the Milky Way. Globular clusters are also common near giant elliptical galaxies.

Open clusters are groups of closely grouped stars that are usually located along the spiral disk of a galaxy. Newly formed open clusters have many bright blue stars, as shown in **Figure 2.** There may be a few hundred to a few thousand stars in an open cluster.

Reading Check What is the difference between a globular cluster and an open cluster?

nebula a large cloud of dust and gas in interstellar space; a region in space where stars are born or where stars explode at the end of their lives

globular cluster a tight group of stars that looks like a ball and contains up to 1 million stars

open cluster a group of stars that are close together relative to surrounding stars

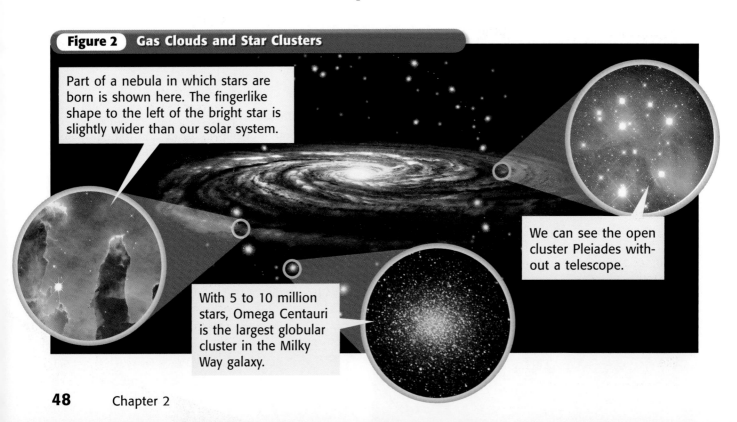

Figure 2 Gas Clouds and Star Clusters

Part of a nebula in which stars are born is shown here. The fingerlike shape to the left of the bright star is slightly wider than our solar system.

With 5 to 10 million stars, Omega Centauri is the largest globular cluster in the Milky Way galaxy.

We can see the open cluster Pleiades without a telescope.

Origin of Galaxies

Scientists investigate the early universe by observing objects that are extremely far away in space. Because it takes time for light to travel through space, looking through a telescope is like looking back in time. Looking at distant galaxies reveals what early galaxies looked like. This information gives scientists an idea of how galaxies change over time and may give them insight about what caused the galaxies to form.

Quasars

Among the most distant objects are quasars. **Quasars** are starlike sources of light that are extremely far away. They are among the most powerful energy sources in the universe. Some scientists think that quasars may be caused by massive black holes in the cores of some galaxies. **Figure 3** shows a quasar that is 6 billion light-years away.

✓ **Reading Check** What are quasars? What do some scientists think quasars might be?

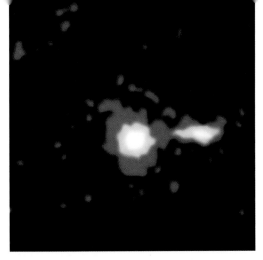

Figure 3 *The quasar known as PKS 0637-752 is as massive as 10 billion suns.*

quasar a very luminous, starlike object that generates energy at a high rate; quasars are thought to be the most distant objects in the universe

---

SECTION Review

Summary

● Edwin Hubble classified galaxies according to their shape including spiral, elliptical, and irregular galaxies.

● Some galaxies consist of nebulas and star clusters.

● Nebulas are large clouds of gas and dust. Globular clusters are tightly grouped stars. Open clusters are closely grouped stars.

● Scientists look at distant galaxies to learn what early galaxies looked like.

Using Key Terms

1. Use the following terms in the same sentence: *nebula, globular cluster,* and *open cluster.*

Understanding Key Ideas

2. Arrange the following galaxies in order of decreasing size: spiral, giant elliptical, dwarf elliptical, and irregular.

3. All of the following are shapes used to classify galaxies EXCEPT
   a. elliptical.
   b. irregular.
   c. spiral.
   d. triangular.

Critical Thinking

4. **Making Comparisons** Describe the difference between an elliptical galaxy and a globular cluster.

5. **Identifying Relationships** Explain how looking through a telescope is like looking back in time.

Math Skills

6. The quasar known as PKS 0637-752 is 6 billion light-years away from Earth. The North Star is 431 light-years away from Earth. What is the ratio of the distances in kilometers these two celestial objects are from Earth? (Hint: One light-year is equal to 9.46 trillion km.)

SCiLINKS.

NSTA
Developed and maintained by the
National Science Teachers Association

For a variety of links related to this chapter, go to www.scilinks.org

Topic: Galaxies
SciLinks code: HSM0632

49

Formation of the Universe

Imagine explosions, bright lights, and intense energy. Does that scene sound like an action movie? This scene could also describe a theory about the formation of the universe.

The study of the origin, structure, and future of the universe is called **cosmology.** Like other scientific theories, theories about the beginning and end of the universe must be tested by observations or experiments.

Universal Expansion

To understand how the universe formed, scientists study the movement of galaxies. Careful measurements have shown that most galaxies are moving apart.

A Raisin-Bread Model

To understand how the galaxies are moving, imagine a loaf of raisin bread before it is baked. Inside the dough, each raisin is a certain distance from every other raisin. As the dough gets warm and rises, it expands and all of the raisins begin to move apart. No matter which raisin you observe, the other raisins are moving farther away from it. The universe, like the rising bread dough, is expanding. Think of the raisins as galaxies. As the universe expands, the galaxies move farther apart.

The Big Bang Theory

With the discovery that the universe is expanding, scientists began to wonder what it would be like to watch the formation of the universe in reverse. The universe would appear to be contracting, not expanding. All matter would eventually come together at a single point. Thinking about what would happen if all of the matter in the universe were squeezed into such a small space led scientists to the big bang theory.

READING WARM-UP

Objectives

● Describe the big bang theory.

● Explain evidence used to support the big bang theory.

● Describe the structure of the universe.

● Describe two ways scientists calculate the age of the universe.

● Explain what will happen if the universe expands forever.

Terms to Learn

cosmology
big bang theory

READING STRATEGY

Prediction Guide Before reading this section, write the title of each heading in this section. Next, under each heading, write what you think you will learn.

cosmology the study of the origin, properties, processes, and evolution of the universe

Figure 1 *Some astronomers think the big bang caused the universe to expand in all directions.*

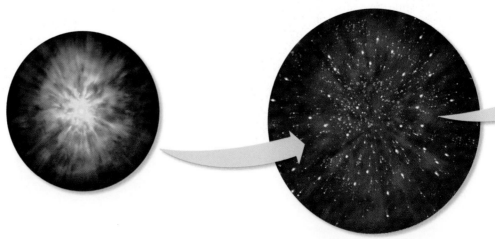

A Tremendous Explosion

The theory that the universe began with a tremendous explosion is called the **big bang theory.** According to the theory, 13.7 billion years ago all the contents of the universe was compressed under extreme pressure, temperature, and density in a very tiny spot. Then, the universe rapidly expanded, and matter began to come together and form galaxies. **Figure 1** illustrates what the big bang might have looked like.

Cosmic Background Radiation

In 1964, two scientists using a huge antenna accidentally found radiation coming from all directions in space. One explanation for this radiation is that it is *cosmic background radiation* left over from the big bang. To understand the connection between the big bang theory and cosmic background radiation, think about a kitchen oven. When an oven door is left open after the oven has been used, thermal energy is transferred throughout the kitchen and the oven cools. Eventually, the room and the oven are the same temperature. According to the big bang theory, the thermal energy from the original explosion was distributed in every direction as the universe expanded. This cosmic background radiation now fills all of space.

✓ Reading Check Explain the relationship between cosmic background radiation and the big bang theory. (*See the Appendix for answers to Reading Checks.*)

big bang theory the theory that states the universe began with a tremendous explosion 13.7 billion years ago

Structure of the Universe

From our home on Earth, the universe stretches out farther than astronomers can see with their most advanced instruments. The universe contains a variety of objects. But these objects in the universe are not simply scattered through the universe in a random pattern. The universe has a structure that is loosely repeated over and over again.

A Cosmic Repetition

Every object in the universe is part of a larger system. As illustrated in **Figure 2,** a cluster or group of galaxies can be made up of smaller star clusters and galaxies. Galaxies, such as the Milky Way, can include planetary systems, such as our solar system. Earth is part of our solar system. Although our solar system is the planetary system that we are most familiar with, other planets have been detected in orbit around other stars. Scientists think that planetary systems are common in the universe.

How Old Is the Universe?

One way scientists can calculate the age of the universe is to measure the distance from Earth to various galaxies. By using these distances, scientists can estimate the age of the universe and predict its rate of expansion.

Another way to estimate the age of the universe is to calculate the ages of old, nearby stars. Because the universe must be at least as old as the oldest stars it contains, the ages of the stars provide a clue to the age of the universe.

✓ *Reading Check* What is one way that scientists calculate the age of the universe?

Figure 2 *Every object in the universe is part of a larger system. Earth is part of our solar system, which is in turn part of the Milky Way galaxy.*

A Forever Expanding Universe

What will happen to the universe? As the galaxies move farther apart, they get older and stop forming stars. The farther galaxies move apart from each other, the less visible to us they will become. The expansion of the universe depends on how much matter the universe contains. Scientists predict that if there is enough matter, gravity could eventually stop the expansion of the universe. If the universe stops expanding, it could start collapsing to its original state. This process would be a reverse of what might have happened during the big bang.

However, scientists now think that there may not be enough matter in the universe, so the universe will continue to expand forever. Therefore, stars will age and die, and the universe will probably become cold and dark after many billions of years. Even after the universe becomes cold and dark, it will continue to expand forever.

Reading Check If the universe expanded to the point at which gravity stopped the expansion, what would happen? What will happen if the expansion of the universe continues forever?

CONNECTION TO Physics

WRITING SKILL **Origin of the Universe** The big bang theory is one scientific theory about the origin of the universe. Use library resources to research these other scientific theories. In your **science journal,** describe in your own words the different theories of the origin of the universe. Use charts or tables to examine and evaluate these differences.

SECTION Review

Summary

● Observations show that the universe is expanding.

● The big bang theory states that the universe began with an explosion about 13.7 billion years ago.

● Cosmic background radiation helps support the big bang theory.

● Scientists use different ways to calculate the age of the universe.

● Scientists think that the universe may expand forever.

Using Key Terms

1. In your own words, write a definition for the following terms: *cosmology* and *big bang theory*.

Understanding Key Ideas

2. Describe two ways scientists calculate the age of the universe.

3. The expansion of the universe can be compared to
   a. cosmology.
   b. raisin bread baking in an oven.
   c. thermal energy leaving an oven as the oven cools.
   d. bread pudding.

4. How does cosmic background radiation support the big bang theory?

5. What do scientists think will eventually happen to the universe?

Math Skills

6. The North Star is 4.08×10^{12} km from Earth. What is this number written in its long form?

Critical Thinking

7. **Applying Concepts** Explain how every object in the universe is part of a larger system.

8. **Analyzing Ideas** Why do scientists think that the universe will expand forever?

SCiLINKS **NSTA**
Developed and maintained by the National Science Teachers Association

For a variety of links related to this chapter, go to www.scilinks.org

Topic: Structure of the Universe
SciLinks code: HSM1469

Skills Practice Lab

Red Hot, or Not?

When you look at the night sky, some stars are brighter than others. Some are even different colors. For example, Betelgeuse, a bright star in the constellation Orion, glows red. Sirius, one of the brightest stars in the sky, glows bluish white. Astronomers use color to estimate the temperature of stars. In this activity, you will experiment with a light bulb and some batteries to discover what the color of a glowing object reveals about the temperature of the object.

Discover what the color of a glowing object reveals about the temperature of the object.

Describe how the color and temperature of a star are related.

- battery, D cell (2)
- battery, D cell, weak
- flashlight bulb
- tape, electrical
- wire, insulated copper, with ends stripped, 20 cm long (2)

Ask a Question

1 How are the color and temperature of a star related?

Form a Hypothesis

2 On a sheet of paper, change the question above into a statement that gives your best guess about the relationship between a star's color and temperature.

Test the Hypothesis

3 Tape one end of an insulated copper wire to the positive pole of the weak D cell. Tape one end of the second wire to the negative pole.

4 Touch the free end of each wire to the light bulb. Hold one of the wires against the bottom tip of the light bulb. Hold the second wire against the side of the metal portion of the bulb. The bulb should light.

5 Record the color of the filament in the light bulb. Carefully touch your hand to the bulb. Observe the temperature of the bulb. Record your observations.

6 Repeat steps 3–5 with one of the two fresh D cells.

7 Use the electrical tape to connect two fresh D cells so that the positive pole of the first cell is connected to the negative pole of the second cell.

8 Repeat steps 3–5 using the fresh D cells that are taped together.

Analyze the Results

1 **Describing Events** What was the color of the filament in each of the three trials? For each trial, compare the bulb temperature to the temperature of the bulb in the other two trials.

2 **Analyzing Results** What information does the color of a star tell you about the star?

3 **Classifying** What color are stars that have relatively high surface temperatures? What color are stars that have relatively low surface temperatures?

Draw Conclusions

4 **Applying Conclusions** Arrange the following stars in order from highest to lowest surface temperature: Sirius, which is bluish white; Aldebaran, which is orange; Procyon, which is yellow-white; Capella, which is yellow; and Betelgeuse, which is red.

Chapter Review

USING KEY TERMS

The statements below are false. For each statement, replace the underlined term to make a true statement.

1 The distance that light travels in space in 1 year is called <u>apparent magnitude</u>.

2 <u>Globular clusters</u> are groups of stars that are usually located along the spiral disk of a galaxy.

3 Galaxies that have very bright centers and very little dust and gas are called <u>spiral galaxies</u>.

4 When you look at white light through a glass prism, you see a rainbow of colors called a <u>supernova</u>.

UNDERSTANDING KEY IDEAS

Multiple Choice

5 A scientist can identify a star's composition by looking at

a. the star's prism.

b. the star's continuous spectrum.

c. the star's absorption spectrum.

d. the star's color.

6 If the universe expands forever,

a. the universe will collapse.

b. the universe will repeat itself.

c. the universe will remain just as it is today.

d. stars will age and die and the universe will become cold and dark.

7 The majority of stars in our galaxy are

a. blue stars.

b. white dwarfs.

c. main-sequence stars.

d. red giants.

8 Which of the following is used to measure the distance between objects in space?

a. parallax   c. zenith

b. magnitude   d. altitude

9 Which of the following stars would be seen as the brightest star?

a. Alcyone, which has an apparent magnitude of 3

b. Alpheratz, which has an apparent magnitude of 2

c. Deneb, which has an apparent magnitude of 1

d. Rigel, which has an apparent magnitude of 0

Short Answer

10 Describe how scientists classify stars.

11 Describe the structure of the universe.

12 Explain how stars at different stages in their life cycle appear on the H-R diagram.

13 Explain the difference between the apparent motion and actual motion of stars.

14 Describe how color indicates the temperature of a star.

15 Describe two ways that scientists calculate the age of the universe.

CRITICAL THINKING

16 Concept Mapping Use the following terms to create a concept map: *main-sequence star, nebula, red giant, white dwarf, neutron star,* and *black hole.*

17 Evaluating Conclusions While looking through a telescope, you see a galaxy that doesn't appear to contain any blue stars. What kind of galaxy is it most likely to be? Explain your answer.

18 Making Comparisons Explain the differences between main-sequence stars, giant stars, supergiant stars, and white dwarfs.

19 Evaluating Data Why do astronomers use absolute magnitudes to plot stars? Why don't astronomers use apparent magnitudes to plot stars?

20 Evaluating Sources According to the big bang theory, how did the universe begin? What evidence supports this theory?

21 Evaluating Data If a certain star displayed a large parallax, what could you say about the star's distance from Earth?

The graph below shows Hubble's law, which relates how far galaxies are from Earth and how fast they are moving away from Earth. Use the graph below to answer the questions that follow.

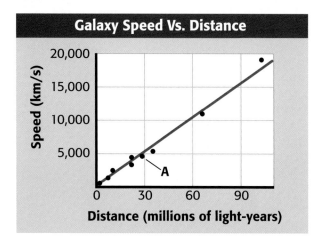

Galaxy Speed Vs. Distance

22 Look at the point that represents galaxy A in the graph. How far is galaxy A from Earth, and how fast is it moving away from Earth?

23 If a galaxy is moving away from Earth at 15,000 km/s, how far is the galaxy from Earth?

24 If a galaxy is 90,000,000 light-years from Earth, how fast is it moving away from Earth?

Chapter Review **57**

Standardized Test Preparation

Read each of the passages below. Then, answer the questions that follow each passage.

Passage 1 Quasars are some of the most puzzling objects in the sky. If viewed through an optical telescope, a quasar appears as a small, dim star. Quasars are the most distant objects that have been observed from Earth. But many quasars are hundreds of times brighter than the brightest galaxy. Because quasars are so far away from Earth and yet are very bright, they most likely emit a large amount of energy. Scientists do not yet understand exactly how quasars can emit so much energy.

1. Based on the passage, which of the following statements is a fact?
   A Quasars, unlike galaxies, include billions of bright objects.
   B Galaxies are brighter than quasars.
   C Quasars are hundreds of times brighter than the brightest galaxy.
   D Galaxies are the most distant objects observed from Earth.

2. Based on the information in the passage, what can the reader conclude?
   F Quasars are the same as galaxies.
   G Quasars appear as small, dim stars, but they emit a large amount of energy.
   H Quasars can be viewed only by using an optical telescope.
   I Quasars will never be understood.

3. Why do scientists think that quasars emit a large amount of energy?
   A because quasars are the brightest stars in the universe
   B because quasars can be viewed only through an optical telescope
   C because quasars are very far away and are still bright
   D because quasars are larger than galaxies

Passage 2 If you live away from bright outdoor lights, you may be able to see a faint, narrow band of light and dark patches across the sky. This band is called the Milky Way. Our galaxy, the Milky Way, consists of stars, gases, and dust. Between the stars of the Milky Way are clouds of gas and dust called <u>interstellar matter</u>. These clouds provide materials that form new stars.

Every star that you can see in the night sky is a part of the Milky Way, because our solar system is inside the Milky Way. Because we are inside the galaxy, we cannot see the entire galaxy. But scientists can use astronomical data to create a picture of the Milky Way.

1. In the passage, what does the term *interstellar matter* mean?
   A stars in the Milky Way
   B the Milky Way
   C a narrow band of light and dark patches across the sky
   D the clouds of gas and dust between the stars in the Milky Way

2. Based on the information in the passage, what can the reader conclude?
   F The Milky Way can be seen in the night sky near a large city.
   G The entire Milky Way can be seen all at once.
   H Every star that is seen in the night sky is a part of the Milky Way.
   I Scientists have no idea what the entire Milky Way looks like.

The graph below shows the relationship between a star's age and mass. Use the graph below to answer the questions that follow.

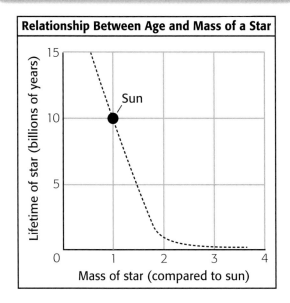

Relationship Between Age and Mass of a Star

Y-axis: Lifetime of star (billions of years)
X-axis: Mass of star (compared to sun)

1. How long does a star that has 1.2 times the mass of the sun live?

   A 10 billion years

   B 8 billion years

   C 6 billion years

   D 5 billion years

2. How long does a star that has 2 times the mass of the sun live?

   F 4 billion years

   G 1 billion years

   H 10 billion years

   I 5 billion years

3. If the sun's mass was reduced by half, how long would the sun live?

   A 2 billion years

   B 8 billion years

   C 10 billion years

   D more than 15 billion years

4. According to the graph, how long is the sun predicted to live?

   F 15 billion years

   G 10 billion years

   H 5 billion years

   I 2 billion years

Read each question below, and choose the best answer.

1. How many kilometers away from Earth is an object that is 8 light-years away from Earth? (Hint: One light-year is equal to 9.46 trillion kilometers.)

   A 77 trillion kilometers

   B 76 trillion kilometers

   C 7.66 trillion kilometers

   D 7.6 trillion kilometers

2. An astronomer observes two stars of about the same temperature and size. Alpha Centauri B is about 4 light-years away from Earth, and Sigma 2 Eridani A is about 16 light-years away from Earth. How many times as bright as Sigma 2 Eridani A does Alpha Centauri B appear? (Hint: One light-year is equal to 9.46 trillion kilometers.)

   F 2 times as bright

   G 4 times as bright

   H 16 times as bright

   I 32 times as bright

3. Star A is 5 million kilometers from Star B. What is this distance expressed in meters?

   A 0.5 m

   B 5,000 m

   C 5×10^6 m

   D 5×10^9 m

4. In the vacuum of space, light travels 3×10^8 m/s. How far does light travel in 1 h in space?

   F 3,600 m

   G 1.80×10^{10} m

   H 1.08×10^{12} m

   I 1.08×10^{16} m

5. The mass of the known universe is about 10^{23} solar masses, which is 10^{50} metric tons. How many metric tons is one solar mass?

   A 10^{27} solar masses

   B 10^{27} metric tons

   C 10^{73} solar masses

   D 10^{73} metric tons

Science in Action

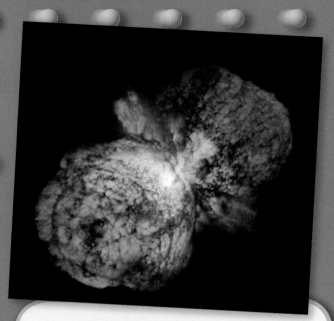

Weird Science

Holes Where Stars Once Were

An invisible phantom lurks in space, ready to swallow everything that comes near it. Once trapped in its grasp, matter is stretched, torn, and crushed into oblivion. Does this tale sound like a horror story? Guess again! Scientists call this phantom a *black hole*. As a star runs out of fuel, it cools and eventually collapses under the force of its own gravity. If the collapsing star is massive enough, it may shrink to become a black hole. The resulting gravitational attraction is so strong that even light cannot escape! Many astronomers think that black holes lie at the heart of many galaxies. Some scientists suggest that there is a giant black hole at the center of our own Milky Way.

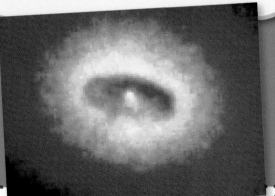

Scientific Discoveries

Eta Carinae: The Biggest Star Ever Discovered

In 1841, Eta Carinae was the second-brightest star in the night sky. Why is this observation a part of history? Eta Carinae's brightness is historic because before 1837, Eta Carinae wasn't even visible to the naked eye! Strangely, a few years later Eta Carinae faded again and disappeared from the night sky. Something unusual was happening to Eta Carinae, and scientists wanted to know what it was. As soon as scientists had telescopes with which they could see far into space, they took a closer look at Eta Carinae. Scientists discovered that this star is highly unstable and prone to violent outbursts. These outbursts, the last of which was seen in 1841, can be seen on Earth. Scientists also discovered that Eta Carinae is 150 times as big as our sun and about 4 million times as bright. Eta Carinae is the biggest and brightest star ever found!

Language Arts ACTiViTY

WRITING SKILL Can you imagine traveling through a black hole? Write a short story that describes what you would see if you led a space mission to a black hole.

Math ACTiViTY

If Eta Carinae is 8,000 light-years from our solar system, how many kilometers is Eta Carinae from our solar system? (Hint: One light-year is equal to 9.46 trillion kilometers.)

Jocelyn Bell-Burnell

Astrophysicist Imagine getting a signal from far out in space and not knowing what or whom it's coming from. That's what happened to astrophysicist Jocelyn Bell-Burnell. Bell-Burnell is known for discovering pulsars, objects in space that emit radio waves at short, regular intervals. But before she and her advisor discovered that the signals came from pulsars, they thought that the signals may have come from aliens!

Born in 1943 in Belfast, Northern Ireland, Jocelyn Bell-Burnell became interested in astronomy at an early age. At Cambridge University in 1967, Bell-Burnell, who was a graduate student, and her advisor, Anthony Hewish, completed work on a huge radio telescope designed to pick up signals from quasars. Bell-Burnell's job was to operate the telescope and analyze its chart paper recordings on a graph. Each day, the telescope recordings used 29.2 m of chart paper! After a month, Bell-Burnell noticed that the recordings showed a few "bits of scruff"—very short, pulsating radio signals—that she could not explain. Bell-Burnell and Hewish struggled to find the source of the mysterious signal. They checked the equipment and began eliminating possible sources of the signal, such as satellites, television, and radar. Shortly after finding the first signal, Bell-Burnell discovered a second. The second signal was similar to the first but came from a different position in the sky. By January 1968, Bell-Burnell had discovered two more pulsating signals. In March of 1968, her findings that the signals were from a new kind of star were published and amazed the scientific community. The scientific press named the newly discovered stars *pulsars*.

Today, Bell-Burnell is a leading expert in the field of astrophysics and the study of stars. She is currently head of the physics department at the Open University, in Milton Keynes, England.

Social Studies ACTIVITY

Use the Internet or library resources to research historical events that occurred during 1967 and 1968. Find out if the prediction that the signals from pulsars were coming from aliens affected historical events during this time.

To learn more about these Science in Action topics, visit **go.hrw.com** and type in the keyword **HZ5UNVF.**

Current Science

Check out Current Science® articles related to this chapter by visiting **go.hrw.com**. Just type in the keyword **HZ5CS19.**

Formation of the Solar System

About the PHOTO

The Orion Nebula, a vast cloud of dust and gas that is 35 trillion miles wide, is part of the familiar Orion constellation. Here, swirling clouds of dust and gas give birth to systems like our own solar system.

PRE-READING ACTiViTY

Graphic **Organizer**

Chain-of-Events Chart Before you read the chapter, create the graphic organizer entitled "Chain-of-Events Chart" described in the **Study Skills** section of the Appendix. As you read the chapter, fill in the chart with details about each step of the formation of the solar system.

START-UP ACTIVITY

Strange Gravity

If you drop a heavy object, will it fall faster than a lighter one? According to the law of gravity, the answer is no. In 1971, *Apollo 15* astronaut David Scott stood on the moon and dropped a feather and a hammer. Television audiences were amazed to see both objects strike the moon's surface at the same time. Now, you can perform a similar experiment.

Procedure

1. Select **two pieces of identical notebook paper.** Crumple one piece of paper into a ball.

2. Place the flat piece of paper on top of a **book** and the paper ball on top of the flat piece of paper.

3. Hold the book waist high, and then drop it to the floor.

Analysis

1. Which piece of paper reached the bottom first? Did either piece of paper fall slower than the book? Explain your observations.

2. Now, hold the crumpled paper in one hand and the flat piece of paper in the other. Drop both pieces of paper at the same time. Besides gravity, what affected the speed of the falling paper? Record your observations.

A Solar System Is Born

As you read this sentence, you are traveling at a speed of about 30 km/s around an incredibly hot star shining in the vastness of space!

Earth is not the only planet orbiting the sun. In fact, Earth has eight fellow travelers in its cosmic neighborhood. The solar system includes a star we call the sun, nine planets, and many moons and small bodies that travel around the sun. For almost 5 billion years, planets have been orbiting the sun. But how did the solar system come to be?

The Solar Nebula

All of the ingredients for building planets, moons, and stars are found in the vast, seemingly empty regions of space between the stars. Just as there are clouds in the sky, there are clouds in space. These clouds are called nebulas. **Nebulas** (or nebulae) are mixtures of gases—mainly hydrogen and helium—and dust made of elements such as carbon and iron. Although nebulas are normally dark and invisible to optical telescopes, they can be seen when nearby stars illuminate them. So, how can a cloud of gas and dust such as the Horsehead Nebula, shown in **Figure 1,** form planets and stars? To answer this question, you must explore two forces that interact in nebulas—gravity and pressure.

Gravity Pulls Matter Together

The gas and dust that make up nebulas are made of matter. The matter of a nebula is held together by the force of gravity. In most nebulas, there is a lot of space between the particles. In fact, nebulas are less dense than air! Thus, the gravitational attraction between the particles in a nebula is very weak. The force is just enough to keep the nebula from drifting apart.

nebula a large cloud of gas and dust in interstellar space; a region in space where stars are born or where stars explode at the end of their lives

Figure 1 *The Horsehead Nebula is a cold, dark cloud of gas and dust. But observations suggest that it is also a site where stars form.*

Figure 2 **Gravity and Pressure in a Nebula**

1 Gravity causes the particles in a nebula to be attracted to each other.

2 As particles move closer together, collisions cause pressure to increase and particles are pushed apart.

3 If the inward force of gravity is balanced by outward pressure, the nebula becomes stable.

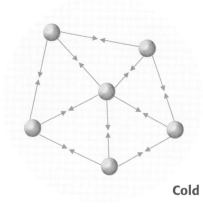

Cold

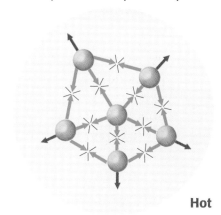

Hot

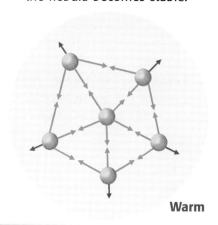

Warm

Pressure Pushes Matter Apart

If gravity pulls on all of the particles in a nebula, why don't nebulas slowly collapse? The answer has to do with the relationship between temperature and pressure in a nebula. *Temperature* is a measure of the average kinetic energy, or the energy of motion, of the particles in an object. If the particles in a nebula have little kinetic energy, they move slowly and the temperature of the cloud is very low. If the particles move fast, the temperature of the cloud is high. As particles move around, they sometimes crash into each other. As shown in **Figure 2,** these collisions cause particles to push away from each other, which creates *pressure*. If you have ever blown up a balloon, you understand how pressure works—pressure keeps a balloon from collapsing. In a nebula, outward pressure balances the inward gravitational pull and keeps the cloud from collapsing.

Upsetting the Balance

The balance between gravity and pressure in a nebula can be upset if two nebulas collide or a nearby star explodes. These events compress, or push together, small regions of a nebula called *globules,* or gas clouds. Globules can become so dense that they contract under their own gravity. As the matter in a globule collapses inward, the temperature increases and the stage is set for stars to form. The **solar nebula**—the cloud of gas and dust that formed our solar system—may have formed in this way.

solar nebula the cloud of gas and dust that formed our solar system

✓ Reading Check **What is the solar nebula?** (*See the Appendix for answers to Reading Checks.*)

Figure 3 The Formation of the Solar System

1 The young solar nebula begins to collapse.

2 The solar nebula rotates, flattens, and becomes warmer near its center.

3 Planetesimals begin to form within the swirling disk.

4 As the largest planetesimals grow in size, their gravity attracts more gas and dust.

5 Smaller planetesimals collide with the larger ones, and planets begin to grow.

6 A star is born, and the remaining gas and dust are blown out of the new solar system.

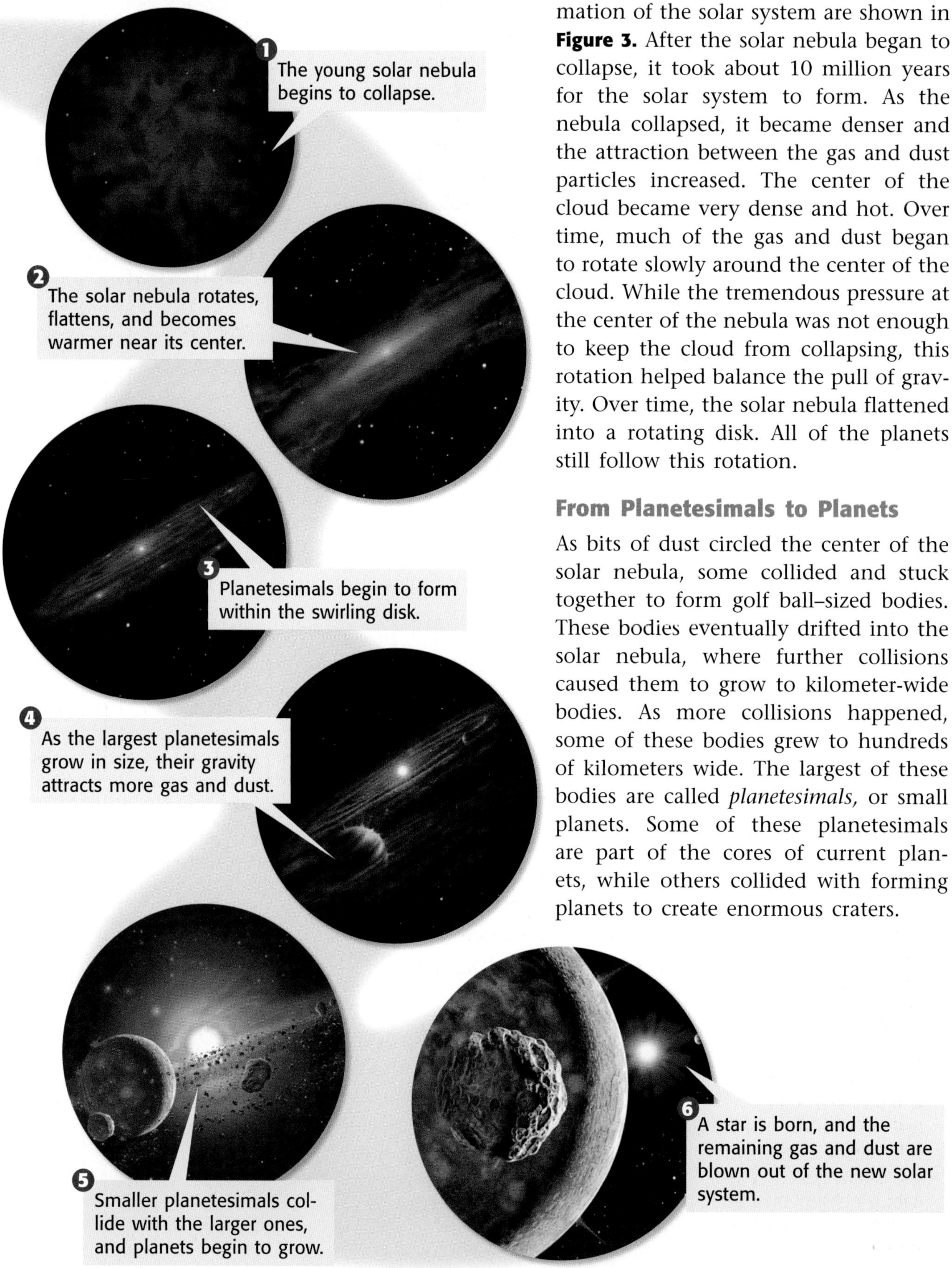

How the Solar System Formed

The events that may have led to the formation of the solar system are shown in **Figure 3.** After the solar nebula began to collapse, it took about 10 million years for the solar system to form. As the nebula collapsed, it became denser and the attraction between the gas and dust particles increased. The center of the cloud became very dense and hot. Over time, much of the gas and dust began to rotate slowly around the center of the cloud. While the tremendous pressure at the center of the nebula was not enough to keep the cloud from collapsing, this rotation helped balance the pull of gravity. Over time, the solar nebula flattened into a rotating disk. All of the planets still follow this rotation.

From Planetesimals to Planets

As bits of dust circled the center of the solar nebula, some collided and stuck together to form golf ball–sized bodies. These bodies eventually drifted into the solar nebula, where further collisions caused them to grow to kilometer-wide bodies. As more collisions happened, some of these bodies grew to hundreds of kilometers wide. The largest of these bodies are called *planetesimals,* or small planets. Some of these planetesimals are part of the cores of current planets, while others collided with forming planets to create enormous craters.

Gas Giant or Rocky Planet?

The largest planetesimals formed near the outside of the rotating solar disk, where hydrogen and helium were located. These planetesimals were far enough from the solar disk that their gravity could attract the nebula gases. These outer planets grew to huge sizes and became the gas giants—Jupiter, Saturn, Uranus, and Neptune. Closer to the center of the nebula, where Mercury, Venus, Earth, and Mars formed, temperatures were too hot for gases to remain. Therefore, the inner planets in our solar system are made mostly of rocky material.

Reading Check Which planets are gas giants?

The Birth of a Star

As the planets were forming, other matter in the solar nebula was traveling toward the center. The center became so dense and hot that hydrogen atoms began to fuse, or join, to form helium. Fusion released huge amounts of energy and created enough outward pressure to balance the inward pull of gravity. At this point, when the gas stopped collapsing, our sun was born and the new solar system was complete!

CONNECTION TO Language Arts

WRITING SKILL **Eyewitness Account** Research information on the formation of the outer planets, inner planets, and the sun. Then, imagine that you witnessed the formation of the planets and sun. Write a short story describing your experience.

SECTION Review

Summary

- The solar system formed out of a vast cloud of gas and dust called the *nebula*.
- Gravity and pressure were balanced until something upset the balance. Then, the nebula began to collapse.
- Collapse of the solar nebula caused heating at the center, while planetesimals formed in surrounding space.
- The central mass of the nebula became the sun. Planets formed from the surrounding materials.

Using Key Terms

1. In your own words, write a definition for each of the following terms: *nebula* and *solar nebula*.

Understanding Key Ideas

2. What is the relationship between gravity and pressure in a nebula?
   a. Gravity reduces pressure.
   b. Pressure balances gravity.
   c. Pressure increases gravity.
   d. None of the above

3. Describe how our solar system formed.

4. Compare the inner planets with the outer planets.

Math Skills

5. If the planets, moons, and other bodies make up 0.15% of the solar system's mass, what percentage does the sun make up?

Critical Thinking

6. **Evaluating Hypotheses** Pluto, the outermost planet, is small and rocky. Some scientists argue that Pluto is a captured asteroid, not a planet. Use what you know about how solar systems form to evaluate this hypothesis.

7. **Making Inferences** Why do all of the planets go around the sun in the same direction, and why do the planets lie on a relatively flat plane?

SCiLINKS **NSTA**
Developed and maintained by the National Science Teachers Association

For a variety of links related to this chapter, go to www.scilinks.org

Topic: The Planets
SciLinks code: HSM1152

The Sun: Our Very Own Star

Can you imagine what life on Earth would be like if there were no sun? Without the sun, life on Earth would be impossible!

READING WARM-UP

Objectives

- Describe the basic structure and composition of the sun.
- Explain how the sun generates energy.
- Describe the surface activity of the sun, and identify how this activity affects Earth.

Terms to Learn

nuclear fusion
sunspot

READING STRATEGY

Reading Organizer As you read this section, create an outline of the section. Use the headings from the section in your outline.

Energy from the sun lights and heats Earth's surface. Energy from the sun even drives the weather. Making up more than 99% of the solar system's mass, the sun is the dominant member of our solar system. The sun is basically a large ball of gas made mostly of hydrogen and helium held together by gravity. But what does the inside of the sun look like?

The Structure of the Sun

Although the sun may appear to have a solid surface, it does not. When you see a picture of the sun, you are really seeing through the sun's outer atmosphere. The visible surface of the sun starts at the point where the gas becomes so thick that you cannot see through it. As **Figure 1** shows, the sun is made of several layers.

Figure 1 The Structure and Atmosphere of the Sun

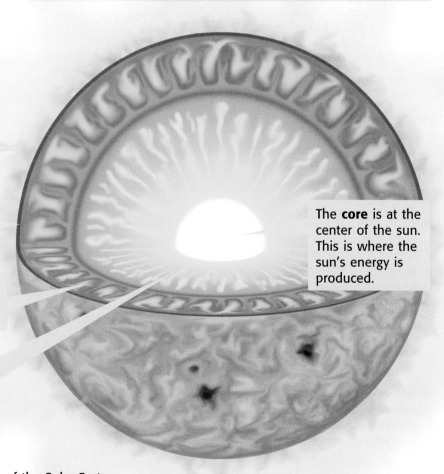

The **corona** forms the sun's outer atmosphere.

The **chromosphere** is a thin region below the corona, only 30,000 km thick.

The **photosphere** is the visible part of the sun that we can see from Earth.

The **convective zone** is a region about 200,000 km thick where gases circulate.

The **radiative zone** is a very dense region about 300,000 km thick.

The **core** is at the center of the sun. This is where the sun's energy is produced.

At first, some type of burning fuel was thought to be the source of the sun's energy.

A shrinking sun was another explanation for solar energy.

Figure 2 *Ideas about the source of the sun's energy have changed over time.*

Energy Production in the Sun

The sun has been shining on Earth for about 4.6 billion years. How can the sun stay hot for so long? And what makes it shine? **Figure 2** shows two theories that were proposed to answer these questions. Many scientists thought that the sun burned fuel to generate its energy. But the amount of energy that is released by burning would not be enough to power the sun. If the sun were simply burning, it would last for only 10,000 years.

Burning or Shrinking?

It eventually became clear to scientists that burning wouldn't last long enough to keep the sun shining. Then, scientists began to think that gravity was causing the sun to slowly shrink. They thought that perhaps gravity would release enough energy to heat the sun. While the release of gravitational energy is more powerful than burning, it is not enough to power the sun. If all of the sun's gravitational energy were released, the sun would last for only 45 million years. However, fossils that have been discovered prove that dinosaurs roamed the Earth more than 65 million years ago, so this couldn't be the case. Therefore, something even more powerful than gravity was needed.

✔ **Reading Check** **Why isn't energy from gravity enough to power the sun?** (*See the Appendix for answers to Reading Checks.*)

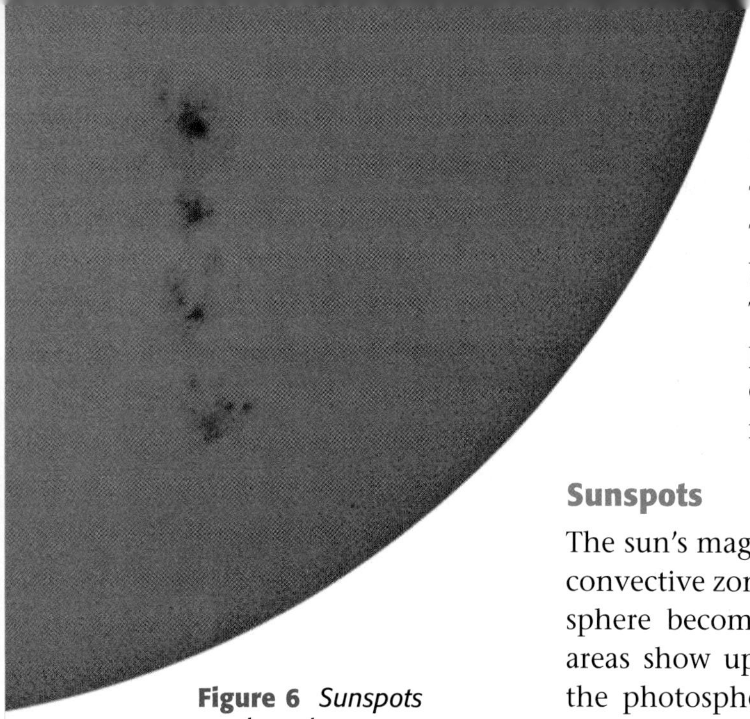

Solar Activity

The photosphere is an ever-changing place. Thermal energy moves from the sun's interior by the circulation of gases in the convective zone. This movement of energy causes the gas in the photosphere to boil and churn. This circulation, combined with the sun's rotation, creates magnetic fields that reach far out into space.

Sunspots

The sun's magnetic fields tend to slow down the activity in the convective zone. When activity slows down, areas of the photosphere become cooler than surrounding areas. These cooler areas show up as sunspots. **Sunspots** are cooler, dark spots of the photosphere of the sun, as shown in **Figure 6.** Sunspots can vary in shape and size. Some sunspots can be as large as 50,000 miles in diameter.

The numbers and locations of sunspots on the sun change in a regular cycle. Scientists have found that the sunspot cycle lasts about 11 years. Every 11 years, the amount of sunspot activity in the sun reaches a peak intensity and then decreases. **Figure 7** shows the sunspot cycle since 1610, excluding the years 1645–1715, which was a period of unusually low sunspot activity.

✓ Reading Check What are sunspots? What causes sunspots to occur?

Climate Confusion

Scientists have found that sunspot activity can affect the Earth. For example, some scientists have linked the period of low sunspot activity, 1645–1715, with the very low temperatures that Europe experienced during that time. This period is known as the "Little Ice Age." Most scientists, however, think that more research is needed to fully understand the possible connection between sunspots and Earth's climate.

Figure 6 *Sunspots mark cooler areas on the sun's surface. They are related to changes in the magnetic properties of the sun.*

sunspot a dark area of the photosphere of the sun that is cooler than the surrounding areas and that has a strong magnetic field

Figure 7 *This graph shows the number of sunspots that have occurred each year since Galileo's first observation in 1610.*

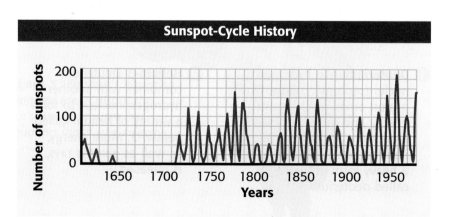

Solar Flares

The magnetic fields that cause sunspots also cause solar flares. *Solar flares,* as shown in **Figure 8,** are regions of extremely high temperature and brightness that develop on the sun's surface. When a solar flare erupts, it sends huge streams of electrically charged particles into the solar system. Solar flares can extend upward several thousand kilometers within minutes. Solar flares are usually associated with sunspots and can interrupt radio communications on Earth and in orbit. Scientists are trying to find ways to give advance warning of solar flares.

Figure 8 *Solar flares are giant eruptions on the sun's surface.*

SECTION Review

Summary

- The sun is a large ball of gas made mostly of hydrogen and helium. The sun consists of many layers.

- The sun's energy comes from nuclear fusion that takes place in the center of the sun.

- The visible surface of the sun, or the photosphere, is very active.

- Sunspots and solar flares are the result of the sun's magnetic fields that reach space.

- Sunspot activity may affect Earth's climate, and solar flares can interact with Earth's atmosphere.

Using Key Terms

1. In your own words, write a definition for each of the following terms: *sunspot* and *nuclear fusion.*

Understanding Key Ideas

2. Which of the following statements describes how energy is produced in the sun?
   a. The sun burns fuels to generate energy.
   b. As hydrogen changes into helium deep inside the sun, a great deal of energy is made.
   c. Energy is released as the sun shrinks because of gravity.
   d. None of the above

3. Describe the composition of the sun.

4. Name and describe the layers of the sun.

5. In which area of the sun do sunspots appear?

6. Explain how sunspots form.

7. Describe how sunspots can affect the Earth.

8. What are solar flares, and how do they form?

Math Skills

9. If the equatorial diameter of the sun is 1.39 million kilometers, how many kilometers is the sun's radius?

Critical Thinking

10. **Applying Concepts** If nuclear fusion in the sun's core suddenly stopped today, would the sky be dark in the daytime tomorrow? Explain.

11. **Making Comparisons** Compare the theories that scientists proposed about the source of the sun's energy with the process of nuclear fusion in the sun.

SCILINKS®

NSTA
Developed and maintained by the
National Science Teachers Association

For a variety of links related to this chapter, go to www.scilinks.org

Topic: The Sun
SciLinks code: HSM1477

The Earth Takes Shape

In many ways, Earth seems to be a perfect place for life.

We live on the third planet from the sun. The Earth, shown in **Figure 1,** is mostly made of rock, and nearly three-fourths of its surface is covered with water. It is surrounded by a protective atmosphere of mostly nitrogen and oxygen and smaller amounts of other gases. But Earth has not always been such an oasis in the solar system.

Formation of the Solid Earth

The Earth formed as planetesimals in the solar system collided and combined. From what scientists can tell, the Earth formed within the first 10 million years of the collapse of the solar nebula!

The Effects of Gravity

When a young planet is still small, it can have an irregular shape, somewhat like a potato. But as the planet gains more matter, the force of gravity increases. When a rocky planet, such as Earth, reaches a diameter of about 350 km, the force of gravity becomes greater than the strength of the rock. As the Earth grew to this size, the rock at its center was crushed by gravity and the planet started to become round.

The Effects of Heat

As the Earth was changing shape, it was also heating up. Planetesimals continued to collide with the Earth, and the energy of their motion heated the planet. Radioactive material, which was present in the Earth as it formed, also heated the young planet. After Earth reached a certain size, the temperature rose faster than the interior could cool, and the rocky material inside began to melt. Today, the Earth is still cooling from the energy that was generated when it formed. Volcanoes, earthquakes, and hot springs are effects of this energy trapped inside the Earth. As you will learn later, the effects of heat and gravity also helped form the Earth's layers when the Earth was very young.

✓ Reading Check What factors heated the Earth during its early formation? (*See the Appendix for answers to Reading Checks.*)

Figure 1 *When Earth is seen from space, one of its unique features—the presence of water—is apparent.*

How the Earth's Layers Formed

Have you ever watched the oil separate from vinegar in a bottle of salad dressing? The vinegar sinks because it is denser than oil. The Earth's layers formed in much the same way. As rocks melted, denser materials, such as nickel and iron, sank to the center of the Earth and formed the core. Less dense materials floated to the surface and became the crust. This process is shown in **Figure 2.**

The **crust** is the thin, outermost layer of the Earth. It is 5 to 100 km thick. Crustal rock is made of materials that have low densities, such as oxygen, silicon, and aluminum. The **mantle** is the layer of Earth beneath the crust. It extends 2,900 km below the surface. Mantle rock is made of materials such as magnesium and iron and is denser than crustal rock. The **core** is the central part of the Earth below the mantle. It contains the densest materials (nickel and iron) and extends to the center of the Earth—almost 6,400 km below the surface.

crust the thin and solid outermost layer of the Earth above the mantle

mantle the layer of rock between the Earth's crust and core

core the central part of the Earth below the mantle

Figure 2   The Formation of Earth's Layers

❶ All materials in the early Earth are randomly mixed.

❷ Rocks melt, and denser materials sink toward the center. Less dense elements rise and form layers.

❸ According to composition, the Earth is divided into three layers: the crust, the mantle, and the core.

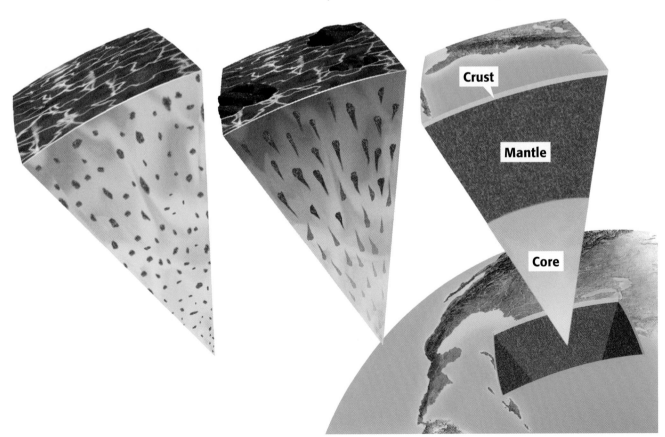

Crust

Mantle

Core

Formation of the Earth's Atmosphere

Today, Earth's atmosphere is 78% nitrogen, 21% oxygen, and about 1% argon. (There are tiny amounts of many other gases.) Did you know that the Earth's atmosphere did not always contain the oxygen that you need to live? The Earth's atmosphere is constantly changing. Scientists think that the Earth's earliest atmosphere was very different than it is today.

Earth's Early Atmosphere

Scientists think that Earth's early atmosphere was a mixture of gases that were released as Earth cooled. During the final stages of the Earth's formation, its surface was very hot—even molten in places—as shown in **Figure 3.** The molten rock released large amounts of carbon dioxide and water vapor. Therefore, scientists think that Earth's early atmosphere was a steamy mixture of carbon dioxide and water vapor.

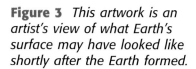 **Reading Check** Describe Earth's early atmosphere.

Figure 3 *This artwork is an artist's view of what Earth's surface may have looked like shortly after the Earth formed.*

Figure 4 *As this volcano in Hawaii shows, a large amount of gas is released during an eruption.*

Earth's Changing Atmosphere

As the Earth cooled and its layers formed, the Earth's atmosphere changed again. This atmosphere probably formed from volcanic gases. Volcanoes, such as the one in **Figure 4,** released chlorine, nitrogen, and sulfur in addition to large amounts of carbon dioxide and water vapor. Some of this water vapor may have condensed to form the Earth's first oceans.

Comets, which are planetesimals made of ice, also may have contributed to this change of Earth's atmosphere. As comets crashed into the Earth, they brought in a range of elements, such as carbon, hydrogen, oxygen, and nitrogen. Comets also may have brought some of the water that helped form the oceans.

The Role of Life

How did this change of Earth's atmosphere become the air you are breathing right now? The answer is related to the appearance of life on Earth.

Ultraviolet Radiation

Scientists think that ultraviolet (UV) radiation, the same radiation that causes sunburns, helped produce the conditions necessary for life. Because UV light has a lot of energy, it can break apart molecules in your skin and in the air. Today, we are shielded from most of the sun's UV rays by Earth's protective ozone layer. But Earth's early atmosphere probably did not have ozone, so many molecules in the air and at Earth's surface were broken apart. Over time, this material collected in the Earth's waters. Water offered protection from the effects of UV radiation. In these sheltered pools of water, chemicals may have combined to form the complex molecules that made life possible. The first life-forms were very simple and did not need oxygen to live.

Comets and Meteors

What is the difference between a comet and a meteor? With a parent, research the difference between comets and meteors. Then, find out if you can view meteor showers in your area!

The Source of Oxygen

Sometime before 3.4 billion years ago, organisms that produced food by photosynthesis appeared. *Photosynthesis* is the process of absorbing energy from the sun and carbon dioxide from the atmosphere to make food. During the process of making food, these organisms released oxygen—a gas that was not abundant in the atmosphere at that time. Scientists think that the descendants of these early life-forms are still around today, as shown in **Figure 5.**

Photosynthetic organisms played a major role in changing Earth's atmosphere to become the mixture of gases you breathe today. Over the next hundreds of millions of years, more and more oxygen was added to the atmosphere. At the same time, carbon dioxide was removed. As oxygen levels increased, some of the oxygen formed a layer of ozone in the upper atmosphere. This ozone blocked most of the UV radiation and made it possible for life, in the form of simple plants, to move onto land about 2.2 billion years ago.

Reading Check How did photosynthesis contribute to Earth's current atmosphere?

Formation of Oceans and Continents

Scientists think that the oceans probably formed during Earth's second atmosphere, when the Earth was cool enough for rain to fall and remain on the surface. After millions of years of rainfall, water began to cover the Earth. By 4 billion years ago, a global ocean covered the planet.

For the first few hundred million years of Earth's history, there may not have been any continents. Given the composition of the rocks that make up the continents, scientists know that these rocks have melted and cooled many times in the past. Each time the rocks melted, the heavier elements sank and the lighter ones rose to the surface.

Figure 5 *Stromatolites, mats of fossilized algae (left), are among the earliest evidence of life. Blue-green algae (right) living today are thought to be similar to the first life-forms on Earth.*

The Growth of Continents

After a while, some of the rocks were light enough to pile up on the surface. These rocks were the beginning of the earliest continents. The continents gradually thickened and slowly rose above the surface of the ocean. These scattered young continents did not stay in the same place, however. The slow transfer of thermal energy in the mantle pushed them around. Approximately 2.5 billion years ago, continents really started to grow. And by 1.5 billion years ago, the upper mantle had cooled and had become denser and heavier. At this time, it was easier for the cooler parts of the mantle to sink. These conditions made it easier for the continents to move in the same way that they do today.

INTERNET ACTIVITY

For another activity related to this chapter, go to **go.hrw.com** and type in the keyword **HZ5SOLW**.

SECTION Review

Summary

● The effects of gravity and heat created the shape and structure of Earth.

● The Earth is divided into three main layers based on composition: the crust, mantle, and core.

● The presence of life dramatically changed Earth's atmosphere by adding free oxygen.

● Earth's oceans formed shortly after the Earth did, when it had cooled off enough for rain to fall. Continents formed when lighter materials gathered on the surface and rose above sea level.

Using Key Terms

1. Use each of the following terms in a separate sentence: *crust, mantle,* and *core.*

Understanding Key Ideas

2. Earth's first atmosphere was mostly made of
   a. nitrogen and oxygen.
   b. chlorine, nitrogen, and sulfur.
   c. carbon dioxide and water vapor.
   d. water vapor and oxygen.

3. Describe the structure of the Earth.

4. Why did the Earth separate into distinct layers?

5. Describe the development of Earth's atmosphere. How did life affect Earth's atmosphere?

6. Explain how Earth's oceans and continents formed.

Critical Thinking

7. **Applying Concepts** How did the effects of gravity help shape the Earth?

8. **Making Inferences** How would the removal of forests affect the Earth's atmosphere?

Interpreting Graphics

Use the illustration below to answer the questions that follow.

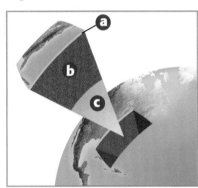

9. Which of the layers is composed mostly of the elements magnesium and iron?

10. Which of the layers is composed mostly of the elements iron and nickel?

SCILINKS

NSTA
Developed and maintained by the
National Science Teachers Association

For a variety of links related to this chapter, go to www.scilinks.org

Topic: The Layers of the Earth; The Oceans
SciLinks code: HSM0862; HSM1069

Planetary Motion

Why do the planets revolve around the sun? Why don't they fly off into space? Does something hold them in their paths?

To answer these questions, you need to go back in time to look at the discoveries made by the scientists of the 1500s and 1600s. Danish astronomer Tycho Brahe (TIE koh BRAH uh) carefully observed the positions of planets for more than 25 years. When Brahe died in 1601, a German astronomer named Johannes Kepler (yoh HAHN uhs KEP luhr) continued Brahe's work. Kepler set out to understand the motions of planets and to describe the solar system.

A Revolution in Astronomy

Each planet spins on its axis. The spinning of a body, such as a planet, on its axis is called **rotation.** As the Earth rotates, only one-half of the Earth faces the sun. The half facing the sun is light (day). The half that faces away from the sun is dark (night).

The path that a body follows as it travels around another body in space is called the **orbit.** One complete trip along an orbit is called a **revolution.** The amount of time a planet takes to complete a single trip around the sun is called a *period of revolution.* Each planet takes a different amount of time to circle the sun. Earth's period of revolution is about 365.25 days (a year), but Mercury orbits the sun in only 88 days. **Figure 1** illustrates the orbit and revolution of the Earth around the sun as well as the rotation of the Earth on its axis.

rotation the spin of a body on its axis

orbit the path that a body follows as it travels around another body in space

revolution the motion of a body that travels around another body in space; one complete trip along an orbit

Figure 1 *A planet rotates on its own axis and revolves around the sun in a path called an* orbit.

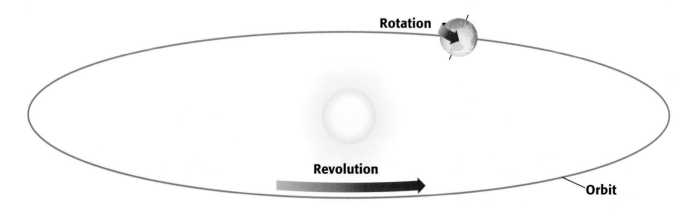

Rotation

Revolution

Orbit

Figure 2 Parts of an Ellipse

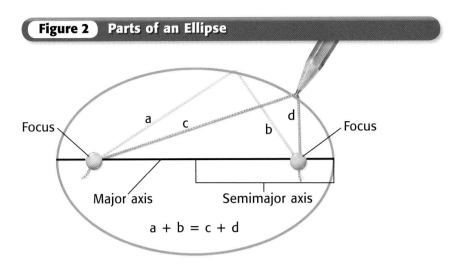

Focus — Major axis — Semimajor axis — Focus

a + b = c + d

Kepler's First Law of Motion

Kepler's first discovery came from his careful study of Mars. Kepler discovered that Mars did not move in a circle around the sun but moved in an elongated circle called an *ellipse*. This finding became Kepler's first law of motion. An ellipse is a closed curve in which the sum of the distances from the edge of the curve to two points inside the ellipse is always the same, as shown in **Figure 2.** An ellipse's maximum length is called its *major axis*. Half of this distance is the *semimajor axis*, which is usually used to describe the size of an ellipse. The semimajor axis of Earth's orbit—the maximum distance between Earth and the sun—is about 150 million kilometers.

Kepler's Second Law of Motion

Kepler's second discovery, or second law of motion, was that the planets seemed to move faster when they are close to the sun and slower when they are farther away. To understand this idea, imagine that a planet is attached to the sun by a string, as modeled in **Figure 3.** When the string is shorter, the planet must move faster to cover the same area.

Kepler's Third Law of Motion

Kepler noticed that planets that are more distant from the sun, such as Saturn, take longer to orbit the sun. This finding was Kepler's third law of motion, which explains the relationship between the period of a planet's revolution and its semimajor axis. Knowing how long a planet takes to orbit the sun, Kepler was able to calculate the planet's distance from the sun.

✓ **Reading Check** Describe Kepler's third law of motion. (*See the Appendix for answers to Reading Checks.*)

MATH PRACTICE

Kepler's Formula

Kepler's third law can be expressed with the formula

$$P^2 = a^3$$

where P is the period of revolution and a is the semimajor axis of an orbiting body. For example, Mars's period is 1.88 years, and its semimajor axis is 1.523 AU. Thus, $1.88^2 = 1.523^3 = 3.53$. Calculate a planet's period of revolution if the semimajor axis is 5.74 AU.

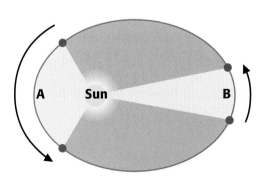

Figure 3 *According to Kepler's second law, to keep the area of A equal to the area of B, the planet must move faster in its orbit when it is closer to the sun.*

Skills Practice Lab

OBJECTIVES

Create a solar-distance measuring device.

Calculate the Earth's distance from the sun.

MATERIALS

- aluminum foil, 5 cm × 5 cm
- card, index
- meterstick
- poster board
- ruler, metric
- scissors
- tape, masking
- thumbtack

SAFETY

How Far Is the Sun?

It doesn't slice, it doesn't dice, but it can give you an idea of how big our universe is! You can build your very own solar-distance measuring device from household items. Amaze your friends by figuring out how many metersticks can be placed between the Earth and the sun.

Ask a Question

1 How many metersticks could I place between the Earth and the sun?

Form a Hypothesis

2 Write a hypothesis that answers the question above.

Test the Hypothesis

3 Measure and cut a 4 cm × 4 cm square from the middle of the poster board. Tape the foil square over the hole in the center of the poster board.

4 Using a thumbtack, carefully prick the foil to form a tiny hole in the center. Congratulations! You have just constructed your very own solar-distance measuring device!

5 Tape the device to a window facing the sun so that sunlight shines directly through the pinhole. **Caution:** Do not look directly into the sun.

6 Place one end of the meterstick against the window and beneath the foil square. Steady the meterstick with one hand.

7 With the other hand, hold the index card close to the pinhole. You should be able to see a circular image on the card. This image is an image of the sun.

8 Move the card back until the image is large enough to measure. Be sure to keep the image on the card sharply focused. Reposition the meterstick so that it touches the bottom of the card.

Analyze the Results

1 **Analyzing Results** According to your calculations, how far from the Earth is the sun? Don't forget to convert your measurements to meters.

Draw Conclusions

2 **Evaluating Data** You could put 150 billion metersticks between the Earth and the sun. Compare this information with your result in step 11. Do you think that this activity was a good way to measure the Earth's distance from the sun? Support your answer.

9 Ask your partner to measure the diameter of the image on the card by using the metric ruler. Record the diameter of the image in millimeters.

10 Record the distance between the window and the index card by reading the point at which the card rests on the meterstick.

11 Calculate the distance between Earth and the sun by using the following formula:

$$\text{distance between the sun and Earth} = \text{sun's diameter} \times \frac{\text{distance to the image}}{\text{image's diameter}}$$

1 cm = 10 mm
1 m = 100 cm
1 km = 1,000 m

(Hint: The sun's diameter is 1,392,000,000 m.)

Chapter Review

USING KEY TERMS

Complete each of the following sentences by choosing the correct term from the word bank.

nebula crust
mantle solar nebula

1 A ___ is a large cloud of gas and dust in interstellar space.

2 The ___ lies between the core and the crust of the Earth.

For each pair of terms, explain how the meanings of the terms differ.

3 *nebula* and *solar nebula*

4 *crust* and *mantle*

5 *rotation* and *revolution*

6 *nuclear fusion* and *sunspot*

UNDERSTANDING KEY IDEAS

Multiple Choice

7 To determine a planet's period of revolution, you must know its
  a. size.
  b. mass.
  c. orbit.
  d. All of the above

8 During Earth's formation, materials such as nickel and iron sank to the
  a. mantle.
  b. core.
  c. crust.
  d. All of the above

9 Planetary orbits are shaped like
  a. orbits.
  b. spirals.
  c. ellipses.
  d. periods of revolution.

10 Impacts in the early solar system
  a. brought new materials to the planets.
  b. released energy.
  c. dug craters.
  d. All of the above

11 Organisms that photosynthesize get their energy from
  a. nitrogen.   **c.** the sun.
  b. oxygen.   **d.** water.

12 Which of the following planets has the shortest period of revolution?
  a. Pluto   **c.** Mercury
  b. Earth   **d.** Jupiter

13 Which gas in Earth's atmosphere suggests that there is life on Earth?
  a. hydrogen   **c.** carbon dioxide
  b. oxygen   **d.** nitrogen

14 Which layer of the Earth has the lowest density?
  a. the core
  b. the mantle
  c. the crust
  d. None of the above

15 What is the measure of the average kinetic energy of particles in an object?
  a. temperature   **c.** gravity
  b. pressure   **d.** force

Short Answer

16 Compare a sunspot with a solar flare.

17 Describe how the Earth's oceans and continents formed.

18 Explain how pressure and gravity may have become unbalanced in the solar nebula.

19 Define *nuclear fusion* in your own words. Describe how nuclear fusion generates the sun's energy.

CRITICAL THINKING

20 **Concept Mapping** Use the following terms to create a concept map: *solar nebula, solar system, planetesimals, sun, photosphere, core, nuclear fusion, planets,* and *Earth*.

21 **Making Comparisons** How did Newton's law of universal gravitation help explain the work of Johannes Kepler?

22 **Predicting Consequences** Using what you know about the relationship between living things and the development of Earth's atmosphere, explain how the formation of ozone holes in Earth's atmosphere could affect living things.

23 **Identifying Relationships** Describe Kepler's three laws of motion in your own words. Describe how each law relates to either the revolution, rotation, or orbit of a planetary body.

INTERPRETING GRAPHICS

Use the illustration below to answer the questions that follow.

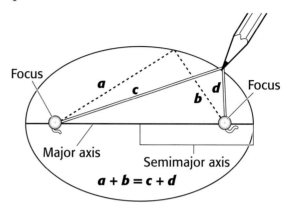

Focus — Focus — *a* *c* *b* *d* — Major axis — Semimajor axis

$$a + b = c + d$$

24 Which of Kepler's laws of motion does the illustration represent?

25 How does the equation shown above support the law?

26 What is an ellipse's maximum length called?

$$E = mc^2$$

READING

Read each of the passages below. Then, answer the questions that follow each passage.

Passage 1 You know that you should not look at the sun, right? But how can we learn anything about the sun if we can't look at it? We can use a solar telescope! About 70 km southwest of Tucson, Arizona, is Kitt Peak National Observatory, where you will find three solar telescopes. In 1958, Kitt Peak was chosen from more than 150 mountain sites to be the site for a national observatory. Located in the Sonoran Desert, Kitt Peak is on land belonging to the Tohono O'odham Indian nation. On this site, the McMath-Pierce Facility houses the three largest solar telescopes in the world. Astronomers come from around the globe to use these telescopes. The largest of the three, the McMath-Pierce solar telescope, produces an image of the sun that is almost 1 m wide!

1. Which of the following is the largest telescope in the world?
   A Kitt Peak
   B Tohono O'odham
   C McMath-Pierce
   D Tucson

2. According to the passage, how can you learn about the sun?
   F You can look at it.
   G You can study it by using a solar telescope.
   H You can go to Kitt Peak National Observatory.
   I You can study to be an astronomer.

3. Which of the following is a fact in the passage?
   A One hundred fifty mountain sites contain solar telescopes.
   B Kitt Peak is the location of the smallest solar telescope in the world.
   C In 1958, Tucson, Arizona, was chosen for a national observatory.
   D Kitt Peak is the location of the largest solar telescope in the world.

Passage 2 Sunlight that has been focused can produce a great amount of thermal energy— enough to start a fire. Now, imagine focusing the sun's rays by using a magnifying glass that is 1.6 m in diameter. The resulting heat could melt metal. If a <u>conventional</u> telescope were pointed directly at the sun, it would melt. To avoid a meltdown, the McMath-Pierce solar telescope uses a mirror that produces a large image of the sun. This mirror directs the sun's rays down a diagonal shaft to another mirror, which is 50 m underground. This mirror is adjustable to focus the sunlight. The sunlight is then directed to a third mirror, which directs the light to an observing room and instrument shaft.

1. In this passage, what does the word *conventional* mean?
   A special
   B solar
   C unusual
   D ordinary

2. What can you infer from reading the passage?
   F Focused sunlight can avoid a meltdown.
   G Unfocused sunlight produces little energy.
   H A magnifying glass can focus sunlight to produce a great amount of thermal energy.
   I Mirrors increase the intensity of sunlight.

3. According to the passage, which of the following statements about solar telescopes is true?
   A Solar telescopes make it safe for scientists to observe the sun.
   B Solar telescopes don't need to use mirrors.
   C Solar telescopes are built 50 m underground.
   D Solar telescopes are 1.6 m in diameter.

The diagram below models the moon's orbit around the Earth. Use the diagram below to answer the questions that follow.

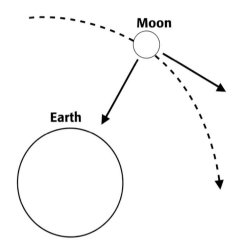

1. Which statement best describes the diagram?

A Orbits are straight lines.

B The force of gravity does not affect orbits.

C Orbits result from a combination of gravitational attraction and inertia.

D The moon moves in three different directions depending on its speed.

2. In which direction does gravity pull the moon?

F toward the Earth

G around the Earth

H away from the Earth

I toward and away from the Earth

3. If the moon stopped moving, what would happen?

A It would fly off into space.

B It would continue to orbit the Earth.

C It would stay where it is in space.

D It would move toward the Earth.

Read each question below, and choose the best answer.

1. An astronomer found 3 planetary systems in the nebula that she was studying. One system had 6 planets, another had 2 planets, and the third had 7 planets. What is the average number of planets in all 3 systems?

A 3

B 5

C 8

D 16

2. A newly discovered planet has a period of rotation of 270 Earth years. How many Earth days are in 270 Earth years?

F 3,240

G 8,100

H 9,855

I 98,550

3. A planet has seven rings. The first ring is 20,000 km from the center of the planet. Each ring is 50,000 km wide and 500 km apart. What is the total radius of the ring system from the planet's center?

A 353,000 km

B 373,000 km

C 373,500 km

D 370,000 km

4. If you bought a telescope for $87.75 and received a $10 bill, two $1 bills, and a quarter as change, how much money did you give the clerk?

F $100

G $99

H $98

I $90

Standardized Test Preparation

Science in Action

Science, Technology, and Society

Don't Look at the Sun!

How can we learn anything about the sun if we can't look at it? The answer is to use a special telescope called a *solar telescope*. The three largest solar telescopes in the world are located at Kitt Peak National Observatory near Tucson, Arizona. The largest of these telescopes, the McMath-Pierce solar telescope, creates an image of the sun that is almost 1 m wide! How is the image created? The McMath-Pierce solar telescope uses a mirror that is more than 2 m in diameter to direct the sun's rays down a diagonal shaft to another mirror, which is 152 m underground. This mirror is adjustable to focus the sunlight. The sunlight is then directed to a third mirror, which directs the light to an observing room and instrument shaft.

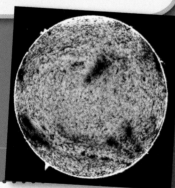

Scientific Discoveries

The Oort Cloud

Have you ever wondered where comets come from? In 1950, Dutch astronomer Jan Oort decided to find out where comets originated. Oort studied 19 comets. He found that none of these comets had orbits indicating that the comets had come from outside the solar system. Oort thought that all of the comets had come from an area at the far edge of the solar system. In addition, he believed that the comets had entered the planetary system from different directions. These conclusions led Oort to theorize that the area from which comets come surrounds the solar system like a sphere and that comets can come from any point within the sphere. Today, this spherical zone at the edge of the solar system is called the *Oort Cloud*. Astronomers believe that billions or even trillions of comets may exist within the Oort Cloud.

Math ACTIVITY

The outer skin of the McMath-Pierce solar telescope consists of 140 copper panels that measure 10.4 m × 2.4 m each. How many square meters of copper were used to construct the outer skin of the telescope?

Social Studies ACTIVITY

WRITING SKILL Before astronomers understood the nature of comets, comets were a source of much fear and misunderstanding among humans. Research some of the myths that humans have created about comets. Summarize your findings in a short essay.

Subrahmanyan Chandrasekhar

From White Dwarfs to Black Holes You may be familiar with the *Chandra X-Ray Observatory*. Launched by NASA in July 1999 to search for x-ray sources in space, the observatory is the most powerful x-ray telescope that has ever been built. However, you may not know how the observatory got its name. The *Chandra X-Ray Observatory* was named after the Indian American astrophysicist Subrahmanyan Chandrasekhar (SOOB ruh MAHN yuhn CHUHN druh SAY kuhr).

One of the most influential astrophysicists of the 20th century, Chandrasekhar was simply known as "Chandra" by his fellow scientists. Chandrasekhar made many contributions to physics and astrophysics. The contribution for which Chandrasekhar is best known was made in 1933, when he was a 23-year-old graduate student at Cambridge University in England. At the time, astrophysicists thought that all stars eventually became planet-sized stars known as *white dwarfs*. But from his calculations, Chandrasekhar believed that not all stars ended their lives as white dwarfs. He determined that the upper limit to the mass of a white dwarf was 1.4 times the mass of the sun. Stars that were more massive would collapse and would become very dense objects. These objects are now known as *black holes*. Chandrasekhar's ideas revolutionized astrophysics. In 1983, at the age of 73, Chandrasekhar was awarded the Nobel Prize in physics for his work on the evolution of stars.

Language Arts ACTiViTY

WRITING SKILL Using the Internet or another source, research the meaning of the word *chandra*. Write a paragraph describing your findings.

go.hrw.com

To learn more about these Science in Action topics, visit go.hrw.com and type in the keyword **HZ5SOLF.**

Current Science

Check out Current Science® articles related to this chapter by visiting go.hrw.com. Just type in the keyword HZ5CS20.

A Family of Planets

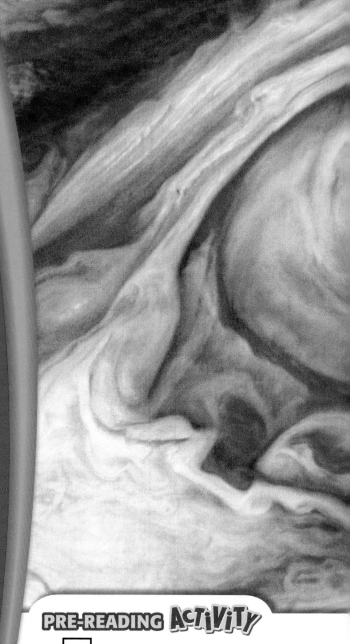

About the PHOTO

These rich swirls of color may remind you of a painting you might see in an art museum. But this photograph is of the planet Jupiter. The red swirl, called the Great Red Spot, is actually a hurricane-like storm system that is 3 times the diameter of Earth!

PRE-READING ACTIVITY

FOLDNOTES **Booklet** Before you read the chapter, create the FoldNote entitled "Booklet" described in the **Study Skills** section of the Appendix. Label each page of the booklet with a name of a planet in our solar system. As you read the chapter, write what you learn about each planet on the appropriate page of the booklet.

START-UP ACTIVITY

Measuring Space

Do the following activity to get a better idea of your solar neighborhood.

Procedure

1. Use a **meterstick** and some **chalk** to draw a line 2 m long on a **chalkboard.** Draw a large dot at one end of the line. This dot represents the sun.

2. Draw smaller dots on the line to represent the relative distances of each of the planets from the sun, based on information in the table.

Analysis

1. What do you notice about how the planets are spaced?

Planet	Distance from sun	
	Millions of km	Scaled to cm
Mercury	57.9	2
Venus	108.2	4
Earth	149.6	5
Mars	227.9	8
Jupiter	778.4	26
Saturn	1,424.0	48
Uranus	2,827.0	97
Neptune	4,499.0	151
Pluto	5,943.0	200

A Family of Planets **93**

The Nine Planets

Did you know that planets, when viewed from Earth, look like stars to the naked eye? Ancient astronomers were intrigued by these "stars" which seemed to wander in the sky.

Ancient astronomers named these "stars" planets, which means "wanderers" in Greek. These astronomers knew planets were physical bodies and could predict their motions. But scientists did not begin to explore these worlds until the 17th century, when Galileo used the telescope to study planets and stars. Now, scientists have completed more than 150 successful missions to moons, planets, comets, and asteroids in our cosmic neighborhood.

Our Solar System

Our *solar system,* shown in **Figure 1,** includes the sun, the planets, and many smaller objects. In some cases, these bodies may be organized into smaller systems of their own. For example, the Saturn system is made of the planet Saturn and the several moons that orbit Saturn. In this way, our solar system is a combination of many smaller systems.

READING WARM-UP

Objectives

- List the planets in the order in which they orbit the sun.
- Explain how scientists measure distances in space.
- Describe how the planets in our solar system were discovered.
- Describe three ways in which the inner planets and outer planets differ.

Terms to Learn

astronomical unit

READING STRATEGY

Paired Summarizing Read this section silently. In pairs, take turns summarizing the material. Stop to discuss ideas that seem confusing.

Figure 1 *These images show the relative diameters of the planets and the sun.*

Mercury
4,879 km

Venus
12,104 km

Earth
12,756 km

Mars
6,794 km

Sun
1,392,000 km

Jupiter
142,984 km

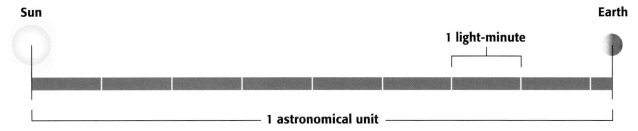

Sun   Earth

1 light-minute

1 astronomical unit

Figure 2 *One astronomical unit equals about 8.3 light-minutes.*

Measuring Interplanetary Distances

One way that scientists measure distances in space is by using the astronomical unit. One **astronomical unit** (AU) is the average distance between the sun and Earth, or approximately 150,000,000 km. Another way to measure distances in space is by using the speed of light. Light travels at about 300,000 km/s in space. This means that in 1 s, light travels 300,000 km.

In 1 min, light travels nearly 18,000,000 km. This distance is also called a *light-minute*. Look at **Figure 2.** Light from the sun takes 8.3 min to reach Earth. So, the distance from Earth to the sun, or 1 AU, is 8.3 light-minutes. Distances in the solar system can be measured in light-minutes and light-hours.

Reading Check **How far does light travel in 1 s?** (*See the Appendix for answers to Reading Checks.*)

astronomical unit the average distance between the Earth and the sun; approximately 150 million kilometers (symbol, AU)

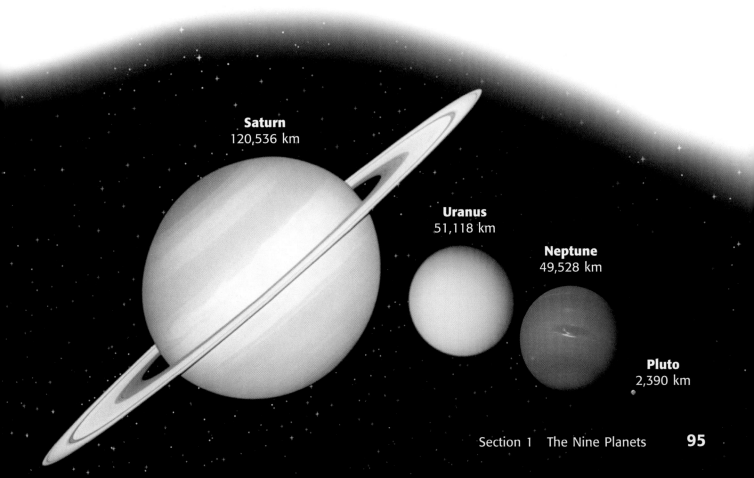

Saturn
120,536 km

Uranus
51,118 km

Neptune
49,528 km

Pluto
2,390 km

For another activity related to this chapter, go to **go.hrw.com** and type in the keyword **HZ5FAMW.**

The Discovery of the Solar System

Up until the 17th century, the universe was thought to have only eight bodies. These bodies included the planets Earth, Mercury, Venus, Mars, Jupiter, and Saturn, the sun, and the Earth's moon. These bodies are the only ones that can be seen from Earth without using a telescope.

After the telescope was invented in the 17th century, however, more discoveries were made. By the end of the 17th century, nine more large bodies were discovered. These bodies were moons of Jupiter and Saturn.

By the 18th century, the planet Uranus, along with two of its moons and two more of Saturn's moons, was discovered. In the 19th century, Neptune, as well as moons of several other planets, was discovered. Finally, in the 20th century, the ninth planet, Pluto, was discovered.

The Inner and Outer Solar Systems

The solar system is divided into two main parts: the inner solar system and the outer solar system. The inner solar system contains the four planets that are closest to the sun. The outer solar system contains the planets that are farthest from the sun.

The Inner Planets

The planets of the inner solar system, shown in **Figure 3,** are more closely spaced than the planets of the outer solar system. The inner planets are also known as the *terrestrial planets* because their surfaces are dense and rocky. However, each of the inner planets is unique.

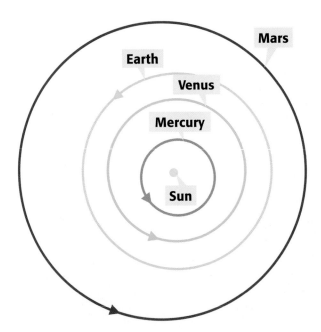

Figure 3 *The inner planets are the planets that are closest to the sun.*

The Outer Planets

The planets of the outer solar system include Jupiter, Saturn, Uranus, Neptune, and Pluto. The outer planets are very different from the inner planets, as you will soon find out.

Unlike the inner planets, the outer planets, except for Pluto, are large and are composed mostly of gases. Because of this, Jupiter, Saturn, Uranus, and Neptune are known as gas giants. The atmospheres of these planets blend smoothly into the denser layers of their interiors. The icy planet Pluto is the only planet of the outer solar system that is small, dense, and rocky. You can see a diagram of the outer solar system in **Figure 4.**

Reading Check Which planets are in the outer solar system?

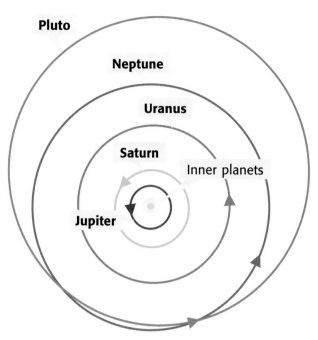

Figure 4 The planets of the outer solar system are the farthest from the sun.

SECTION Review

Summary

- In the order in which they orbit the sun, the nine planets are Mercury, Venus, Earth, Mars, Jupiter, Saturn, Uranus, Neptune, and Pluto.

- Two ways in which scientists measure distances in space are to use astronomical units and to use light-years.

- The inner planets are spaced more closely together, are smaller, and are rockier than the outer planets.

Using Key Terms

1. In your own words, write a definition for the term *astronomical unit*.

Understanding Key Ideas

2. When was the planet Uranus discovered?
   a. before the 17th century
   b. in the 18th century
   c. in the 19th century
   d. in the 20th century

3. The invention of what instrument helped early scientists discover more bodies in the solar system?

4. Which of the nine planets are included in the outer solar system?

5. Describe how the inner planets are different from the outer planets.

Math Skills

6. If Venus is 6.0 light-minutes from the sun, what is Venus's distance from the sun in astronomical units?

Critical Thinking

7. **Analyzing Methods** The distance between Earth and the sun is measured in light-minutes, but the distance between Pluto and the sun is measured in light-hours. Explain why.

Developed and maintained by the National Science Teachers Association

For a variety of links related to this chapter, go to www.scilinks.org

Topic: The Nine Planets
SciLinks code: HSM1033

SECTION 2

The Inner Planets

In the inner solar system, you will find one of the hottest places in our solar system as well as the only planet known to support life.

READING WARM-UP

Objectives

- Explain the difference between a planet's period of rotation and period of revolution.
- Describe the difference between prograde and retrograde rotation.
- Describe the individual characteristics of Mercury, Venus, Earth, and Mars.
- Identify the characteristics that make Earth suitable for life.

Terms to Learn

terrestrial planet
prograde rotation
retrograde rotation

READING STRATEGY

Reading Organizer As you read this section, create an outline of the section. Use the headings from the section in your outline.

The inner planets are also called **terrestrial planets** because, like Earth, they are very dense and rocky. The inner planets are smaller, denser, and rockier than the outer planets. In this section, you will learn more about the individual characteristics of Mercury, Venus, Earth, and Mars.

terrestrial planet one of the highly dense planets nearest to the sun; Mercury, Venus, Mars, and Earth

Mercury: Closest to the Sun

If you visited the planet Mercury, shown in **Figure 1,** you would find a very strange world. For one thing, on Mercury you would weigh only 38% of what you weigh on Earth. The weight you have on Earth is due to surface gravity, which is less on less massive planets. Also, because of Mercury's slow rotation, a day on Mercury is almost 59 Earth days long! The amount of time that an object takes to rotate once is called its *period of rotation.* So, Mercury's period of rotation is almost 59 Earth days long.

A Year on Mercury

Another curious thing about Mercury is that its year is only 88 Earth days long. As you know, a *year* is the time that a planet takes to go around the sun once. The motion of a body orbiting another body in space is called *revolution.* The time an object takes to revolve around the sun once is called its *period of revolution.* Every 88 Earth days, or 1.5 Mercurian days, Mercury revolves once around the sun.

Figure 1 *This image of Mercury was taken by the* Mariner 10 *spacecraft on March 24, 1974, from a distance of 5,380,000 km.*

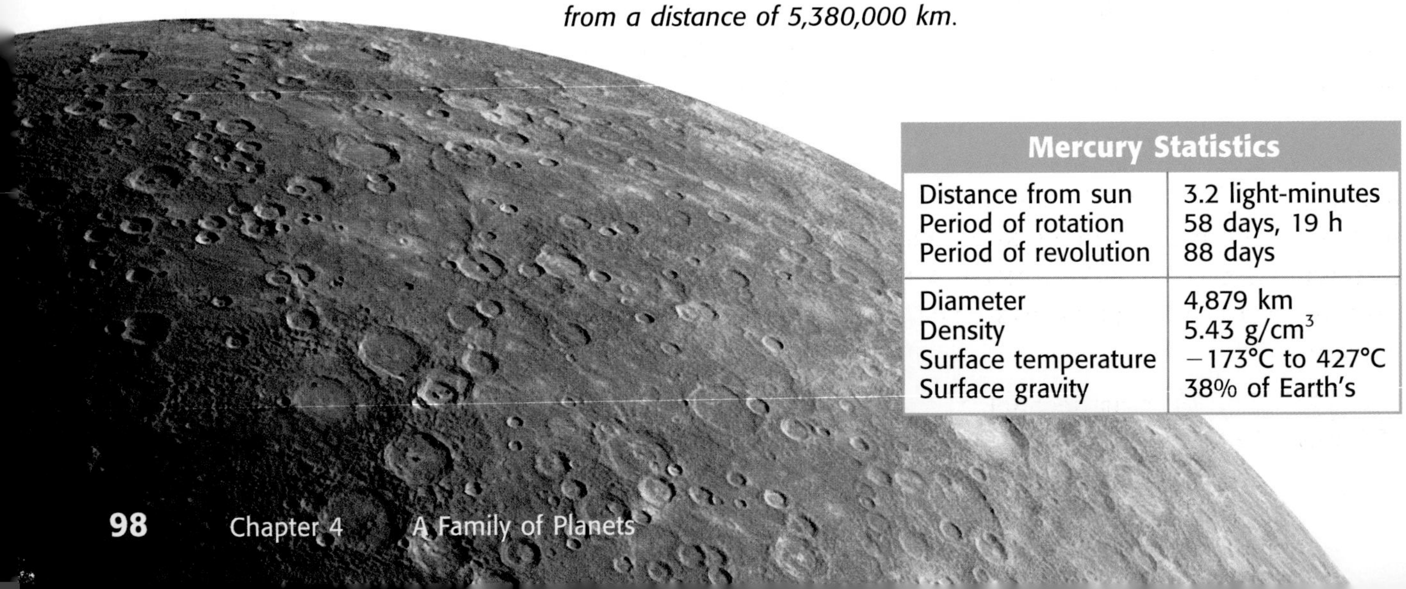

Mercury Statistics	
Distance from sun	3.2 light-minutes
Period of rotation	58 days, 19 h
Period of revolution	88 days
Diameter	4,879 km
Density	5.43 g/cm^3
Surface temperature	−173°C to 427°C
Surface gravity	38% of Earth's

Venus Statistics	
Distance from sun	6.0 light-minutes
Period of rotation	243 days, 16 h (R)*
Period of revolution	224 days, 17 h
Diameter	12,104 km
Density	5.24 g/cm³
Surface temperature	464°C
Surface gravity	91% of Earth's

*R = retrograde rotation

Figure 2 *This image of Venus was taken by* Mariner 10 *on February 5, 1974. The uppermost layer of clouds contains sulfuric acid.*

Venus: Earth's Twin?

Look at **Figure 2.** In many ways, Venus is more like Earth than any other planet. Venus is only slightly smaller, less massive, and less dense than Earth. But in other ways, Venus is very different from Earth. On Venus, the sun rises in the west and sets in the east. The reason is that Venus and Earth rotate in opposite directions. Earth is said to have **prograde rotation** because it appears to spin in a *counterclockwise* direction when it is viewed from above its North Pole. If a planet spins in a *clockwise* direction, the planet is said to have **retrograde rotation.**

The Atmosphere of Venus

Of the terrestrial planets, Venus has the densest atmosphere. Venus's atmosphere has 90 times the pressure of Earth's atmosphere! The air on Venus is mostly carbon dioxide, but the air is also made of some of the most destructive acids known. The carbon dioxide traps thermal energy from sunlight in a process called the *greenhouse effect.* The greenhouse effect causes Venus's surface temperature to be very high. At 464°C, Venus has the hottest surface of any planet in the solar system.

Mapping Venus's Surface

Between 1990 and 1992, the *Magellan* spacecraft mapped the surface of Venus by using radar waves. The radar waves traveled through the clouds and bounced off the planet's surface. Data gathered from the radar waves showed that Venus, like Earth, has volcanoes.

Reading Check What technology was used to map the surface of Venus? (*See the Appendix for answers to Reading Checks.*)

prograde rotation the counter-clockwise spin of a planet or moon as seen from above the planet's North Pole; rotation in the same direction as the sun's rotation

retrograde rotation the clockwise spin of a planet or moon as seen from above the planet's North Pole

Figure 3 *Earth is the only planet known to support life.*

Earth: An Oasis in Space

As viewed from space, Earth is like a sparkling blue oasis in a black sea of stars. Constantly changing weather patterns create the swirls of clouds that blanket the blue and brown sphere we call home. Look at **Figure 3.** Why did Earth have such good fortune, while its two nearest neighbors, Venus and Mars, are unsuitable for life as we know it?

Water on Earth

Earth formed at just the right distance from the sun. Earth is warm enough to keep most of its water from freezing. But unlike Venus, Earth is cool enough to keep its water from boiling away. Liquid water is a vital part of the chemical processes that living things depend on for survival.

The Earth from Space

The picture of Earth shown in **Figure 4** was taken from space. You might think that the only goal of space exploration is to make discoveries beyond Earth. But the National Aeronautics and Space Administration (NASA) has a program to study Earth by using satellites in the same way that scientists study other planets. This program is called the Earth Science Enterprise. Its goal is to study the Earth as a global system that is made of smaller systems. These smaller systems include the atmosphere, land, ice, the oceans, and life. The program will also help us understand how humans affect the global environment. By studying Earth from space, scientists hope to understand how different parts of the global system interact.

Reading Check What is the Earth Science Enterprise?

Earth Statistics	
Distance from sun	8.3 light-minutes
Period of rotation	23 h, 56 min
Period of revolution	365 days, 6 h
Diameter	12,756 km
Density	5.52 g/cm^3
Surface temperature	−13°C to 37°C
Surface gravity	100% of Earth's

Figure 4 *This image of Earth was taken on December 7, 1972, by the crew of the* Apollo 17 *spacecraft while on their way to the moon.*

Mars Statistics	
Distance from sun	12.7 light-minutes
Period of rotation	24 h, 40 min
Period of revolution	1 year, 322 days
Diameter	6,794 km
Density	3.93 g/cm³
Surface temperature	−123°C to 37°C
Surface gravity	38% of Earth's

Mars: Our Intriguing Neighbor

Mars, shown in **Figure 5,** is perhaps the most studied planet in the solar system other than Earth. Much of our knowledge of Mars has come from information gathered by spacecraft. *Viking 1* and *Viking 2* landed on Mars in 1976, and *Mars Pathfinder* landed on Mars in 1997.

The Atmosphere of Mars

Because of its thinner atmosphere and greater distance from the sun, Mars is a cold planet. Midsummer temperatures recorded by the *Mars Pathfinder* range from –13°C to –77°C. Martian air is so thin that the air pressure on the surface of Mars is about the same as it is 30 km above Earth's surface. This distance is about 3 times higher than most planes fly! The air pressure is so low that any liquid water would quickly boil away. The only water found on the surface of Mars is in the form of ice.

Figure 5 *This Viking orbiter image shows the eastern hemisphere of Mars. The large circular feature in the center is the impact crater Schiaparelli, which has a diameter of 450 km.*

Water on Mars

Even though liquid water cannot exist on Mars's surface today, there is strong evidence that it existed there in the past. **Figure 6** shows an area on Mars with features that might have resulted from deposition of sediment in a lake. This finding means that in the past Mars might have been a warmer place and had a thicker atmosphere.

Figure 6 *The origin of the features shown in this image is unknown. The features might have resulted from deposition of sediment in a lake.*

The Outer Planets

What do all the outer planets except for Pluto have in common?

Except for Pluto, the outer planets are very large planets that are made mostly of gases. These planets are called gas giants. **Gas giants** are planets that have deep, massive atmospheres rather than hard and rocky surfaces like those of the inner planets.

Jupiter: A Giant Among Giants

Jupiter is the largest planet in our solar system. Like the sun, Jupiter is made mostly of hydrogen and helium. The outer part of Jupiter's atmosphere is made of layered clouds of water, methane, and ammonia. The beautiful colors you see in **Figure 1** are probably due to small amounts of organic compounds. At a depth of about 10,000 km into Jupiter's atmosphere, the pressure is high enough to change hydrogen gas into a liquid. Deeper still, the pressure changes the liquid hydrogen into a liquid, metallic state. Unlike most planets, Jupiter radiates much more energy into space than it receives from the sun. The reason is that Jupiter's interior is very hot. Another striking feature of Jupiter is the Great Red Spot, a storm system that is more than 400 years old and is about 3 times the diameter of Earth!

NASA Missions to Jupiter

NASA has sent five missions to Jupiter. These include two Pioneer missions, two Voyager missions, and the recent Galileo mission. The *Voyager 1* and *Voyager 2* spacecraft sent back images that revealed a thin, faint ring around Jupiter. The Voyager missions also gave us the first detailed images of Jupiter's moons. The *Galileo* spacecraft reached Jupiter in 1995 and sent a probe into Jupiter's atmosphere. The probe sent back data on Jupiter's composition, temperature, and pressure.

Figure 1 *This* Voyager 2 *image of Jupiter was taken at a distance of 28.4 million kilometers. Io, one of Jupiter's largest moons, can also be seen in this image.*

Jupiter Statistics	
Distance from sun	43.3 light-minutes
Period of rotation	9 h, 54 min
Period of revolution	11 years, 313 days
Diameter	142,984 km
Density	1.33 g/cm^3
Temperature	−110°C
Gravity	236% of Earth's

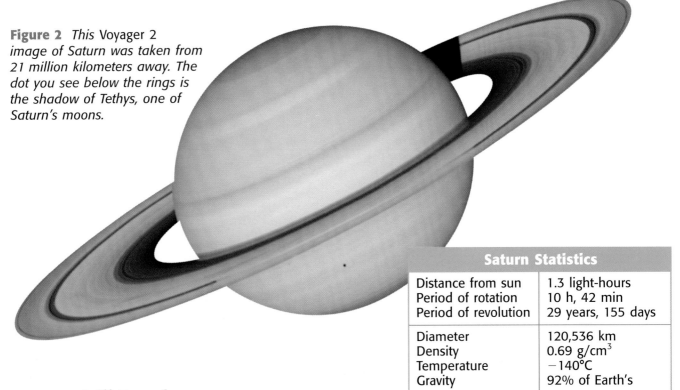

Figure 2 *This* Voyager 2 *image of Saturn was taken from 21 million kilometers away. The dot you see below the rings is the shadow of Tethys, one of Saturn's moons.*

Saturn Statistics	
Distance from sun	1.3 light-hours
Period of rotation	10 h, 42 min
Period of revolution	29 years, 155 days
Diameter	120,536 km
Density	0.69 g/cm^3
Temperature	−140°C
Gravity	92% of Earth's

Saturn: Still Forming

Saturn, shown in **Figure 2,** is the second-largest planet in the solar system. Saturn has roughly 764 times the volume of Earth and is 95 times more massive than Earth. Its overall composition, like Jupiter's, is mostly hydrogen and helium. But methane, ammonia, and ethane are found in the upper atmosphere. Saturn's interior is probably much like Jupiter's. Also, like Jupiter, Saturn gives off much more energy than it receives from the sun. Scientists think that Saturn's extra energy comes from helium falling out of the atmosphere and sinking to the core. In other words, Saturn is still forming!

The Rings of Saturn

Although all of the gas giants have rings, Saturn's rings are the largest. Saturn's rings have a total diameter of 272,000 km. Yet, Saturn's rings are only a few hundred meters thick. The rings are made of icy particles that range in size from a few centimeters to several meters wide. **Figure 3** shows a close-up view of Saturn's rings.

Reading Check What are Saturn's rings made of? (*See the Appendix for answers to Reading Checks.*)

NASA's Exploration of Saturn

Launched in 1997, the *Cassini* spacecraft is designed to study Saturn's rings, moons, and atmosphere. The spacecraft is also designed to return more than 300,000 color images of Saturn.

Figure 3 *The different colors in this* Voyager 2 *image of Saturn's rings show differences in the rings' chemical composition.*

Uranus Statistics	
Distance from sun	2.7 light-hours
Period of rotation	17 h, 12 min (R)*
Period of revolution	83 years, 273 days
Diameter	51,118 km
Density	1.27 g/cm^3
Temperature	−195°C
Gravity	89% of Earth's

*R = retrograde rotation

Figure 4 *This image of Uranus was taken by* Voyager 2 *at a distance of 9.1 million kilometers.*

Uranus: A Small Giant

Uranus (YOOR uh nuhs) was discovered by the English amateur astronomer William Herschel in 1781. The atmosphere of Uranus is mainly hydrogen and methane. Because these gases absorb the red part of sunlight very strongly, Uranus appears blue-green in color, as shown in **Figure 4.** Uranus and Neptune have much less mass than Jupiter, but their densities are similar. This suggests that their compositions are different from Jupiter's. They may have lower percentages of light elements and a greater percentage of water.

A Tilted Planet

Figure 5 *Uranus's axis of rotation is tilted so that the axis is nearly parallel to the plane of Uranus's orbit. In contrast, the axes of most other planets are closer to being perpendicular to the plane of the planets' orbits.*

Unlike most other planets, Uranus is tipped over on its side. So, its axis of rotation is tilted by almost 90° and lies almost in the plane of its orbit, as shown in **Figure 5.** For part of a Uranus year, one pole points toward the sun while the other pole is in darkness. At the other end of Uranus's orbit, the poles are reversed. Some scientists think that early in its history, Uranus may have been hit by a massive object that tipped the planet over.

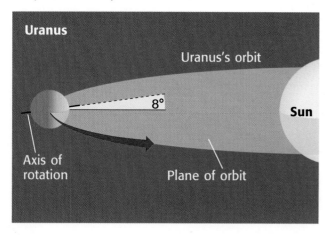

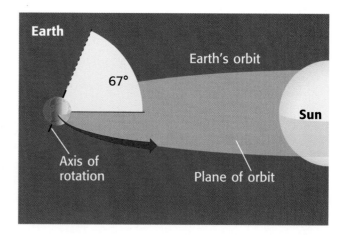

Neptune: The Blue World

Irregularities in the orbit of Uranus suggested to early astronomers that there must be another planet beyond it. They thought that the gravity of this new planet pulled Uranus off its predicted path. By using the predictions of the new planet's orbit, astronomers discovered the planet Neptune in 1846. Neptune is shown in **Figure 6.**

The Atmosphere of Neptune

The *Voyager 2* spacecraft sent back images that provided much new information about Neptune's atmosphere. Although the composition of Neptune's atmosphere is similar to that of Uranus's atmosphere, Neptune's atmosphere has belts of clouds that are much more visible. At the time of *Voyager 2*'s visit, Neptune had a Great Dark Spot like the Great Red Spot on Jupiter. And like the interiors of Jupiter and Saturn, Neptune's interior releases thermal energy to its outer layers. This release of energy helps the warm gases rise and the cool gases sink, which sets up the wind patterns in the atmosphere that create the belts of clouds. *Voyager 2* images also revealed that Neptune has a set of very narrow rings.

Reading Check What characteristic of Neptune's interior accounts for the belts of clouds in Neptune's atmosphere?

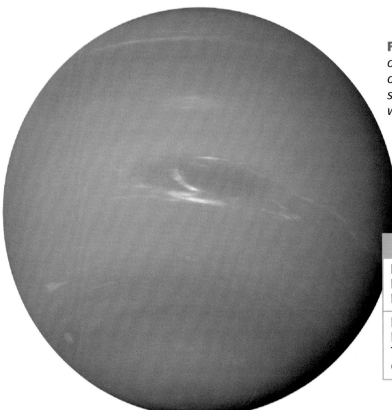

Figure 6 *This* Voyager 2 *image of Neptune, taken at a distance of more than 7 million kilometers, shows the Great Dark Spot as well as some bright cloud bands.*

Neptune Statistics	
Distance from sun	4.2 light-hours
Period of rotation	16 h, 6 min
Period of revolution	163 years, 263 days
Diameter	49,528 km
Density	1.64 g/cm^3
Temperature	−200°C
Gravity	112% of Earth's

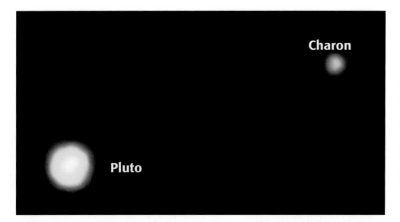

Pluto Statistics	
Distance from sun	5.4 light-hours
Period of rotation	6 days, 10 h (R)*
Period of revolution	248 years, 4 days
Diameter	2,390 km
Density	1.75 g/cm^3
Surface temperature	−225°C
Surface gravity	6% of Earth's

*R = retrograde rotation

Figure 7 *This Hubble Space Telescope image is one of the clearest ever taken of Pluto (left) and its moon, Charon (right).*

Pluto: The Mystery Planet

Further study of Neptune showed some irregularities in Neptune's orbit. This finding led many scientists to believe there was yet another planet beyond Neptune. The mystery planet was finally discovered in 1930.

A Small World

The mystery planet, now called Pluto, is the farthest planet from the sun. Less than half the size of Mercury, Pluto is also the smallest planet. Pluto's moon, Charon (KER uhn), is more than half its size! In fact, Charon is the largest satellite relative to its planet in the solar system. **Figure 7** shows Pluto and Charon together. From Earth, it is hard to separate the images of Pluto and Charon because the bodies are so far away. **Figure 8** shows how far from the sun Pluto and Charon really are. From Pluto, the sun looks like a very distant bright star.

From calculations of Pluto's density, scientists know that Pluto must be made of rock and ice. Pluto is covered by frozen nitrogen, but Charon is covered by frozen water. Scientists believe Pluto has a thin atmosphere of methane.

Figure 8 *An artist's view of the sun and Charon from Pluto shows just how little light and heat Pluto receives from the sun.*

A True Planet?

Because Pluto is so small and is so unusual, some scientists think that it should not be classified as a planet. In fact, some scientists agree that Pluto could be considered a large asteroid or comet—large enough to have its own satellite. However, because Pluto was historically classified as a planet, it most likely will remain so.

Pluto is the only planet that has not been visited by a NASA mission. However, plans are underway to visit Pluto and Charon in 2006. During this mission, scientists hope to learn more about this unusual planet and map the surface of both Pluto and Charon.

SCHOOL to HOME

Surviving Space

WRITING SKILL Imagine it is the year 2150 and you are flying a spacecraft to Pluto. Suddenly, your systems fail, giving you only one chance to land safely. You can't head back to Earth. With a parent, write a paragraph explaining which planet you would choose to land on.

ACTIVITY

SECTION Review

Summary

- Jupiter is the largest planet in our solar system. Energy from the interior of Jupiter is transferred to its exterior.

- Saturn is the second-largest planet and, in some ways, is still forming as a planet.

- Uranus's axis of rotation is tilted by almost 90°.

- Neptune has a faint ring, and its atmosphere contains belts of clouds.

- Pluto is the smallest planet, and its moon, Charon, is more than half its size.

Using Key Terms

1. In your own words, write a definition for the term *gas giant*.

Understanding Key Ideas

2. The many colors of Jupiter's atmosphere are probably caused by _____ in the atmosphere.
   a. clouds of water
   b. methane
   c. ammonia
   d. organic compounds

3. Why do scientists claim that Saturn, in a way, is still forming?

4. Why does Uranus have a blue green color?

5. What is unusual about Pluto's moon, Charon?

6. What is the Great Red Spot?

7. Explain why Jupiter radiates more energy into space than it receives from the sun.

8. How do the gas giants differ from the terrestrial planets?

9. What is so unusual about Uranus's axis of rotation?

Math Skills

10. Pluto is 5.5 light-hours from the sun. How far is Pluto from the sun in astronomical units? (Hint: 1 AU = 8.3 light-minutes)

11. If Jupiter is 43.3 light-minutes from the sun and Neptune is 4.2 light-hours from the sun, how far from Jupiter is Neptune?

Critical Thinking

12. **Evaluating Data** What conclusions can your draw about the properties of a planet just by knowing how far it is from the sun?

13. **Applying Concepts** Why isn't the word *surface* included in the statistics for the gas giants?

SCILINKS

NSTA
Developed and maintained by the National Science Teachers Association

For a variety of links related to this chapter, go to www.scilinks.org

Topic: The Outer Planets
SciLinks code: HSM1091

Moons

If you could, which moon would you visit? With volcanoes, craters, and possible underground oceans, the moons in our solar system would be interesting places to visit.

Natural or artificial bodies that revolve around larger bodies such as planets are called **satellites.** Except for Mercury and Venus, all of the planets have natural satellites called *moons.*

Luna: The Moon of Earth

Scientists have learned a lot from studying Earth's moon, which is also called *Luna.* The lunar rocks brought back during the Apollo missions were found to be about 4.6 billion years old. Because these rocks have hardly changed since they formed, scientists know the solar system itself is about 4.6 billion years old.

The Surface of the Moon

As you can see in **Figure 1,** the moon's history is written on its face. The surfaces of bodies that have no atmospheres preserve a record of almost all of the impacts that the bodies have had. Because scientists now know the age of the moon, they can count the number of impact craters to find the rate of cratering since the birth of our solar system. By knowing the rate of cratering, scientists are able to use the number of craters on any body to estimate how old the body's surface is. That way, scientists don't need to bring back rock samples.

READING WARM-UP

Objectives

● Describe the current theory of the origin of Earth's moon.

● Explain what causes the phases of Earth's moon.

● Describe the difference between a solar eclipse and a lunar eclipse.

● Describe the individual characteristics of the moons of other planets.

Terms to Learn

satellite
phase
eclipse

READING STRATEGY

Reading Organizer As you read this section, make a table comparing solar eclipses and lunar eclipses.

Figure 1 *This image of the moon was taken by the* Galileo *spacecraft while on its way to Jupiter. The large, dark areas are lava plains called* maria.

Moon Statistics	
Period of rotation	27 days, 9 hours
Period of revolution	27 days, 7 hours
Diameter	3,475 km
Density	3.34 g/cm^3
Surface temperature	−170 to 134°C
Surface gravity	16% of Earth's

Lunar Origins

Before scientists had rock samples from the moon, there were three popular explanations for the moon's formation: (1) The moon was a separate body captured by Earth's gravity, (2) the moon formed at the same time and from the same materials as the Earth, and (3) the newly formed Earth was spinning so fast that a piece flew off and became the moon.

When rock samples of the moon were brought back from the Apollo mission, the mystery was solved. Scientists found that the composition of the moon was similar to that of Earth's mantle. This evidence from the lunar rock samples supported the third explanation for the moon's formation.

The current theory is that a large, Mars-sized object collided with Earth while the Earth was still forming, as shown in **Figure 2.** The collision was so violent that part of the Earth's mantle was blasted into orbit around Earth to form the moon.

satellite a natural or artificial body that revolves around a planet

✓ **Reading Check** What is the current explanation for the formation of the moon? (*See the Appendix for answers to Reading Checks.*)

Figure 2 **Formation of the Moon**

❶ **Impact**
About 4.6 billion years ago, when Earth was still mostly molten, a large body collided with Earth. Scientists reason that the object must have been large enough to blast part of Earth's mantle into space, because the composition of the moon is similar to that of Earth's mantle.

❷ **Ejection**
The resulting debris began to revolve around the Earth within a few hours of the impact. This debris consisted of mantle material from Earth and from the impacting body as well as part of the iron core of the impacting body.

❸ **Formation**
Soon after the giant impact, the clumps of material ejected into orbit around Earth began to join together to form the moon. Much later, as the moon cooled, additional impacts created deep basins and fractured the moon's surface. Lunar lava flowed from those cracks and flooded the basins to form the lunar maria that we see today.

Phases of the Moon

From Earth, one of the most noticeable aspects of the moon is its continually changing appearance. Within a month, the moon's Earthward face changes from a fully lit circle to a thin crescent and then back to a circle. These different appearances of the moon result from its changing position relative to Earth and the sun. As the moon revolves around Earth, the amount of sunlight on the side of the moon that faces Earth changes. The different appearances of the moon due to its changing position are called **phases.** The phases of the moon are shown in **Figure 3.**

phase the change in the sunlit area of one celestial body as seen from another celestial body

Waxing and Waning

When the moon is *waxing,* the sunlit fraction that we can see from Earth is getting larger. When the moon is *waning,* the sunlit fraction is getting smaller. Notice in **Figure 3** that even as the phases of the moon change, the total amount of sunlight that the moon gets remains the same. Half the moon is always in sunlight, just as half the Earth is always in sunlight. But because the moon's period of rotation is the same as its period of revolution, on Earth you always see the same side of the moon. If you lived on the far side of the moon, you would see the sun for half of each lunar day, but you would never see the Earth!

Figure 3 *The positions of the moon, sun, and Earth determine which phase the moon is in. The photo insets show how the moon looks from Earth at each phase.*

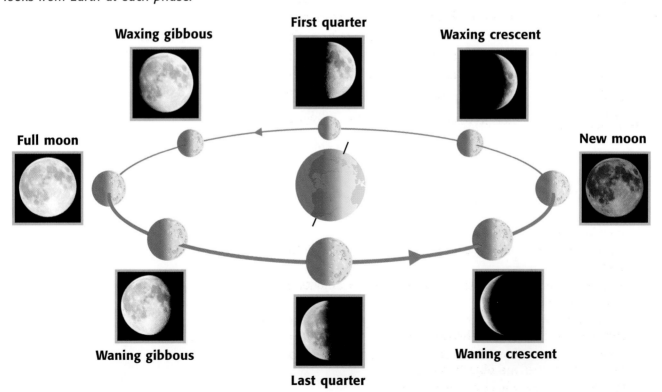

Waxing gibbous

First quarter

Waxing crescent

Full moon

New moon

Waning gibbous

Last quarter

Waning crescent

Solar eclipse

NEVER look directly at the sun! You can permanently damage your eyes.

Eclipses

When the shadow of one celestial body falls on another, an **eclipse** occurs. A *solar eclipse* happens when the moon comes between Earth and the sun and the shadow of the moon falls on part of Earth. A *lunar eclipse* happens when Earth comes between the sun and the moon and the shadow of Earth falls on the moon.

Solar Eclipses

Because the moon's orbit is elliptical, the distance between the moon and the Earth changes. During an *annular eclipse*, the moon is farther from the Earth. The disk of the moon does not completely cover the disk of the sun. A thin ring of the sun shows around the moon's outer edge. When the moon is closer to the Earth, the moon appears to be the same size as the sun. During a *total solar eclipse*, the disk of the moon completely covers the disk of the sun, as shown in **Figure 4.**

✓ **Reading Check** Describe what happens during a solar eclipse.

Figure 4 *On the left is a diagram of the positions of the Earth and the moon during a solar eclipse. On the right is a picture of the sun's outer atmosphere, or corona, which is visible only when the entire disk of the sun is blocked by the moon.*

eclipse an event in which the shadow of one celestial body falls on another

Clever Insight

1. Cut out a circle of **heavy, white paper**. This circle will represent Earth.
2. Find **two spherical objects** and **several other objects** of different shapes.
3. Hold up each object in front of a **lamp** (which represents the sun) so that the object's shadow falls on the white paper circle.
4. Rotate your objects in all directions, and record the shapes of the shadows that the objects make.
5. Which objects always cast a curved shadow?

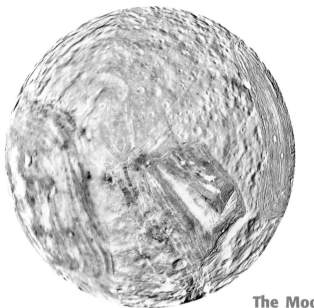

Figure 8 *This* Voyager 2 *image shows Miranda, the most unusual moon of Uranus. Its patchwork terrain indicates that it has had a violent history.*

The Moons of Uranus

Uranus has several moons. Like the moons of Saturn, Uranus's largest moons are made of ice and rock and are heavily cratered. The small moon Miranda, shown in **Figure 8,** has some of the strangest features in the solar system. Miranda's surface has smooth, cratered plains as well as regions that have grooves and cliffs. Scientists think that Miranda may have been hit and broken apart in the past. Gravity pulled the pieces together again, leaving a patchwork surface.

The Moons of Neptune

Neptune has several known moons, only one of which is large. This large moon, Triton, is shown in **Figure 9.** It revolves around the planet in a *retrograde,* or "backward," orbit. This orbit suggests that Triton may have been captured by Neptune's gravity. Triton has a very thin atmosphere made mostly of nitrogen gas. Triton's surface is mostly frozen nitrogen and methane. *Voyager 2* images reveal that Triton is geologically active. "Ice volcanoes," or geysers, eject nitrogen gas high into the atmosphere. The other moons of Neptune are small, rocky worlds much like the smaller moons of Saturn and Jupiter.

The Moon of Pluto

Pluto's only known moon, Charon, was discovered in 1978. Charon's period of revolution is the same as Pluto's period of rotation—about 6.4 days. So, one side of Pluto always faces Charon. In other words, if you stood on the surface of Pluto, Charon would always occupy the same place in the sky. Charon's orbit around Pluto is tilted relative to Pluto's orbit around the sun. As a result, Pluto, as seen from Earth, is sometimes eclipsed by Charon. But don't hold your breath; this eclipse happens only once every 120 years!

✓ Reading Check How often is Pluto eclipsed by Charon?

Figure 9 *This* Voyager 2 *image shows Neptune's largest moon, Triton. The polar icecap currently facing the sun may have a slowly evaporating layer of nitrogen ice, adding to Triton's thin atmosphere.*

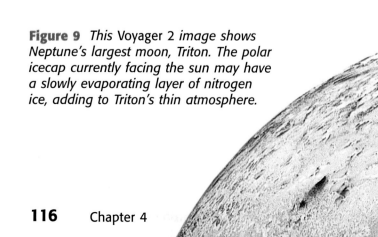

Summary

- Scientists reason that the moon formed from the debris that was created after a large body collided with Earth.
- As the moon revolves around Earth, the amount of sunlight on the side of the moon changes. Because the amount of sunlight on the side of the moon changes, the moon's appearance from Earth changes. These changes in appearance are the phases of the moon.
- A solar eclipse happens when the shadow of the moon falls on Earth.

- A lunar eclipse happens when the shadow of Earth falls on the moon.
- Mars has 2 moons: Phobos and Deimos.
- Jupiter has dozens of moons. Ganymede, Io, Callisto, and Europa are the largest.
- Saturn has dozens of moons. Titan is the largest.
- Uranus has several moons.
- Neptune has several moons. Triton is the largest.
- Pluto has 1 known moon, Charon.

Using Key Terms

Complete each of the following sentences by choosing the correct term from the word bank.

> satellite   eclipse

1. A(n) _____, or a body that revolves around a larger body, can be either artificial or natural.

2. A(n) _____ occurs when the shadow of one body in space falls on another body.

Understanding Key Ideas

3. Which of the following is a Galilean satellite?
   a. Phobos
   b. Deimos
   c. Ganymede
   d. Charon

4. Describe the current theory for the origin of Earth's moon.

5. What is the difference between a solar eclipse and a lunar eclipse?

6. What causes the phases of Earth's moon?

Critical Thinking

7. **Analyzing Methods** How can astronomers use the age of a lunar rock to estimate the age of the surface of a planet such as Mercury?

8. **Identifying Relationships** Charon stays in the same place in Pluto's sky, but the moon moves across Earth's sky. What causes this difference?

Interpreting Graphics

Use the diagram below to answer the questions that follow.

9. What type of eclipse is shown in the diagram?

10. Describe what is happening in the diagram.

11. Make a sketch of the type of eclipse that is not shown in the diagram.

SCiLINKS®
NSTA
Developed and maintained by the National Science Teachers Association

For a variety of links related to this chapter, go to www.scilinks.org

Topic: Moons of Other Planets
SciLinks code: HSM0993

Small Bodies in the Solar System

Imagine you are traveling in a spacecraft to explore the edge of our solar system. You see several small bodies, as well as the planets and their satellites, moving through space.

The solar system contains not only planets and moons but other small bodies, including comets, asteroids, and meteoroids. Scientists study these objects to learn about the composition of the solar system.

Comets

A small body of ice, rock, and cosmic dust loosely packed together is called a **comet**. Some scientists refer to comets as "dirty snowballs" because of their composition. Comets formed in the cold, outer solar system. Nothing much has happened to comets since the birth of the solar system 4.6 billion years ago. Comets are probably left over from the time when the planets formed. As a result, each comet is a sample of the early solar system. Scientists want to learn more about comets to piece together the history of our solar system.

Comet Tails

When a comet passes close enough to the sun, solar radiation heats the ice so that the comet gives off gas and dust in the form of a long tail, as shown in **Figure 1.** Sometimes, a comet has two tails—an *ion tail* and a *dust tail*. The ion tail is made of electrically charged particles called *ions*. The solid center of a comet is called its *nucleus*. Comet nuclei can range in size from less than half a kilometer to more than 100 km in diameter.

Figure 1 *This image shows the physical features of a comet when it is close to the sun. The nucleus of a comet is hidden by brightly lit gases and dust.*

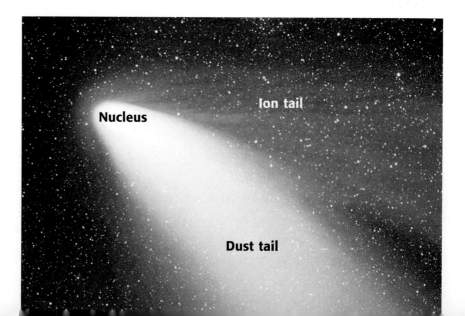

Nucleus

Ion tail

Dust tail

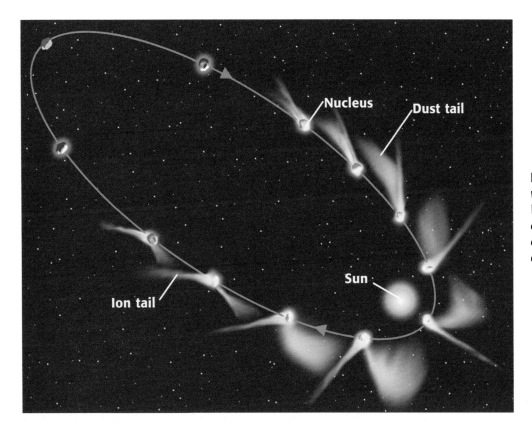

Figure 2 *Comets have very elongated orbits. When a comet gets close to the sun, the comet can develop one or two tails.*

Nucleus
Dust tail
Ion tail
Sun

Comet Orbits

The orbits of all bodies that move around the sun are ellipses. *Ellipses* are circles that are somewhat stretched out of shape. The orbits of most planets are close to perfect circles, but the orbits of comets are very elongated.

Notice in **Figure 2** that a comet's ion tail always points away from the sun. The reason is that the ion tail is blown away from the sun by *solar wind*, which is also made of ions. The dust tail tends to follow the comet's orbit around the sun. Dust tails do not always point away from the sun. When a comet is close to the sun, its tail can extend millions of kilometers through space!

Comet Origins

Where do comets come from? Many scientists think that comets come from the Oort (AWRT) cloud, a spherical region that surrounds the solar system. When the gravity of a passing planet or star disturbs part of this cloud, comets can be pulled toward the sun. Another recently discovered region where comets exist is the Kuiper (KIE puhr) belt, which is the region outside the orbit of Neptune.

Reading Check **From which two regions do comets come?**
(See the Appendix for answers to Reading Checks.)

comet a small body of ice, rock, and cosmic dust that follows an elliptical orbit around the sun and that gives off gas and dust in the form of a tail as it passes close to the sun

CONNECTION TO
Language Arts

WRITING SKILL **Interplanetary Journalist** In 1994, the world watched in awe as parts of the comet Shoemaker-Levy 9 collided with Jupiter, which caused enormous explosions. Imagine you were an interplanetary journalist who traveled through space to observe the comet during this time. Write an article describing your adventure.

Asteroids

Small, rocky bodies that revolve around the sun are called **asteroids.** They range in size from a few meters to more than 900 km in diameter. Asteroids have irregular shapes, although some of the larger ones are spherical. Most asteroids orbit the sun in the asteroid belt. The **asteroid belt** is a wide region between the orbits of Mars and Jupiter. Like comets, asteroids are thought to be material left over from the formation of the solar system.

Types of Asteroids

The composition of asteroids varies depending on where they are located within the asteroid belt. In the outermost region of the asteroid belt, asteroids have dark reddish brown to black surfaces. This coloring may indicate that the asteroids are rich in organic material. Asteroids that have dark gray surfaces are rich in carbon. In the innermost part of the asteroid belt are light gray asteroids that have either a stony or metallic composition. **Figure 3** shows three asteroids: Hektor, Ceres, and Vesta.

asteroid a small, rocky object that orbits the sun, usually in a band between the orbits of Mars and Jupiter

asteroid belt the region of the solar system that is between the orbits of Mars and Jupiter and in which most asteroids orbit

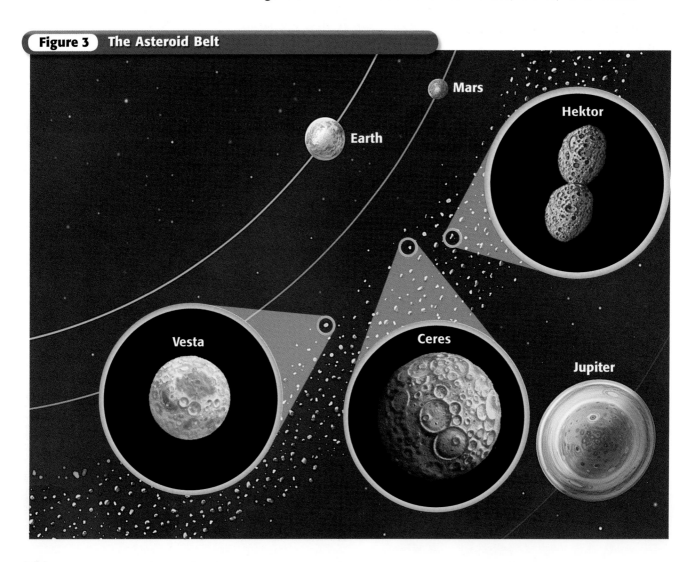

Figure 3 The Asteroid Belt

Meteoroids

Meteoroids are similar to but much smaller than asteroids. A **meteoroid** is a small, rocky body that revolves around the sun. Most meteoroids are probably pieces of asteroids. A meteoroid that enters Earth's atmosphere and strikes the ground is called a **meteorite.** As a meteoroid falls into Earth's atmosphere, the meteoroid moves so fast that its surface melts. As the meteoroid burns up, it gives off an enormous amount of light and thermal energy. From the ground, you see a spectacular streak of light, or a shooting star. A **meteor** is the bright streak of light caused by a meteoroid or comet dust burning up in the atmosphere.

meteoroid a relatively small, rocky body that travels through space

meteorite a meteoroid that reaches the Earth's surface without burning up completely

meteor a bright streak of light that results when a meteoroid burns up in the Earth's atmosphere

Meteor Showers

Many of the meteors that we see come from very small (dust-sized to pebble-sized) rocks. Even so, meteors can be seen on almost any night if you are far enough away from a city to avoid the glare of its lights. At certain times of the year, you can see large numbers of meteors, as shown in **Figure 4.** These events are called *meteor showers.* Meteor showers happen when Earth passes through the dusty debris that comets leave behind.

Types of Meteorites

Like their asteroid relatives, meteorites have different compositions. The three major types of meteorites—stony, metallic, and stony-iron meteorites—are shown in **Figure 5.** Many of the stony meteorites probably come from carbon-rich asteroids. Stony meteorites may contain organic materials and water. Scientists use meteorites to study the early solar system. Like comets and asteroids, meteorites are some of the building blocks of planets.

Figure 4 *Meteors are the streaks of light caused by meteoroids as they burn up in Earth's atmosphere.*

✓ **Reading Check** What are the major types of meteorites?

Figure 5 **Three Major Types of Meteorites**

| **Stony meteorite** rocky material | **Metallic meteorite** iron and nickel | **Stony-iron meteorite** rocky material, iron, and nickel |

WRITING SKILL **Mass Extinctions** Throughout Earth's history, there have been times when large numbers of species suddenly became extinct. Many scientists think that these mass extinctions may have been caused by impacts of large objects on Earth. However, other scientists are not so sure. Use the Internet or another source to research this idea. In your **science journal,** write a paragraph describing the different theories scientists have for past mass extinctions.

The Role of Impacts in the Solar System

An impact happens when an object in space collides with another object in space. Often, the result of such a collision is an impact crater. Many planets and moons have visible impact craters. In fact, several planets and moons have many more impact craters than Earth does. Planets and moons that do not have atmospheres have more impact craters than do planets and moons that have atmospheres.

Look at **Figure 6.** Earth's moon has many more impact craters than the Earth does because the moon has no atmosphere to slow objects down. Fewer objects strike Earth because Earth's atmosphere acts as a shield. Smaller objects burn up before they ever reach the surface. Also, most craters left on Earth are no longer visible because of weathering, erosion, and tectonic activity.

Future Impacts on Earth?

Most objects that come close to Earth are small and usually burn up in the atmosphere. However, larger objects are more likely to strike Earth's surface. Scientists estimate that impacts that are powerful enough to cause a natural disaster might happen once every few thousand years. An impact that is large enough to cause a global catastrophe is estimated to happen once every few hundred thousand years, on average.

Reading Check How often do large objects strike Earth?

Figure 6 *The surface of the moon preserves a record of billions of years of cosmic impacts.*

The Torino Scale

The Torino scale is a system that allows scientists to rate the hazard level of an object moving toward Earth. The object is carefully observed and then assigned a number from the scale. The scale ranges from 0 to 10. Zero indicates that the object has a very small chance of striking Earth. Ten indicates that the object will definitely strike Earth and cause a global disaster. The Torino scale is also color coded. White represents 0, and green represents 1. White and green objects rarely strike Earth. Yellow represents 2, 3, and 4 and indicates a higher chance that objects will hit Earth. Orange, which represents 5, 6, and 7, refers to objects highly likely to hit Earth. Red refers to objects that will definitely hit Earth.

SECTION Review

Summary

- Studying comets, asteroids, and meteoroids can help scientists understand more about the formation of the solar system.

- Asteroids are small bodies that orbit the sun. Meteoroids are similar to but smaller than asteroids. Most meteoroids come from asteroids.

- Most objects that collide with Earth burn up in the atmosphere. Large impacts, however, may cause a global catastrophe.

Using Key Terms

For each pair of terms, explain how the meanings of the terms differ.

1. *comet* and *asteroid*

2. *meteor* and *meteorite*

Understanding Key Ideas

3. Which of the following is NOT a type of meteorite?
   a. stony meteorite
   b. rocky-iron meteorite
   c. stony-iron meteorite
   d. metallic meteorite

4. Why is the study of comets, asteroids, and meteoroids important in understanding the formation of the solar system?

5. Why do a comet's two tails often point in different directions?

6. How can a cosmic impact affect life on Earth?

7. What is the difference between an asteroid and a meteoroid?

8. Where is the asteroid belt located?

9. What is the Torino scale?

10. Describe why we see several impact craters on the moon but few on Earth.

Math Skills

11. The diameter of comet A's nucleus is 55 km. If the diameter of comet B's nucleus is 30% larger than comet A's nucleus, what is the diameter of comet B's nucleus?

Critical Thinking

12. **Expressing Opinions** Do you think the government should spend money on programs to search for asteroids and comets that have Earth-crossing orbits? Explain.

13. **Making Inferences** What is the likelihood that scientists will discover an object belonging in the red category of the Torino scale in the next 500 years? Explain your answer.

For a variety of links related to this chapter, go to www.scilinks.org

Topic: Comets, Asteroids, and Meteoroids

SciLinks code: HSM0317

Inquiry Lab

OBJECTIVES

Create a calendar based on the Martian cycles of rotation and revolution.

Describe why it is useful to have a calendar that matches the cycles of the planet on which you live.

MATERIALS

- calculator (optional)
- marker
- pencils, assorted colors
- poster board
- ruler, metric

Create a Calendar

Imagine that you live in the first colony on Mars. You have been trying to follow the Earth calendar, but it just isn't working anymore. Mars takes almost 2 Earth years to revolve around the sun—almost 687 Earth days to be exact! That means that there are only two Martian seasons for every Earth calendar year. On Mars, in one Earth year, you get winter and spring, but the next year, you get only summer and fall! And Martian days are longer than Earth days. Mars takes 24.6 Earth hours to rotate on its axis. Although they are similar, Earth days and Martian days just don't match. You need a new calendar!

Ask a Question

1 How can I create a calendar based on the Martian cycles of rotation and revolution that includes months, weeks, and days?

Form a Hypothesis

2 Write a few sentences that answer your question.

Test the Hypothesis

3 Use the following formulas to determine the number of Martian days in a Martian year:

$$\frac{687 \text{ Earth days}}{1 \text{ Martian year}} \times \frac{24 \text{ Earth hours}}{1 \text{ Earth day}} = \text{Earth hours per Martian year}$$

$$\text{Earth hours per Martian year} \times \frac{1 \text{ Martian day}}{24.6 \text{ Earth hours}} = \text{Martian days per Martian year}$$

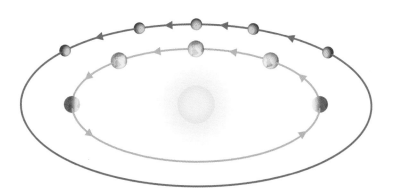

4. Decide how to divide your calendar into a system of Martian months, weeks, and days. Will you have a leap day, a leap week, a leap month, or a leap year? How often will it occur?

5. Choose names for the months and days of your calendar. Explain why you chose each name. If you have time, explain how you would number the Martian years. For instance, would the first year correspond to a certain Earth year?

6. Follow your design to create your own calendar for Mars. Construct your calendar by using a computer to help organize your data. Draw the calendar on your piece of poster board. Make sure it is brightly colored and easy to follow.

7. Present your calendar to the class. Explain how you chose your months, weeks, and days.

Analyze the Results

1. **Analyzing Results** What advantages does your calendar design have? Are there any disadvantages to your design?

2. **Classifying** Which student or group created the most original calendar? Which design was the most useful? Explain.

3. **Analyzing Results** What might you do to improve your calendar?

Draw Conclusions

4. **Evaluating Models** Take a class vote to decide which design should be chosen as the new calendar for Mars. Why was this calendar chosen? How did it differ from the other designs?

5. **Drawing Conclusions** Why is it useful to have a calendar that matches the cycles of the planet on which you live?

Chapter Review

USING KEY TERMS

For each pair of terms, explain how the meanings of the terms differ.

1 *terrestrial planet* and *gas giant*

2 *asteroid* and *comet*

3 *meteor* and *meteorite*

Complete each of the following sentences by choosing the correct term from the word bank.

astronomical unit   meteorite
meteoroid   prograde
retrograde   satellite

4 The average distance between the sun and Earth is 1 ___.

5 A small rock in space is called a(n) ___.

6 When viewed from above its north pole, a body that moves in a counterclockwise direction is said to have ___ rotation.

7 A(n) ___ is a natural or artificial body that revolves around a planet.

UNDERSTANDING KEY IDEAS

Multiple Choice

8 Of the following, which is the largest body?

  a. the moon

  b. Pluto

  c. Mercury

  d. Ganymede

9 Which of the following planets have retrograde rotation?

  a. the terrestrial planets

  b. the gas giants

  c. Mercury, Venus, and Uranus

  d. Venus, Uranus, and Pluto

10 Which of the following planets does NOT have any moons?

  a. Mercury

  b. Mars

  c. Uranus

  d. None of the above

11 Why can liquid water NOT exist on the surface of Mars?

  a. The temperature is too high.

  b. Liquid water once existed there.

  c. The gravity of Mars is too weak.

  d. The atmospheric pressure is too low.

Short Answer

12 List the names of the planets in the order the planets orbit the sun.

13 Describe three ways in which the inner planets are different from the outer planets.

14 What are the gas giants? How are the gas giants different from the terrestrial planets?

15 What is the difference between asteroids and meteoroids?

16 What is the difference between a planet's period of rotation and period of revolution?

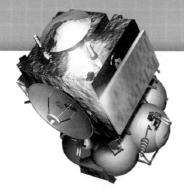

17 Explain the difference between prograde rotation and retrograde rotation.

18 Which characteristics of Earth make it suitable for life?

19 Describe the current theory for the origin of Earth's moon.

20 What causes the phases of the moon?

CRITICAL THINKING

21 **Concept Mapping** Use the following terms to create a concept map: *solar system, terrestrial planets, gas giants, moons, comets, asteroids,* and *meteoroids.*

22 **Applying Concepts** Even though we haven't yet retrieved any rock samples from Mercury's surface for radiometric dating, scientists know that the surface of Mercury is much older than that of Earth. How do scientists know this?

23 **Making Inferences** Where in the solar system might scientists search for life, and why?

24 **Analyzing Ideas** Is the far side of the moon always dark? Explain your answer.

25 **Predicting Consequences** If scientists could somehow bring Europa as close to the sun as the Earth is, 1 AU, how do you think Europa would be affected?

26 **Identifying Relationships** How did variations in the orbit of Uranus help scientists discover Neptune?

INTERPRETING GRAPHICS

The graph below shows density versus mass for Earth, Uranus, and Neptune. Mass is given in Earth masses—the mass of Earth is equal to 1 Earth mass. The relative volumes for the planets are shown by the size of each circle. Use the graph below to answer the questions that follow.

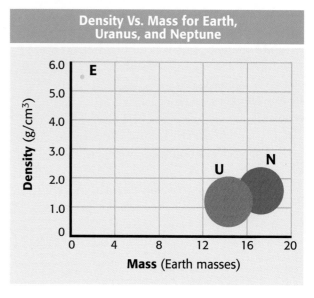

Density Vs. Mass for Earth, Uranus, and Neptune

27 Which planet is denser, Uranus or Neptune? How can you tell?

28 You can see that although Earth has the smallest mass, it has the highest density of the three planets. How can Earth be the densest of the three when Uranus and Neptune have so much more mass than Earth does?

READING

Read each of the passages below. Then, answer the questions that follow each passage.

Passage 1 Imagine that it is 200 BCE and you are an apprentice to a Greek astronomer. After years of observing the sky, the astronomer knows all of the constellations as well as the back of his hand. He shows you how the stars all move together—the whole sky spins slowly as the night goes on. He also shows you that among the thousands of stars in the sky, some of the brighter ones slowly change their position relative to the other stars. He names these stars *planetai*, the Greek word for "wanderers." Building on the observations of the ancient Greeks, we now know that the *planetai* are actually planets, not wandering stars.

1. Which of the following did the ancient Greeks know to be true?
   A All planets have at least one moon.
   B The planets revolve around the sun.
   C The planets are much smaller than the stars.
   D The planets appear to move relative to the stars.

2. What can you infer from the passage about the ancient Greek astronomers?
   F They were patient and observant.
   G They knew much more about astronomy than we do.
   H They spent all their time counting stars.
   I They invented astrology.

3. What does the word *planetai* mean in Greek?
   A planets
   B wanderers
   C stars
   D moons

Passage 2 To explain the source of short-period comets (comets that have a relatively short orbit), the Dutch-American astronomer Gerard Kuiper proposed in 1949 that a belt of icy bodies must lie beyond the orbits of Pluto and Neptune. Kuiper argued that comets were icy <u>planetesimals</u> that formed from the condensation that happened during the formation of our galaxy. Because the icy bodies are so far from any large planet's gravitational field (30 to 100 AU), they can remain on the fringe of the solar system. Some theorists speculate that the large moons Triton and Charon were once members of the Kuiper belt before they were captured by Neptune and Pluto. These moons and short-period comets have similar physical and chemical properties.

1. According to the passage, why can icy bodies remain at the edge of the solar system?
   A The icy bodies are so small that they naturally float to the edge of the solar system.
   B The icy bodies have weak gravitational fields and therefore do not orbit individual planets.
   C The icy bodies are short-period comets, which can reside only at the edge of the solar system.
   D The icy bodies are so far away from any large planet's gravitational field that they can remain at the edge of the solar system.

2. According to the passage, which of the following best describes the meaning of the word *planetesimal*?
   F a small object that existed during the early development of the solar system
   G an extremely tiny object in space
   H a particle that was once part of a planet
   I an extremely large satellite that was the result of a collision of two objects

Use the diagrams below to answer the questions that follow.

Planet A 115 craters/km²

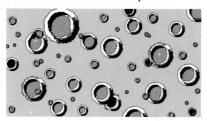

Planet B 75 craters/km²

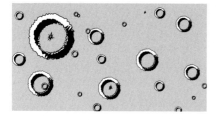

Planet C 121 craters/km²

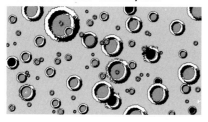

Planet D 97 craters/km²

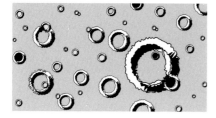

1. According to the information above, which planet has the oldest surface?

A planet A

B planet B

C planet C

D planet D

2. How many more craters per square kilometer are there on planet C than on planet B?

F 46 craters per square kilometer

G 24 craters per square kilometer

H 22 craters per square kilometer

I 6 craters per square kilometer

Read each question below, and choose the best answer.

1. Venus's surface gravity is 91% of Earth's. If an object weighs 12 N on Earth, how much would it weigh on Venus?

A 53 N

B 13 N

C 11 N

D 8 N

2. Earth's overall density is 5.52 g/cm³, while Saturn's density is 0.69 g/cm³. How many times denser is Earth than Saturn?

F 8 times

G 9 times

H 11 times

I 12 times

3. If Earth's history spans 4.6 billion years and the Phanerozoic eon was 543 million years, what percentage of Earth's history does the Phanerozoic eon represent?

A about 6%

B about 12%

C about 18%

D about 24%

4. The diameter of Venus is 12,104 km. The diameter of Mars is 6,794 km. What is the difference between the diameter of Venus and the diameter of Mars?

F 5,400 km

G 5,310 km

H 4,890 km

I 890 km

Standardized Test Preparation

Science in Action

Science Fiction

"The Mad Moon" by Stanley Weinbaum

The third largest moon of Jupiter, called Io, can be a hard place to live. Grant Calthorpe is finding this out the hard way. Although living comfortably is possible in the small cities at the polar regions of Io, Grant has to spend most of his time in the moon's hot and humid jungles. Grant treks into the jungles of Io to gather ferva leaves so that they can be converted into useful medications for humans. During Grant's quest, he encounters loonies and slinkers, and he has to avoid blancha, a kind of tropical fever that causes hallucinations, weakness, and vicious headaches. Without proper medication a person with blancha can go mad or even die. In "The Mad Moon," you'll discover a dozen adventures with Grant Calthorpe as he struggles to stay alive—and sane.

Language Arts ACTiViTY

WRITING SKILL Read "The Mad Moon" by Stanley Weinbaum. Write a short story describing the adventures that you would have on Io if you were chosen as Grant Calthorpe's assistant.

Scientific Debate

Is Pluto a Planet?

Is it possible that Pluto isn't a planet? Some scientists think so! Since 1930, Pluto has been included as one of the nine planets in our solar system. But observations in the 1990s led many astronomers to refer to Pluto as an object, not a planet. Other astronomers disagree with this change. Astronomers that refer to Pluto as an object do not think that it fits well with the other outer planets. Unlike the other outer planets, which are large and gaseous, Pluto is small and made of rock and ice. Pluto also has a very elliptical orbit that is unlike its neighboring planets. Astronomers that think Pluto is a planet point out that Pluto, like all other planets, has its own atmosphere and its own moon, called Charon. These and other factors have fueled a debate as to whether Pluto should be classified as a planet.

Math ACTiViTY

How many more kilometers is Earth's diameter compared to Pluto's diameter if Earth's diameter is 12,756 km and Pluto's diameter is 2,390 km?

Adriana C. Ocampo

Planetary Geologist Sixty-five million years ago, in what is now Mexico, a giant meteor at least six miles wide struck Earth. The meteor made a hole nine miles deep and over 100 miles wide. The meteor sent billions of tons of dust into Earth's atmosphere. This dust formed thick clouds. After forming, these clouds may have left the planet in total darkness for six months, and the temperature near freezing for ten years. Some scientists think that this meteor crash and its effect on the Earth's climate led to the extinction of the dinosaurs. Adriana Ocampo studies the site in Mexico made by the crater known as the Chicxulub (cheeks OO loob) impact crater. Ocampo is a planetary geologist and has been interested in space exploration since she was young. Ocampo's specialty is studying "impact craters." "Impact craters are formed when an asteroid or a comet collides with the Earth or any other terrestrial planet," explains Ocampo. Ocampo visits crater sites around the world to collect data. She also uses computers to create models of how the impact affected the planet. Ocampo has worked for NASA and has helped plan space exploration missions to Mars, Jupiter, Saturn, and Mercury. Ocampo currently works for the European Space Agency (ESA) and is part of the team getting ready to launch the next spacecraft that will go to Mars.

Social Studies ACTiViTY

Research information about impact craters. Find the different locations around the world where impact craters have been found. Make a world map that highlights these locations.

The circle on the map shows the site in Mexico made by the Chicxulub impact crater.

go.hrw.com

To learn more about these Science in Action topics, visit go.hrw.com and type in the keyword HZ5FAMF.

Current Science

Check out Current Science® articles related to this chapter by visiting go.hrw.com. Just type in the keyword HZ5CS21.

5

Exploring Space

About the PHOTO

Although the astronauts in the photo appear to be motionless, they are orbiting the Earth at almost 28,000 km/h! The astronauts reached orbit—about 300 km above the Earth's surface—in a space shuttle. Space shuttles are the first vehicles in a new generation of reusable spacecraft. They have opened an era of space exploration in which missions to space are more common than ever before.

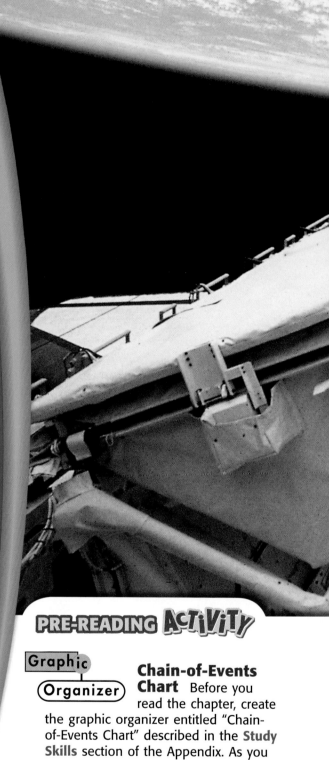

PRE-READING ACTIVITY

Graphic
Organizer

Chain-of-Events Chart Before you read the chapter, create the graphic organizer entitled "Chain-of-Events Chart" described in the **Study Skills** section of the Appendix. As you read the chapter, fill in the chart with a timeline that describes the exploration of space from the theories of Konstantin Tsiolkovsky to the future of space exploration.

START-UP ACTIVITY

Balloon Rockets

In this activity you will launch a balloon "rocket" to learn about how rockets move.

Procedure

1. Insert a **2 m thread** through a **drinking straw,** and tie it between two objects that won't move, such as **chairs.** Make sure that the thread is tight.

2. Inflate a **large balloon.** Do not tie the neck of the balloon closed. Hold the neck of the balloon closed, and **tape** the balloon firmly to the straw, parallel to the thread.

3. Move the balloon to one end of the thread, and then release the neck of the balloon. Use a **meterstick** to record the distance the balloon traveled.

4. Repeat steps 2–3. This time, hold a piece of **poster board** behind the balloon.

Analysis

1. Did the poster board affect the distance that the balloon traveled? Explain your answer.

2. Newton's third law of motion states that for every action there is an equal and opposite reaction. Apply this idea and your observations of the balloon to explain how rockets accelerate. Do rockets move by "pushing off" a launch pad? Explain your answer.

How Rockets Work

If you are sitting in a chair that has wheels and you want to move, you would probably push away from a table or kick yourself along with your feet. Many people think that rockets move in a similar way—by pushing off of a launch pad. But if rockets moved in this way, how would they accelerate in the vacuum of space where there is nothing to push against?

For Every Action . . .

As you saw in the Start-Up Activity, the balloon moved according to Newton's third law of motion. This law states that for every action there is an equal and opposite reaction. For example, the air rushing backward from a balloon (the action) results in the forward motion of the balloon (the reaction). Rockets work in the same way. In fact, rockets were once called *reaction devices*.

However, in the case of rockets, the action and the reaction may not be obvious. The mass of a rocket—including all of the fuel it carries—is much greater than the mass of the hot gases that come out of the bottom of the rocket. But because the exhaust gases are under extreme pressure, they exert a huge amount of force. The force that accelerates a rocket is called **thrust**. Look at **Figure 4** to learn more about how rockets work.

You Need More Than Rocket Fuel

Rockets burn fuel to provide the thrust that propels them. In order for something to burn, oxygen must be present. Although oxygen is plentiful at the Earth's surface, there is little or no oxygen in the upper atmosphere and in outer space. For this reason, rockets that go into outer space must carry enough oxygen with them to be able to burn their fuel. The space shuttles, for example, carry hundreds of thousands of gallons of liquid oxygen. This oxygen is needed to burn the shuttle's rocket fuel.

Reading Check Why do rockets carry oxygen in addition to fuel?

thrust the pushing or pulling force exerted by the engine of an aircraft or rocket

Figure 4 *Rockets move according to Newton's third law of motion.*

Reaction
Gas at the top of the combustion chamber pushes the rocket upward.

Action
Gas at the bottom of the combustion chamber pushes the exhaust downward.

How to Leave the Earth

The gravitational pull of the Earth is the main factor that a rocket must overcome. As shown in **Figure 5,** a rocket must reach a certain *velocity*, or speed and direction, to orbit or escape the Earth.

Orbital Velocity and Escape Velocity

For a rocket to orbit the Earth, it must have enough thrust to reach orbital velocity. *Orbital velocity* is the speed and direction a rocket must travel in order to orbit a planet or moon. The lowest possible speed a rocket may go and still orbit the Earth is about 8 km/s (17,927 mi/h). If the rocket goes any slower, it will fall back to Earth. For a rocket to travel beyond Earth orbit, the rocket must achieve escape velocity. *Escape velocity* is the speed and direction a rocket must travel to completely break away from a planet's gravitational pull. The speed a rocket must reach to escape the Earth is about 11 km/s (24,606 mi/h).

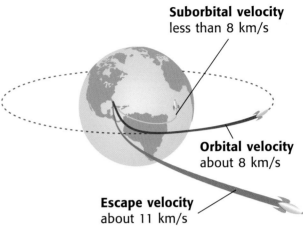

Suborbital velocity
less than 8 km/s

Orbital velocity
about 8 km/s

Escape velocity
about 11 km/s

Figure 5 *A rocket must travel very fast to escape the gravitational pull of the Earth.*

SECTION Review

Summary

- Tsiolkovsky and Goddard were pioneers of rocket science.

- The outcome of WWII and the political pressures of the Cold War helped advance rocket science.

- Rockets work according to Newton's third law of motion—for every action there is an equal and opposite reaction.

- Rockets need to reach different velocities to attain orbit and to escape a planet's gravitational attraction.

Using Key Terms

1. Use each of the following terms in a separate sentence: *rocket, thrust,* and *NASA*.

Understanding Key Ideas

2. What factor must a rocket overcome to reach escape velocity?
   a. Earth's axial tilt
   b. Earth's gravity
   c. the thrust of its engines
   d. Newton's third law of motion

3. Describe the contributions of Tsiolkovsky and Goddard to modern rocketry.

4. Use Newton's third law of motion to describe how rockets work.

5. What is the difference between orbital and escape velocity?

6. How did the Cold War accelerate the U.S. space program?

Math Skills

7. If you travel at 60 mi/h, it takes about 165 days to reach the moon. Approximately how far away is the moon?

Critical Thinking

8. **Applying Concepts** How do rockets accelerate in space?

9. **Making Inferences** Why does escape velocity vary depending on the planet from which a rocket is launched?

Artificial Satellites

You are watching TV, and suddenly a weather bulletin interrupts your favorite show. There is a HURRICANE WARNING! You grab a cell phone and call your friend— the hurricane is headed straight for where she lives!

In the story above, the TV show, the weather bulletin, and perhaps even the phone call were all made possible by artificial satellites orbiting thousands of miles above Earth! An **artificial satellite** is any human-made object placed in orbit around a body in space.

There are many kinds of artificial satellites. Weather satellites provide continuous updates on the movement of gases in the atmosphere so that we can predict weather on Earth's surface. Communications satellites relay TV programs, phone calls, and computer data. Remote-sensing satellites monitor changes in the environment. Perhaps more than the exploration of space, satellites have changed the way we live.

The First Satellites

The first artificial satellite, *Sputnik 1,* was launched by the Soviets in 1957. **Figure 1** shows a model of *Sputnik 1,* which orbited for 57 days before it fell back to Earth and burned up in the atmosphere. Two months later, *Sputnik 2* carried the first living being into space—a dog named Laika. The United States followed with the launch of its first satellite, *Explorer 1,* in 1958. The development of new satellites increased quickly. By 1964, communications satellite networks were able to send messages around the world. Today, thousands of satellites orbit the Earth, and more are launched every year.

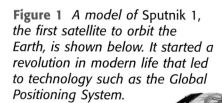

Figure 1 *A model of* Sputnik 1, *the first satellite to orbit the Earth, is shown below. It started a revolution in modern life that led to technology such as the Global Positioning System.*

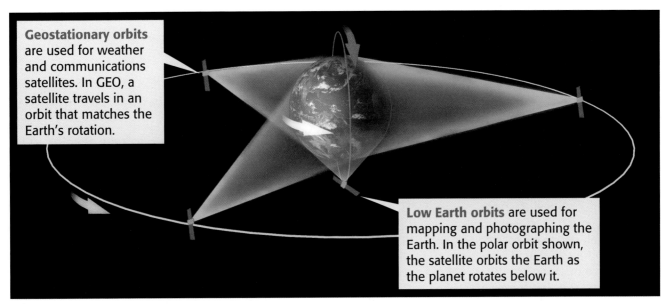

Geostationary orbits are used for weather and communications satellites. In GEO, a satellite travels in an orbit that matches the Earth's rotation.

Low Earth orbits are used for mapping and photographing the Earth. In the polar orbit shown, the satellite orbits the Earth as the planet rotates below it.

Choosing Your Orbit

Satellites are placed in different types of orbits, as shown in **Figure 2**. All of the early satellites were placed in **low Earth orbit** (LEO), which is a few hundred kilometers above the Earth's surface. A satellite in LEO moves around the Earth very quickly and can provide clear images of Earth. However, this motion can place a satellite out of contact much of the time.

Most communications satellites and weather satellites orbit much farther from Earth. In this orbit, called a **geostationary orbit** (GEO), a satellite travels in an orbit that exactly matches the Earth's rotation. Thus, the satellite is always above the same spot on Earth. Ground stations are in continuous contact with these satellites so that TV programs and other communications will not be interrupted.

✓ **Reading Check** What is the difference between GEO and LEO? (*See the Appendix for answers to Reading Checks.*)

Figure 2 *Low Earth orbits are in the upper reaches of Earth's atmosphere, while geostationary orbits are about 36,000 km from Earth's surface.*

artificial satellite any human-made object placed in orbit around a body in space

low Earth orbit an orbit less than 1,500 km above the Earth's surface

geostationary orbit an orbit that is about 36,000 km above the Earth's surface and in which a satellite is above a fixed spot on the equator

Modeling LEO and GEO

1. Use a **length of thread** to measure 300 km on the scale of a **globe**.

2. Use another **length of thread** to measure 36,000 km on the globe's scale.

3. Use the short thread to measure the distance of LEO from the surface of the globe and the long thread to measure the distance of GEO from the surface of the globe.

4. Your teacher will turn off the lights. One student will spin the globe, while other students will hold **penlights** at LEO and GEO orbits.

5. Was more of the globe illuminated by the penlights in LEO or GEO?

6. Which orbit is better for communications satellites? Which orbit is better for spy satellites?

Military Satellites

Some satellites placed in LEO are equipped with cameras that can photograph the Earth's surface in amazing detail. It is possible to photograph objects as small as this book from LEO. While photographs taken by satellites are now used for everything from developing real estate to tracking the movements of dolphins, the technology was first developed by the military. Because satellites can take very detailed photos from hundreds of kilometers above the Earth's surface, they are ideal for defense purposes. The United States and the Soviet Union developed satellites to spy on each other right up to the end of the Cold War. **Figure 3,** for example, is a photo of San Francisco taken by a Soviet spy satellite in 1989. Even though the Cold War is over, spy satellites continue to play an important role in the military defense of many countries.

The Global Positioning System

In the past, people invented very complicated ways to keep from getting lost. Now, for less than $100, people can find out their exact location on Earth by using a Global Positioning System (GPS) receiver. GPS is another example of military satellite technology that has become a part of everyday life. The GPS consists of 27 solar-powered satellites that continuously send radio signals to Earth. From the amount of time it takes the signals to reach Earth, the hand-held receiver can calculate its distance from the satellites. Using the distance from four satellites, a GPS receiver can determine a person's location with great accuracy.

Triangulation

GPS uses the principle of triangulation. To practice triangulation, use a drawing compass and a photocopy of a U.S. map that has a scale. Try to find a city that is 980 km from Detroit and Miami, and 950 km from Baltimore. For each city named, adjust the compass to the correct distance on the map's scale. Then, place the compass point on the city's location. Draw a circle with a radius equal to the given distance. Where do the circles overlap? Once you have solved this riddle, write one for a friend!

Figure 3 *This photo was taken in 1989 by a Soviet spy satellite in LEO about 220 km above San Francisco. Can you identify any objects on the ground?*

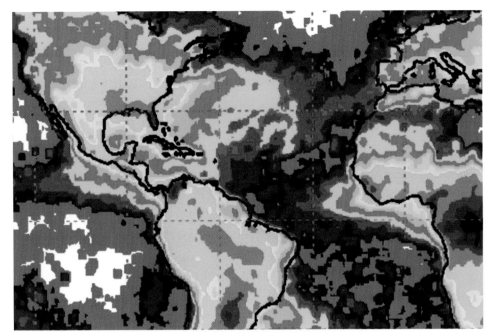

Figure 4 *This map shows average annual lightning strikes around the world. Red and black indicate a high number of strikes. Cooler colors, such as purple and blue, indicate fewer strikes.*

Weather Satellites

It is hard to imagine life without reliable weather forecasts. Every day, millions of people make decisions based on information provided by weather satellites. Weather satellites in GEO provide a big-picture view of the Earth's atmosphere. These satellites constantly monitor the atmosphere for the "triggers" that lead to severe weather conditions. Weather satellites in GEO created the map of world lightning strikes shown in **Figure 4.** Weather satellites in LEO are usually placed in polar orbits. Satellites in polar orbits revolve around the Earth in a north or south direction as the Earth rotates beneath them. These satellites, which orbit between 830 km and 870 km above the Earth, provide a much closer look at weather patterns.

Communications Satellites

Many types of modern communications use radio waves or microwaves to relay messages. Radio waves and microwaves are ideal for communications because they can travel through the air. The problem is that the Earth is round, but the waves travel in a straight line. So how do you send a message to someone on the other side of the Earth? Communications satellites in GEO solve this problem by relaying information from one point on Earth's surface to another. The signals are transmitted to a satellite and then sent to receivers around the world. Communications satellites relay computer data, and some television and radio broadcasts.

Reading Check How do communications satellites relay information from one point on Earth's surface to another?

Tracking Satellites

A comfortable lawn chair and a clear night sky are all you need to track satellites. Just after sunset or before sunrise, satellites in LEO are easy to track. They look like slow-moving stars, and they generally move in a west to east direction. With a little practice, you should be able to find one or two satellites a minute. A pair of binoculars will help you get a closer look. Satellites in GEO are difficult to see because they do not appear to move. You and a parent can find out more about how to track specific satellites and space stations on the Internet.

ACTIVITY

Remote Sensing and Environmental Change

Using satellites, scientists have been able to study the Earth in ways that were never before possible. Satellites gather information by *remote sensing*. Remote sensing is the gathering of images and data from a distance. Remote-sensing satellites measure light and other forms of energy that are reflected from Earth. Some satellites use radar, which bounces high-frequency radio waves off the Earth and measures the returned signal.

Landsat: Monitoring the Earth from Orbit

One of the most successful remote-sensing projects is the Landsat program, which began in 1972 and continues today. It has given us the longest continuous record of Earth's surface as seen from space. Landsat satellites gather images in several wavelengths—from visible light to infrared. **Figure 5** shows Landsat images of part of the Mississippi Delta. One image was taken in 1973, and the other was taken in 2003. The two images reveal a pattern of environmental change over a 30-year period. The main change is a dramatic reduction in the amount of silt that is reaching the delta. A comparison of the images also reveals a large-scale loss of wetlands in the bottom left of the delta in 2003. The loss of wetlands affects plants and animals living on the delta and the fishing industry.

Figure 5 **The Loss of Wetlands in the Mississippi Delta**

Silt reaching the Mississippi Delta is shown in blue. In 1973 (left), the amount of silt reaching the delta was much greater than in 2003 (right). This reduction led to the rapid loss of wetlands, which are green in this image. Notice the lower left corner of the delta in both images. Areas of wetland loss are black.

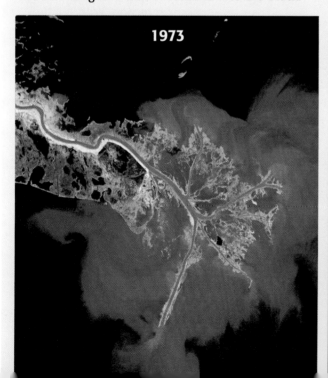
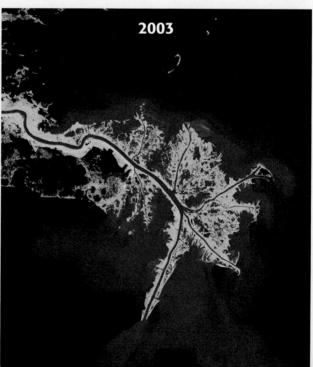

A New Generation of Remote-Sensing Satellites

The Landsat program has produced millions of images that are used to identify and track environmental change on Earth. Satellite remote sensing allows scientists to perform large-scale mapping, look at changes in patterns of vegetation growth, map the spread of urban development, and study the effect of humans on the global environment. In 1999, NASA launched *Terra 1*, the first satellite in NASA's Earth Observing System (EOS) program. Satellites in the EOS program are designed to work together so that they can gather integrated data on environmental change on the land, in the atmosphere, in the oceans, and on the icecaps.

Reading Check What is unique about the EOS program?

INTERNET ACTIVITY

For another activity related to this chapter, go to **go.hrw.com** and type in the keyword **HZ5EXPW.**

SECTION Review

Summary

- *Sputnik 1* was the first artificial satellite. *Explorer 1* was the first U.S. satellite.

- Low Earth orbits are used for making detailed images of the Earth.

- Geostationary orbits are used for communications, navigation, and weather satellites.

- Satellites with remote sensing technology have helped us understand the Earth as a global system.

Using Key Terms

1. Use each of the following terms in a separate sentence: *artificial satellite, low Earth orbit,* and *geostationary orbit.*

Understanding Key Ideas

2. In a low Earth orbit, the speed of a satellite is
   a. slower than the rotational speed of the Earth.
   b. equal to the rotational speed of the Earth.
   c. faster than the rotational speed of the Earth.
   d. None of the above

3. What was the name of the first satellite placed in orbit?

4. List three ways that satellites benefit human society.

5. What was the *Explorer 1*?

6. Explain the differences between LEO and GEO satellites.

7. How does the Global Positioning System work?

8. How do communications satellites relay signals around the curved surface of Earth?

Math Skills

9. The speed required to reach Earth orbit is 8 km/s. What does this equal in *meters per hour*?

Critical Thinking

10. **Applying Concepts** The *Hubble Space Telescope* is located in LEO. Does the telescope move faster or slower around the Earth compared with a geostationary weather satellite? Explain.

11. **Applying Concepts** To triangulate your location on a map, you need to know your distance from three points. If you knew your distance from two points, how many possible places could you occupy?

SCiLINKS

NSTA
Developed and maintained by the National Science Teachers Association

For a variety of links related to this chapter, go to www.scilinks.org

Topic: Artificial Satellites
SciLinks code: HSM0101

Space Probes

What does the surface of Mars look like? Does life exist anywhere else in the solar system?

To answer questions like these, scientists send space probes to explore the solar system. A **space probe** is an uncrewed vehicle that carries scientific instruments to planets or other bodies in space. Unlike satellites, which stay in Earth orbit, space probes travel away from the Earth. Space probes are valuable because they can complete missions that would be very dangerous and expensive for humans to undertake.

Visits to the Inner Solar System

Because Earth's moon and the inner planets are much closer than the other planets and moons in the solar system, they were the first to be explored by space probes. Let's take a closer look at some missions to the moon, Venus, and Mars.

Luna and Clementine: Missions to the Moon

Luna 1, the first space probe, was launched by the Soviets in 1959 to fly past the moon. In 1966, *Luna 9* made the first soft landing on the moon's surface. During the next 10 years, the United States and the Soviet Union completed more than 30 lunar missions. Thousands of images of the moon's surface were taken. In 1994, the United States probe *Clementine* discovered that craters of the moon may contain water left by comet impacts. In 1998, the *Lunar Prospector* confirmed that frozen water exists on the moon. This ice would be very valuable to a human colony on the moon.

READING WARM-UP

Objectives

● Describe five discoveries made by space probes.

● Explain how space-probe missions help us better understand the Earth.

● Describe how NASA's new strategy of "faster, cheaper, and better" relates to space probes.

Terms to Learn

space probe

READING STRATEGY

Reading Organizer As you read this section, make a concept map showing the space probes, the planetary bodies they visited, and their discoveries.

space probe an uncrewed vehicle that carries scientific instruments into space to collect scientific data

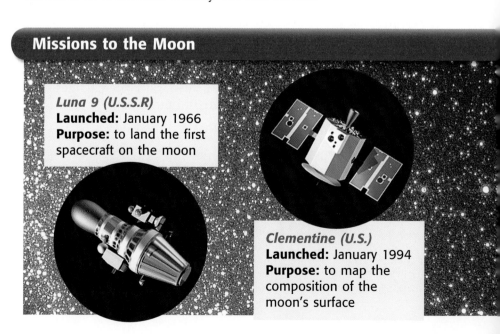

Missions to the Moon

Luna 9 (U.S.S.R)
Launched: January 1966
Purpose: to land the first spacecraft on the moon

Clementine (U.S.)
Launched: January 1994
Purpose: to map the composition of the moon's surface

Venera 9: The First Probe to Land on Venus

The Soviet probe *Venera 9* was the first probe to land on Venus. The probe parachuted into Venus's atmosphere and transmitted images of the surface to Earth. *Venera 9* found that the surface temperature and atmospheric pressure on Venus are much higher than on Earth. The surface temperature of Venus is an average of 464°C—hot enough to melt lead! *Venera 9* also found that the chemistry of the surface rocks on Venus is similar to that of Earth rocks. Perhaps most important, *Venera 9* and earlier missions revealed that Venus has a severe greenhouse effect. Scientists study Venus's atmosphere to learn about the effects of increased greenhouse gases in Earth's atmosphere.

The Magellan Mission: Mapping Venus

In 1989, the United States launched the *Magellan* probe, which used radar to map 98% of the surface of Venus. The radar data were transmitted back to Earth where computers used the data to generate three-dimensional images like the one shown in **Figure 1.** The Magellan mission showed that, in many ways, the geology of Venus is similar to that of Earth. Venus has features that suggest plate tectonics occurs there, as it does on Earth. Venus also has volcanoes, and some of them may be active.

✓ **Reading Check** What discoveries were made by *Magellan*? (*See the Appendix for answers to Reading Checks.*)

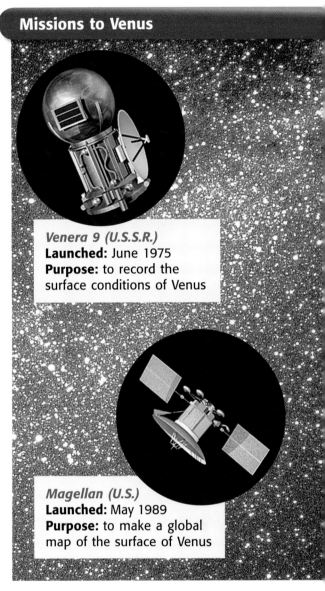

Missions to Venus

Venera 9 (U.S.S.R.)
Launched: June 1975
Purpose: to record the surface conditions of Venus

Magellan (U.S.)
Launched: May 1989
Purpose: to make a global map of the surface of Venus

Figure 1 *This false-color image of volcanoes on the surface of Venus was made with radar data transmitted to Earth by* Magellan.

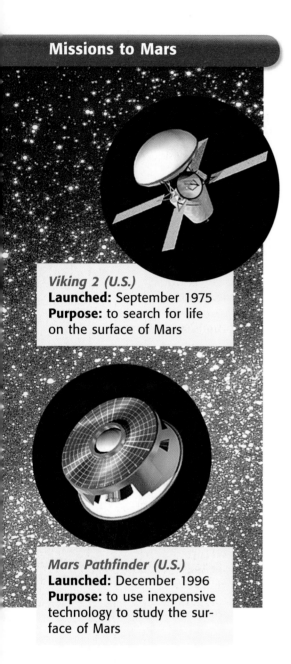

Missions to Mars

Viking 2 (U.S.)
Launched: September 1975
Purpose: to search for life on the surface of Mars

Mars Pathfinder (U.S.)
Launched: December 1996
Purpose: to use inexpensive technology to study the surface of Mars

The Viking Missions: Exploring Mars

In 1975, the United States sent a pair of probes—*Viking 1* and *Viking 2*—to Mars. The surface of Mars is more like the Earth's surface than that of any other planet. For this reason, one of the main goals of the Viking missions was to look for signs of life. The probes contained instruments designed to gather soil and test it for evidence of life. However, no hard evidence was found. The Viking missions did find evidence that Mars was once much warmer and wetter than it is now. This discovery led scientists to ask even more questions about Mars. Did the Martian climate once support life? Why and when did the Martian climate change?

The Mars Pathfinder Mission: Revisiting Mars

More than 20 years later, in 1997, the surface of Mars was visited again by a NASA space probe. The goal of the Mars Pathfinder mission was to show that Martian exploration is possible at a much lower cost than the Viking missions. The probe sent back detailed images of dry water channels on the planet's surface. These images, such as the one shown in **Figure 2,** suggest that massive floods flowed across the surface of Mars relatively recently in the planet's past. The *Mars Pathfinder* successfully landed on Mars and deployed the *Sojourner* rover. *Sojourner* traveled across the surface of Mars for almost three months, collecting data and recording images. The European Space Agency and NASA have many more Mars missions planned for the near future. These missions will pave the way for a crewed mission to Mars that may occur in your lifetime!

Reading Check What discoveries were made by the Mars Pathfinder mission?

Figure 2 *The* Mars Pathfinder *took detailed photographs of the Martian surface. Photographs, such as this one, revealed evidence of massive flooding.*

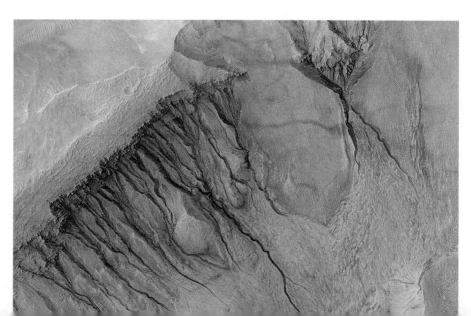

Visits to the Outer Solar System

The planets in the outer solar system—Jupiter, Saturn, Uranus, Neptune, and Pluto—are very far away. Probes such as those described below can take 10 years or more to complete their missions.

Pioneer and Voyager: To Jupiter and Beyond

The *Pioneer 10* and *Pioneer 11* space probes were the first to visit the outer planets. Among other things, these probes sampled the *solar wind*—the flow of particles coming from the sun. The Pioneer probes also found that the dark belts on Jupiter provide deep views into Jupiter's atmosphere. In 1983, *Pioneer 10* became the first probe to travel past the orbit of Pluto, the outermost planet.

The Voyager space probes were the first to detect Jupiter's faint rings, and *Voyager 2* was the first probe to fly by the four gas giants—Jupiter, Saturn, Uranus, and Neptune. The paths of the Pioneer and Voyager space probes are shown in **Figure 3.** Today, they are near the solar system's edge and some are still sending back data.

The Galileo Mission: A Return to Jupiter

The *Galileo* probe arrived at Jupiter in 1995. While *Galileo* itself began a long tour of Jupiter's moons, it sent a smaller probe into Jupiter's atmosphere to measure its composition, density, temperature, and cloud structure. *Galileo* gathered data about the geology of Jupiter's major moons and Jupiter's magnetic properties. The moons of Jupiter proved to be far more exciting than the earlier Pioneer and Voyager images had suggested. *Galileo* discovered that two of Jupiter's moons have magnetic fields and that one of its moons, Europa, may have an ocean of liquid water under its icy surface.

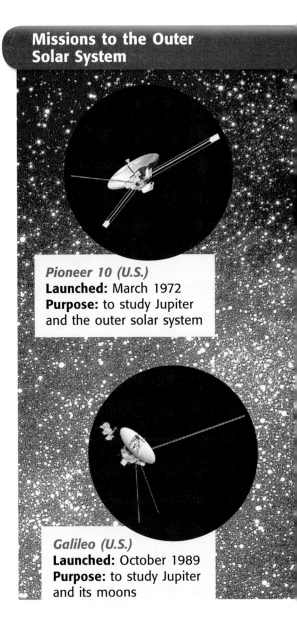

Missions to the Outer Solar System

Pioneer 10 (U.S.)
Launched: March 1972
Purpose: to study Jupiter and the outer solar system

Galileo (U.S.)
Launched: October 1989
Purpose: to study Jupiter and its moons

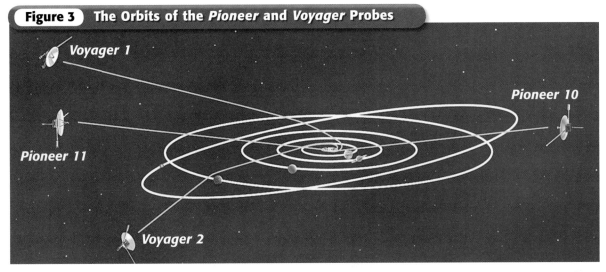

Figure 3 The Orbits of the *Pioneer* and *Voyager* Probes

Voyager 1

Pioneer 10

Pioneer 11

Voyager 2

Figure 4 *This artist's view shows the* Huygens *probe parachuting to the surface of Saturn's moon Titan. Saturn and* Cassini *are in the background.*

CONNECTION TO
Social Studies

Cosmic Message in a Bottle
When the Voyager space probes were launched in 1977, they carried a variety of messages intended for alien civilizations that might find them. In addition to greetings spoken in 55 different languages, a variety of songs, nature sounds, a diagram of the solar system, and photographs of life on Earth were included. Find out more about the message carried by the Voyager missions, and then create your own cosmic message in a bottle.

ACTIVITY

The Cassini Mission: Exploring Saturn's Moons

In 1997, the *Cassini* space probe was launched on a seven-year journey to Saturn where it will make a grand tour of Saturn's moons. As shown in **Figure 4,** a smaller probe, called the *Huygens* probe, will detach itself from *Cassini* and descend into the atmosphere of Saturn's moon Titan. Scientists are interested in Titan's atmosphere because it may be similar to the Earth's early atmosphere. Titan's atmosphere may reveal clues about how life developed on Earth.

Faster, Cheaper, and Better

The early space probe missions were very large and costly. Probes such as *Voyager 2* and *Galileo* took years to develop. Now, NASA has a vision for missions that are "faster, cheaper, and better." One new program, called Discovery, seeks proposals for smaller science programs. The first six approved Discovery missions include sending small space probes to asteroids, landing on Mars again, studying the moon, and returning comet dust to Earth.

Stardust: Comet Detective

Launched in 1999, the *Stardust* space probe is the first probe to focus only on a comet. The probe will arrive at the comet in 2004 and gather samples of the comet's dust tail. It will return the samples to Earth in 2006. For the first time, pure samples from beyond the orbit of the moon will be brought back to Earth. The comet dust should help scientists better understand how the solar system formed.

✓ Reading Check What is the mission of the *Stardust* probe?

Deep Space 1: Testing Ion Propulsion

Another NASA project is the New Millennium program. Its purpose is to test new technologies that can be used in the future. *Deep Space 1,* shown in **Figure 5,** is the first mission of this program. It is a space probe with an ion-propulsion system. Instead of burning chemical fuel, an ion rocket uses charged particles that exit the vehicle at high speed. An ion rocket follows Newton's third law of motion, but it does so using a unique source of propulsion. Ion propulsion is like sitting on the back of a truck and shooting peas out of a straw. If there were no friction, the truck would gradually accelerate to tremendous speeds.

Figure 5 Deep Space 1 *uses a revolutionary type of propulsion—an ion rocket.*

SECTION Review

Summary

- Exploration with space probes began with missions to the moon. Space probes then explored other bodies in the inner solar system.

- Space-probe missions to Mars have focused on the search for signs of water and life.

- The Pioneer and Voyager programs explored the outer solar system.

- Space probe missions have helped us understand Earth's formation and environment.

- NASA's new strategy of "faster, cheaper, and better" seeks to create space-probe missions that are smaller than those of the past.

Using Key Terms

The statements below are false. For each statement, replace the underlined term to make a true statement.

1. <u>Luna 1</u> discovered evidence of water on the moon.

2. <u>Venera 9</u> helped map 98% of Venus's surface.

3. <u>Stardust</u> uses ion propulsion to accelerate.

Understanding Key Ideas

4. What is the significance of the discovery of evidence of water on the moon?
   a. Water is responsible for the formation of craters.
   b. Water was left by early space probes.
   c. Water could be used by future moon colonies.
   d. The existence of water proves that there is life on the moon.

5. Describe three discoveries that have been made by space probes.

6. How do missions to Venus, Mars, and Titan help us understand Earth's environment?

Math Skills

7. Traveling at the speed of light, signals from *Voyager 1* take about 12 h to reach Earth. The speed of light is about 299,793 km/s, how far away is the probe?

Critical Thinking

8. **Making Inferences** Why did we need space probes to discover water channels on Mars and evidence of ice on Europa?

9. **Expressing Opinions** What are the advantages of the new Discovery program over the older space-probe missions, and what are the disadvantages?

10. **Applying Concepts** How does *Deep Space 1* use Newton's third law of motion to accelerate?

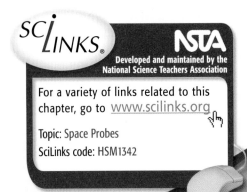

People in Space

One April morning in 1961, a rocket stood on a launch pad in a remote part of the Soviet Union. Inside, a 27-year-old cosmonaut named Yuri Gagarin sat and waited. He was about to do what no human had done before—travel to outer space. No one knew if the human brain would function in space or if he would be instantly killed by radiation.

On April 12, 1961, Yuri Gagarin, shown in **Figure 1,** became the first human to orbit Earth. The flight lasted 108 minutes. An old woman, her granddaughter, and a cow were the first to see Gagarin as he safely parachuted back to Earth, but the news of his success was quickly broadcast around the world.

The Race Is On

The Soviets were first once again, and the Americans were concerned that their rivals were winning the space race. Therefore, on May 25, 1961, President Kennedy announced, "I believe that the nation should commit itself to achieving the goal, before this decade is out, of landing a man on the moon and returning him safely to the Earth. No single project in this period will be more impressive to mankind, or more important for the long range exploration of space."

Kennedy's speech took everyone by surprise—even NASA's leaders. Go to the moon? We had not even reached orbit yet! In response to Kennedy's challenge, a new spaceport called Kennedy Space Center was built in Florida and Mission Control was established in Houston, Texas. In February 1962, John Glenn became the first American to orbit the Earth.

Figure 1 *In 1961, Yuri Gagarin (left) became the first person in space. In 1962, John Glenn (right) became the first American to orbit the Earth.*

"The Eagle Has Landed"

Seven years later, on July 20, 1969, Kennedy's challenge was met. The world watched on television as the *Apollo 11* landing module—the *Eagle,* shown in **Figure 2**—landed on the moon. Neil Armstrong became the first human to set foot on a world other than Earth. This moment forever changed the way we view ourselves and our planet. The Apollo missions also contributed to the advancement of science. *Apollo 11* returned moon rocks to Earth for study. Its crew also put devices on the moon to study moonquakes and the solar wind.

The Space Shuttle

The Saturn V rockets, which carried the Apollo astronauts to the moon, were huge and very expensive. They were longer than a football field, and each could be used only once. To save money, NASA began to develop the space shuttle program in 1972. A **space shuttle** is a reusable space vehicle that takes off like a rocket and lands like an airplane.

The Space Shuttle Gets off the Ground

Columbia, the first space shuttle, was launched on April 12, 1981. Since then, NASA has completed more than 100 successful shuttle missions. If you look at the shuttle *Endeavour* in **Figure 3,** you can see its main parts. The orbiter is about the size of an airplane. It carries the astronauts and payload into space. The liquid-fuel tank is the large red column. Two white solid-fuel booster rockets help the shuttle reach orbit. Then they fall back to Earth along with the fuel tank. The booster rockets are reused, the fuel tank is not. After completing a mission, the orbiter returns to Earth and lands like an airplane.

Reading Check What are the main parts of the shuttle? (*See the Appendix for answers to Reading Checks.*)

Shuttle Tragedies

On January 28, 1986, the booster rocket on the space shuttle *Challenger* exploded just after takeoff, killing all seven of its astronauts. On board was Christa McAuliffe, who would have been the first teacher in space. Investigations found that cold weather on the morning of the launch had caused rubber gaskets in the solid fuel booster rockets to stiffen and fail. The failure of the gaskets led to the explosion. The shuttle program resumed in 1988. In 2003, however, the space shuttle *Columbia* exploded as it reentered the atmosphere. All seven astronauts onboard were killed. These disasters emphasize the dangers of space exploration that continue to challenge scientists and engineers.

Figure 2 *Neil Armstrong took this photo of Edwin "Buzz" Aldrin as Aldrin was about to become the second human to set foot on the moon.*

space shuttle a reusable space vehicle that takes off like a rocket and lands like an airplane

Figure 3 *The space shuttles are the first reusable space vehicles.*

Figure 4 *As this illustration shows, space planes may provide transportation to outer space and around the world.*

Space Planes: The Shuttles of the Future?

NASA is working to develop advanced space systems, such as a space plane. This craft will fly like a normal airplane, but it will have rocket engines for use in space. Once in operation, space planes, such as the one shown in **Figure 4,** may lower the cost of getting material to LEO by 90%. Private companies are also becoming interested in developing space vehicles for commercial use and to make space travel cheaper, easier, and safer.

Space Stations—People Working in Space

A long-term orbiting platform in space is called a **space station.** On April 19, 1971, the Soviets became the first to successfully place a space station in orbit. A crew of three Soviet cosmonauts conducted a 23-day mission aboard the station, which was called *Salyut 1*. By 1982, the Soviets had put up seven space stations. Because of this experience, the Soviet Union became a leader in space-station development and in the study of the effects of weightlessness on humans. Their discoveries will be important for future flights to other planets—journeys that will take years to complete.

Skylab and *Mir*

Skylab, the United States' first space station, was a science and engineering lab used to conduct a wide variety of scientific studies. These studies included experiments in biology and space manufacturing and astronomical observations. Three different crews spent a total of 171 days on *Skylab* before it was abandoned. In 1986, the Soviets began to launch the pieces for a much more ambitious space station called *Mir* (meaning "peace"). Astronauts on *Mir* conducted a wide range of experiments, made many astronomical observations, and studied manufacturing in space. After 15 years, *Mir* was abandoned and it burned up in the Earth's atmosphere in 2001.

space station a long-term orbiting platform from which other vehicles can be launched or scientific research can be carried out

CONNECTION TO Biology

Effects of Weightlessness
When a human body stays in space for long periods of time without having to work against gravity, the bones lose mass and muscles become weaker. Find out about the exercises to reduce the loss of bone mass used by astronauts aboard the *International Space Station.* Create an "Astronaut Exercise Book" to share with your friends.

The *International Space Station*

The *International Space Station (ISS)*, the newest space station, is being constructed in LEO. Russia, the United States, and 14 other countries are designing and building different parts of the station. **Figure 5** shows what the *ISS* will look like when it is completed. The *ISS* is being built with materials brought up on the space shuttles and by Russian rockets. The United States is providing lab modules, the supporting frame, solar panels, living quarters, and a biomedical laboratory. The Russians are contributing a service module, docking modules, life-support and research modules, and transportation to and from the station. Other components will come from Japan, Canada, and several European countries.

✓ Reading Check What contributions are the Americans and Russians making to the *ISS*?

Research on the *International Space Station*

The *ISS* will provide many benefits—some of which we cannot predict. What scientists do know is that it will be a unique, space-based facility to perform space-science experiments and to test new technologies. Much of the space race involved political and military rivalry between the Soviet Union and the United States. Hopefully, the *ISS* will promote cooperation between countries while continuing the pioneering spirit of the first astronauts and cosmonauts.

CONNECTION TO Social Studies

Oral Histories The exciting times of the Apollo moon missions thrilled the nation. Interview adults in your community about their memories of those times. Prepare a list of questions first, and have your questions and contacts approved by your teacher. If possible, use a tape recorder or video camera to record the interviews. As a class, create a library of your oral histories for future students.

ACTIVITY

Figure 5 *When the* International Space Station *is completed, it will be about the size of a soccer field and will weigh about 500 tons.*

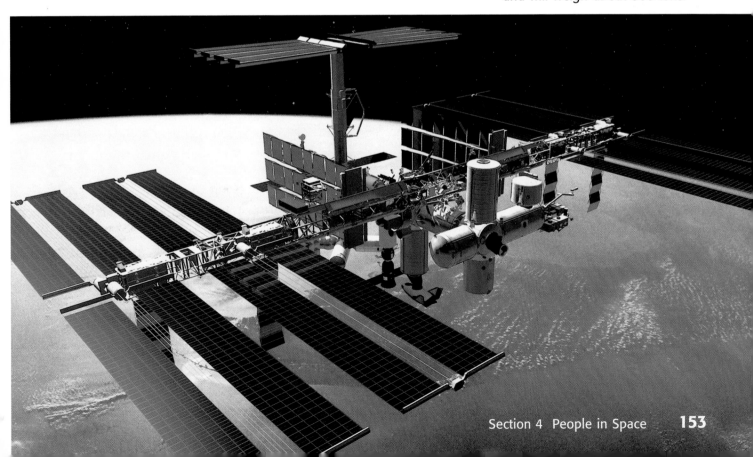

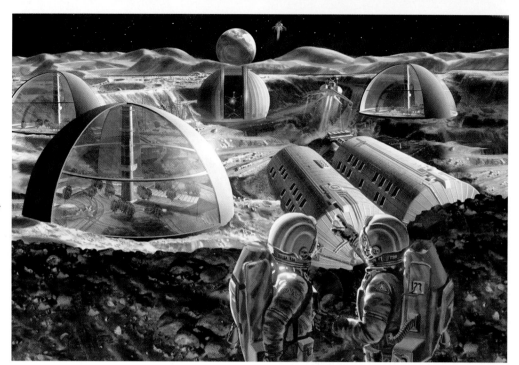

Figure 6 *As shown in this illustration, humans may eventually establish a colony on the moon or on Mars.*

Figure 7 *Aerogel is the lightest solid on Earth. Aerogel is only 3 times heavier than air, and has 39 times the insulating properties of the best fiberglass insulation.*

To the Moon, Mars, and Beyond

We may eventually need resources beyond what Earth can offer. Space offers many such resources. For example, a rare form of helium is found on the moon. If this helium could be used in nuclear fusion reactors, it would produce no radioactive waste! A base on the moon similar to the one shown in **Figure 6** could be used to manufacture materials in low gravity or in a vacuum. A colony on the moon or on Mars could be an important link to bringing space resources to Earth. It would also be a good base for exploring the rest of the solar system. The key will be to make these missions economically worthwhile.

The Benefits of the Space Program

Space exploration is expensive, and it has cost several human lives since the time that Yuri Gagarin and John Glenn first left the Earth more than 40 years ago. We have visited the moon, and we have sent probes outside the solar system. So why should we continue to explore space? There are many answers to this question. Space exploration has expanded our scientific knowledge of everything from the most massive stars to the smallest particles. Life-saving technologies have also resulted from the space missions. For example, artificial heart pumps use a turbine developed to pump fuel in the space shuttles. NASA's aerogel, shown in **Figure 7,** may become an energy-saving replacement for windows in the future. All of the scientific benefits of the space programs cannot be predicted. However, the exploration of space is also a challenge to human courage and a quest for new knowledge of ourselves and the universe.

Space-Age Spinoffs

Technologies that were developed for the space programs but are now used in everyday life are called space-age spinoffs. There are dozens of examples of common items that were first developed for the space programs. Cordless power tools, for example, were first developed for use on the moon by the Apollo astronauts. Hand-held cameras that were developed to study the heat emitted from the space shuttle are used by firefighters to detect dangerous hot spots in fires. A few other examples of space-age spinoffs are shown in **Table 1.**

Reading Check What are space-age spinoffs?

Table 1 Space-Age Spinoffs
smoke detectors
bar coding on merchandise
pacemakers
artificial heart pumps
land mine removal devices
medical lasers
fire fighting equipment
invisible braces
video game joysticks
ear thermometers

SECTION Review

Summary

- In 1961, the Soviet cosmonaut Yuri Gagarin became the first person in space. In 1969, Neil Armstrong became the first person on the moon.

- During the 1970s, the United States focused on developing the space shuttle. The Soviets focused on developing space stations.

- The United States, Russia, and 14 other countries are currently developing the *International Space Station.*

- There have been many scientific, economic, and social benefits of the space programs.

Using Key Terms

1. Use each of the following terms in a separate sentence: *space shuttle* and *space station.*

Using Key Ideas

2. What is the main difference between the space shuttles and other space vehicles?
   a. The space shuttles are powered by liquid rocket fuel.
   b. The space shuttles take off like a plane and land like a rocket.
   c. The space shuttles are reusable.
   d. The space shuttles are not reusable.

3. Describe the history and future of human spaceflight. How was the race to explore space influenced by the Cold War?

4. Describe five "space-age spinoffs."

5. How will space stations help in the exploration of space?

6. In the 1970s, what was the main difference in the focus of the space programs in the United States and in the Soviet Union?

Math Skills

7. When it is fueled, a space shuttle has a mass of about 2,000,000 kg. About 80% of that mass is fuel and oxygen. Calculate the mass of a space shuttle's fuel and oxygen.

Critical Thinking

8. **Making Inferences** Why did the United States stop sending people to the moon after the Apollo program ended?

9. **Expressing Opinions** Imagine that you are a U.S. senator reviewing NASA's proposed budget. Write a two-paragraph position statement expressing your opinion about increasing or decreasing funding for NASA.

SCILINKS®

NSTA
Developed and maintained by the National Science Teachers Association

For a variety of links related to this chapter, go to www.scilinks.org
Topic: Space Exploration and Space Stations
SciLinks code: HSM1340

OBJECTIVES

Predict which design features would improve a rocket's flight.

Design and build a rocket that includes your design features.

Test your rocket design, and evaluate your results.

MATERIALS

- bottle, soda, 2 L
- clay, modeling
- foam board
- rocket launcher
- scissors
- tape, duct
- watch or clock that indicates seconds
- water

SAFETY

Water Rockets Save the Day!

Imagine that for the big Fourth of July celebration, you and your friends had planned a full day of swimming, volleyball, and fireworks at the lake. You've just learned, however, that the city passed a law that bans all fireworks within city limits. But you do not give up so easily on having fun. Last year at summer camp, you learned how to build water rockets. And you have kept the launcher in your garage since then. With a little bit of creativity, you and your friends are going to celebrate with a splash!

Ask a Question

1 What is the most efficient design for a water rocket?

Form a Hypothesis

2 Write a hypothesis that provides a possible answer to the question above.

Test the Hypothesis

3 Decide how your rocket will look, and then draw a sketch.

4 Using only the materials listed, decide how to build your rocket. Write a description of your plan, and have your teacher approve your plan. Keep in mind that you will need to leave the opening of your bottle clear. The bottle opening will be placed over a rubber stopper on the rocket launcher.

5 Fins are often used to stabilize rockets. Do you want fins on your water rocket? Decide on the best shape for the fins, and then decide how many fins your rocket needs. Use the foam board to construct the fins.

6 Your rocket must be heavy enough to fly in a controlled manner. Consider using clay in the body of your rocket to provide some additional weight and stability.

7 Pour water into your rocket until the rocket is one-third to one-half full.

8 Your teacher will provide the launcher and will assist you during blastoff. Attach your rocket to the launcher by placing the opening of the bottle on the rubber stopper.

9 When the rocket is in place, clear the immediate area and begin pumping air into your rocket. Watch the pump gauge, and take note of how much pressure is needed for liftoff. **Caution:** Be sure to step back from the launch site. You should be several meters away from the bottle when you launch it.

10 Use the watch to time your rocket's flight. How long was your rocket in the air?

11 Make small changes in your rocket design that you think will improve the rocket's performance. Consider using different amounts of water and clay or experimenting with different fins. You may also want to compare your design with those of your classmates.

Analyze the Results

1 **Describing Events** How did your rocket perform? If you used fins, do you think they helped your flight? Explain your answer.

2 **Explaining Results** What do you think propelled your rocket? Use Newton's third law of motion to explain your answer.

3 **Analyzing Results** How did the amount of water in your rocket affect the launch?

Draw Conclusions

4 **Drawing Conclusions** What modifications made your rocket fly for the longest time? How did the design help the rockets fly so far?

5 **Evaluating Results** Which group's rocket was the most stable? How did the design help the rocket fly straight?

6 **Making Predictions** How can you improve your design to make your rocket perform even better?

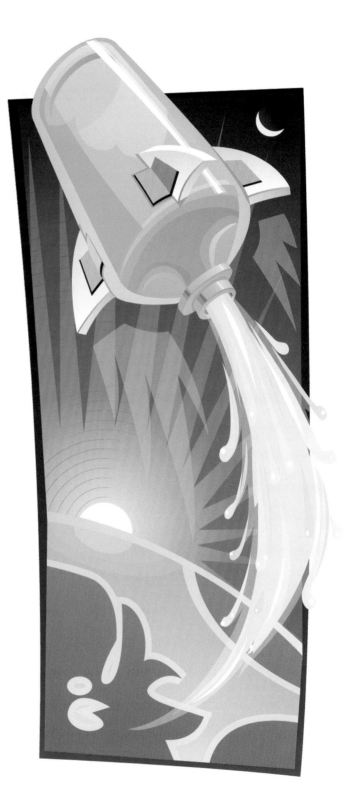

Chapter Review

USING KEY TERMS

For each pair of terms, explain how the meanings of the terms differ.

1 *geostationary orbit* and *low Earth orbit*

2 *space probe* and *space station*

3 *artificial satellite* and *moon*

Complete each of the following sentences by choosing the correct term from the word bank.

escape velocity	oxygen
nitrogen	thrust

4 The force that accelerates a rocket is called ___.

5 Rockets need to have ___ in order to burn fuel.

UNDERSTANDING KEY IDEAS

Multiple Choice

6 Whose rocket research team surrendered to the Americans at the end of World War II?

a. Konstantin Tsiolkovsky's
b. Robert Goddard's
c. Wernher von Braun's
d. Yuri Gargarin's

7 Rockets work according to Newton's

a. first law of motion.
b. second law of motion.
c. third law of motion.
d. law of universal gravitation.

8 The first artificial satellite to orbit the Earth was

a. *Pioneer 4.*   **c.** *Voyager 2.*
b. *Explorer 1.*   **d.** *Sputnik 1.*

9 Communications satellites are able to transfer TV signals between continents because communications satellites

a. are located in LEO.
b. relay signals past the horizon.
c. travel quickly around Earth.
d. can be used during the day and night.

10 GEO is a better orbit for communications satellites because satellites that are in GEO

a. remain in position over one spot.
b. have polar orbits.
c. do not revolve around the Earth.
d. orbit a few hundred kilometers above the Earth.

11 Which space probe discovered evidence of water at the moon's south pole?

a. *Luna 9*
b. *Viking 1*
c. *Clementine*
d. *Magellan*

12 When did humans first set foot on the moon?

a. 1959   **c.** 1969
b. 1964   **d.** 1973

13 Which of the following planets has not yet been visited by space probes?

a. Venus   **c.** Mars
b. Neptune   **d.** Pluto

14 Which of the following space probes has left our solar system?

a. *Galileo*

c. *Viking 10*

b. *Magellan*

d. *Pioneer 10*

15 Based on space-probe data, which of the following is the most likely place in our solar system to find liquid water?

a. the moon

c. Europa

b. Mercury

d. Venus

Short Answer

16 Describe how Newton's third law of motion relates to the movement of rockets.

17 What is one disadvantage that objects in LEO have?

18 Why did the United States develop the space shuttle?

19 How does data from satellites help us understand the Earth's environment?

CRITICAL THINKING

20 **Concept Mapping** Use the following terms to create a concept map: *orbital velocity, thrust, LEO, artificial satellites, escape velocity, space probes, GEO,* and *rockets*.

21 **Making Inferences** What is the difference between speed and velocity?

22 **Applying Concepts** Why must rockets that travel in outer space carry oxygen with them?

23 **Expressing Opinions** What impact has space research had on scientific thought, on society, and on the environment?

INTERPRETING GRAPHICS

The diagram below illustrates suborbital velocity, orbital velocity, and escape velocity. Use the diagram below to answer the questions that follow.

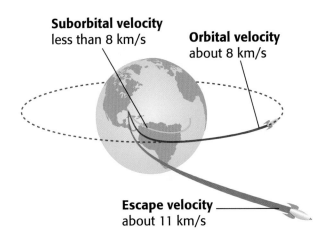

Suborbital velocity
less than 8 km/s

Orbital velocity
about 8 km/s

Escape velocity
about 11 km/s

24 Could a rocket traveling at 6 km/s reach orbital velocity?

25 If a rocket traveled for 3 days at the minimum escape velocity, how far would the rocket travel?

26 How much faster would a rocket traveling in orbital velocity need to travel to reach escape velocity?

27 If the escape velocity for a planet was 9 km/s, would you assume that the mass of the planet was more or less than the mass of Earth?

Standardized Test Preparation

Read each of the passages below. Then, answer the questions that follow each passage.

Passage 1 One of the strange things about living in space is free fall, the reduced effect of gravity. Everything inside the *International Space Station* that is not fastened down will float! The engineers who designed the space station have come up with some <u>intriguing</u> solutions to this problem. For example, each astronaut sleeps in a sack similar to a sleeping bag that is fastened to the module. The sack keeps the astronauts from floating around while they sleep. Astronauts shower with a hand-held nozzle. Afterward, the water droplets are vacuumed up. Other problems that are being studied include how to prepare and serve food, how to design an effective toilet, and how to dispose of waste.

1. What is the main idea of the passage?
   A There is no gravity in space.
   B Astronauts will stay aboard the space station for long periods of time.
   C Living in free fall presents interesting problems.
   D Sleeping bags are needed to keep astronauts warm in space.

2. Which of the following is a problem mentioned in the passage?
   F how to dissipate the heat of reentry
   G how to maintain air pressure
   H how to serve food
   I how to listen to music

3. Which of the following words is the best antonym for *intriguing*?
   A authentic
   B boring
   C interesting
   D unsolvable

Passage 2 In 1999, the crew of the space station *Mir* tried to place a large, umbrella-like mirror in orbit. The mirror was designed to reflect sunlight to Siberia. The experiment failed because the crew was unable to unfold the mirror. If things had gone as planned, the beam of reflected sunlight would have been 5 to 10 times brighter than the light from the moon! If the first space mirror had worked, Russia was planning to place many more mirrors in orbit to lengthen winter days in Siberia, extend the growing season, and even reduce the amount of electricity needed for lighting. Luckily, the experiment failed. If it had succeeded, the environmental effects of extra daylight in Siberia would have been catastrophic. Astronomers were concerned that the mirrors would cause light pollution and obstruct their view of the universe. Outer space should belong to all of humanity, and any project of this kind, including placing advertisements on the moon, should be banned.

1. Which of the following is a statement of opinion?
   A Astronomers were concerned about the effects of the space mirror.
   B Outer space should belong to all of humanity.
   C The experiment failed because the mirror could not unfold.
   D Russia was planning to place many more mirrors in orbit.

2. What can you infer about the location of Siberia?
   F It is near the equator.
   G It is closer to the equator than it is to the North Pole.
   H It is closer to the North Pole than it is to the equator.
   I It is the same distance from the equator as it is from the North Pole.

The diagram below shows the location of satellites in LEO and GEO. Use the diagram below to answer the questions that follow.

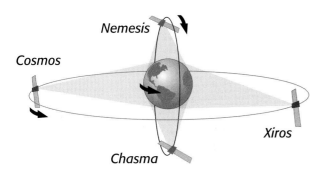

1. Which satellites are always located over the same spot on Earth?
   A *Xiros* and *Chasma*
   B *Xiros* and *Cosmos*
   C *Nemesis* and *Cosmos*
   D *Chasma* and *Nemesis*

2. Which satellites are likely to be spy satellites?
   F *Xiros* and *Cosmos*
   G *Xiros* and *Chasma*
   H *Chasma* and *Nemesis*
   I *Nemesis* and *Cosmos*

3. Which satellites are likely to be communications satellites?
   A *Chasma* and *Nemesis*
   B *Nemesis* and *Cosmos*
   C *Xiros* and *Cosmos*
   D *Xiros* and *Chasma*

4. Which satellites are traveling in an orbit that is 90° with respect to the direction of Earth's rotation?
   F *Nemesis* and *Cosmos*
   G *Xiros* and *Chasma*
   H *Nemesis* and *Chasma*
   I *Xiros* and *Cosmos*

Read each question below, and choose the best answer.

1. To escape Earth's gravity, a rocket must travel at least 11 km/s. About how many hours would it take to get to the moon at this speed? (On average, the moon is about 384,500 km away from Earth.)
   A 1 h
   B 7 h
   C 8 h
   D 10 h

2. The Saturn V launch vehicle, which carried the Apollo astronauts into space, had a mass of about 2.7 million kilograms and carried about 2.5 million kilograms of propellant. What percentage of Saturn V's mass was propellant?
   F 9.25%
   G 9%
   H 92.5%
   I 90%

3. Scientists discovered that when a person is in orbit, bone mass in the lower hip and spine is lost at a rate of 1.2% per month. At that rate, how long would it take for 7.2% of bone mass to be lost?
   A 4 months
   B 6 months
   C 7.2 months
   D 8 months

4. The space shuttle can carry 25,400 kg of cargo into orbit. Assume that the average astronaut has a mass of 75 kg and that each satellite has a mass of 4,300 kg. If a shuttle mission is already carrying 9,000 kg of equipment and 10 astronauts, how many satellites can the shuttle carry?
   F 2
   G 3
   H 4
   I 5

Standardized Test Preparation

Science in Action

Science, Technology, and Society

Mission to Mars

In spring 2003, two cutting-edge NASA rovers were sent on a mission to Mars. When they reach their destination, they will parachute through the thin Martian atmosphere and land on the surface. First, the rovers will use video and infrared cameras to look around. Then, for at least 92 Earth days (90 Martian days), the rovers will explore the surface of Mars. They will gather geologic evidence of liquid water because liquid water may have enabled Mars to support life in the past. Each rover will carry five scientific tools and a Rock Abrasion Tool, or "RAT," which will grind away rock surfaces to expose the rock interiors for scientific tests. Stay tuned for more news from Mars!

Weird Science

Flashline Mars Arctic Research Station

If you wanted to visit a place on Earth that is like the surface of Mars, where would you go? You might head to an impact crater on Devon Island, close to the Arctic circle. The rugged terrain and harsh weather there resemble what explorers will find on Mars, although Mars has no breathable air and is a lot colder. In the summer, volunteers from the Mars Society live in an experimental base in the crater and test technology that might be used on Mars. The volunteers try to simulate the experience of explorers on Mars. For example, the volunteers wear spacesuits when they go outside, and they explore the landscape by using rovers. They even communicate with the outside world using types of technology likely to be used on Mars. These dedicated volunteers have already made discoveries that will help NASA plan a crewed mission to Mars!

Language Arts ACTiViTY

Watch for stories about this mission in newspapers and magazines. If you read about a discovery on Mars, bring a copy of the article to share with your class. As a class, compile a scrapbook entitled "Mars in the News."

Social Studies ACTiViTY

A Mars mission could require astronauts to endure nearly two years of extreme isolation. Research how NASA would prepare astronauts for the psychological pressures of a mission to Mars.

Franklin Chang-Diaz

Astronaut You have to wear a suit, but the commute is not too long. In fact, it is only about eight and a half minutes, and what a view on your way to work! Astronauts, such as Franklin Chang-Diaz, have one of the most exciting jobs on Earth—or in space. Chang-Diaz has flown on seven space shuttle missions and has completed three space walks. Since the time he became an astronaut in 1981, Chang-Diaz has spent more than 1,601 hours (66 days) in space.

Chang-Diaz was born in San Jose, Costa Rica. He earned a degree in mechanical engineering in 1973 and received a doctorate in applied plasma physics from the Massachusetts Institute of Technology (MIT) in 1977. His work in physics attracted the attention of NASA, and he began training at the Johnson Space Center in Houston, Texas. In addition to doing research on the space shuttle, Chang-Diaz has worked on developing plasma propulsion systems for long space flights. He has also helped create closer ties between astronauts and scientists by starting organizations such as the Astronaut Science Colloquium Program and the Astronaut Science Support Group. If you want to find out more about what it takes to be an astronaut, look on NASA's Web site.

Math Activity

If 1 out of 120 people interviewed by NASA is selected for astronaut training, how many people will be selected for training if 10,680 people are interviewed?

As this mission patch shows, Chang-Diaz flew on the 111th space shuttle mission.

To learn more about these Science in Action topics, visit go.hrw.com and type in the keyword HZ5EXPF.

Current Science

Check out Current Science® articles related to this chapter by visiting go.hrw.com. Just type in the keyword HZ5CS22.

Skills Practice Lab

The Sun's Yearly Trip Through the Zodiac

MATERIALS

- ball, inflated
- box, cardboard, large
- cards, index (12)
- chairs (12)
- tape, masking (1 roll)

During the course of a year, the sun appears to move through a circle of 12 constellations in the sky. The 12 constellations make up a "belt" in the sky called the *zodiac.* Each month, the sun appears to be in a different constellation. The ancient Babylonians developed a 12-month calendar based on the idea that the sun moved through this circle of constellations as it revolved around the Earth. They believed that the constellations of stars were fixed in position and that the sun and planets moved past the stars. Later, Copernicus developed a model of the solar system in which the Earth and the planets revolve around the sun. But how can Copernicus's model of the solar system be correct when the sun appears to move through the zodiac?

Ask a Question

1. If the sun is at the center of the solar system, why does it appear to move with respect to the stars in the sky?

Form a Hypothesis

2. Write a possible answer to the question above. Explain your reasoning.

Test the Hypothesis

3. Set the chairs in a large circle so that the backs of the chairs all face the center of the circle. Make sure that the chairs are equally spaced, like the numbers on the face of a clock.

4. Write the name of each constellation in the zodiac on the index cards. You should have one card for each constellation.

5. Stand inside the circle with the masking tape and the index cards. Moving counterclockwise, attach the cards to the backs of the chairs in the following order: Aries, Taurus, Gemini, Cancer, Leo, Virgo, Libra, Scorpio, Sagittarius, Capricorn, Aquarius, and Pisces.

6. Use masking tape to label the ball "Sun."

7. Place the large, closed box in the center of the circle. Set the roll of masking tape flat on top of the box.

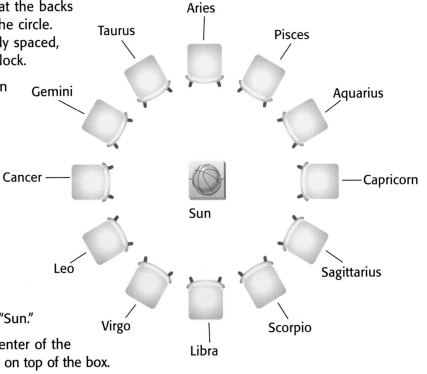

8 Place the ball on top of the roll of masking tape so that the ball stays in place.

9 Stand inside the circle of chairs. You will represent the Earth. As you move around the ball, you will model the Earth's orbit around the sun. Notice that even though only the "Earth" is moving, as seen from the Earth, the sun appears to move through the entire zodiac!

10 Stand in front of the chair labeled "Aries." Look at the ball representing the sun. Then, look past the ball to the chair at the opposite side of the circle. Where in the zodiac does the sun appear to be?

11 Move to the next chair on your right (counterclockwise). Where does the sun appear to be? Is it in the same constellation? Explain your answer.

12 Repeat step 10 until you have observed the position of the sun from each chair in the circle.

Analyze the Results

1 Did the sun appear to move through the 12 constellations, even though the Earth was orbiting around the sun? How can you explain this apparent movement?

Draw Conclusions

2 How does Copernicus's model of the solar system explain the apparent movement of the sun through the constellations of the zodiac?

Skills Practice Lab

I See the Light!

How do you find the distance to an object you can't reach? You can do it by measuring something you can reach, finding a few angles, and using mathematics. In this activity, you'll practice measuring the distances of objects here on Earth. When you get used to it, you can take your skills to the stars!

Ask a Question

1 How can you measure the distance to a star?

Form a Hypothesis

2 Write a hypothesis that might answer this question. Explain your reasoning.

Test the Hypothesis

3 Draw a line 4 cm away from the edge of one side of the piece of poster board. Fold the poster board along this line.

4 Tape the protractor to the poster board with its flat edge against the fold, as shown in the photo below.

5 Use a pencil to carefully punch a hole through the poster board along its folded edge at the center of the protractor.

6 Thread the string through the hole, and tape one end to the underside of the poster board. The other end should be long enough to hang off the far end of the poster board.

7 Carefully punch a second hole in the smaller area of the poster board halfway between its short sides. The hole should be directly above the first hole and should be large enough for the pencil to fit through. This hole is the viewing hole of your new parallax device. This device will allow you to measure the distance of faraway objects.

8 Find a location that is at least 50 steps away from a tall, narrow object, such as the school's flagpole or a tall tree. (This object will represent background stars.) Set the meterstick on the ground with one of its long edges facing the flagpole.

9 Ask your partner, who represents a nearby star, to take 10 steps toward the flagpole, starting at the left end of the meterstick. You will be the observer. When you stand at the left end of the meterstick, which represents the location of the sun, your partner's nose should be lined up with the flagpole.

MATERIALS

- calculator, scientific
- meterstick
- pencil, sharp
- poster board, 16 × 16 cm
- protractor
- ruler, metric
- scissors
- string, 30 cm
- tape measure, metric
- tape, transparent

SAFETY

—Viewing hole

10 Move to the other end of the meterstick, which represents the location of Earth. Does your partner appear to the left or right of the flagpole? Record your observations.

11 Hold the string so that it runs straight from the viewing hole to the 90° mark on the protractor. Using one eye, look through the viewing hole along the string, and point the device at your partner's nose.

12 Holding the device still, slowly move your head until you can see the flagpole through the viewing hole. Move the string so that it lines up between your eye and the flagpole. Make sure the string is taut, and hold it tightly against the protractor.

13 Read and record the angle made by the string and the string's original position at 90° (count the number of degrees between 90° and the string's new position).

14 Use the measuring tape to find and record the distance from the left end of the meterstick to your partner's nose.

15 Now, find a place outside that is at least 100 steps away from the flagpole. Set the meterstick on the ground as before, and repeat steps 9–14.

Analyze the Results

1 The angle you recorded in step 13 is called the *parallax angle*. The distance from one end of the meterstick to the other is called the *baseline*. With this angle and the length of your baseline, you can calculate the distance to your partner.

2 To calculate the distance (*d*) to your partner, use the following equation:

$$d = b/\tan A$$

In this equation, *A* is the parallax angle, and *b* is the length of the baseline (1 m). (Tan *A* means the tangent of angle *A*, which you will learn more about in math classes.)

3 To find *d*, enter 1 (the length of your baseline in meters) into the calculator, press the division key, enter the value of *A* (the parallax angle you recorded), then press the tan key. Finally, press the equals key.

4 Record this result. It is the distance in meters between the left end of the meterstick and your partner. You may want to use a table like the one below.

5 How close is this calculated distance to the distance you measured?

6 Repeat steps 1–3 under Analyze the Results using the angle you found when the flagpole was 100 steps away.

Draw Conclusions

7 At which position, 50 steps or 100 steps from the flagpole, did your calculated distance better match the actual distance as measured?

8 What do you think would happen if you were even farther from the flagpole?

9 When astronomers use parallax, their "flagpoles" are distant stars. Might this affect the accuracy of their parallax readings?

Distance by Parallax Versus Measuring Tape		
	At 50 steps	At 100 steps
Parallax angle °		
Distance (calculated)		
Distance (measured)		

Model-Making Lab

Why Do They Wander?

MATERIALS
- compass, drawing
- paper, white
- pencils, colored
- ruler, metric

SAFETY

Before the discoveries of Nicholas Copernicus in the early 1500s, most people thought that the planets and the sun revolved around the Earth and that the Earth was the center of the solar system. But Copernicus observed that the sun is the center of the solar system and that all the planets, including Earth, revolve around the sun. He also explained a puzzling aspect of the movement of planets across the night sky.

If you watch a planet every night for several months, you'll notice that it appears to "wander" among the stars. While the stars remain in fixed positions relative to each other, the planets appear to move independently of the stars. Mars first travels to the left, then back to the right, and then again to the left.

In this lab, you will make your own model of part of the solar system to find out how Copernicus's model of the solar system explained this zigzag motion of the planets.

Ask a Question

1 Why do the planets appear to move back and forth in the Earth's night sky?

Form a Hypothesis

2 Write a possible answer to the question above.

Test the Hypothesis

3 Use the compass to draw a circle with a diameter of 9 cm on the paper. This circle will represent the orbit of the Earth around the sun. (Note: The orbits of the planets are actually slightly elliptical, but circles will work for this activity.)

4 Using the same center point, draw a circle with a diameter of 12 cm. This circle will represent the orbit of Mars.

5 Using a blue pencil, draw three parallel lines diagonally across one end of your paper, as shown at right. These lines will help you plot the path Mars appears to travel in Earth's night sky. Turn your paper so the diagonal lines are at the top of the page.

6 Place 11 dots 2.5 cm apart from each other on your Earth orbit. Number the dots 1 through 11. These dots will represent Earth's position from month to month.

7 Now, place 11 dots along the top of your Mars orbit 0.5 cm apart from each other. Number the dots as shown. These dots will represent the position of Mars at the same time intervals. Notice that Mars travels slower than Earth.

8 Draw a green line to connect the first dot on Earth's orbit to the first dot on Mars's orbit. Extend this line to the first diagonal line at the top of your paper. Place a green dot where the green line meets the first blue diagonal line. Label the green dot "1."

9 Now, connect the second dot on Earth's orbit to the second dot on Mars's orbit, and extend the line all the way to the first diagonal at the top of your paper. Place a green dot where this line meets the first blue diagonal line, and label this dot "2."

10 Continue drawing green lines from Earth's orbit through Mars's orbit and finally to the blue diagonal lines. Pay attention to the pattern of dots you are adding to the diagonal lines. When the direction of the dots changes, extend the green line to the next diagonal line, and add the dots to that line instead.

11 When you are finished adding green lines, draw a red line to connect all the green dots on the blue diagonal lines in the order you drew them.

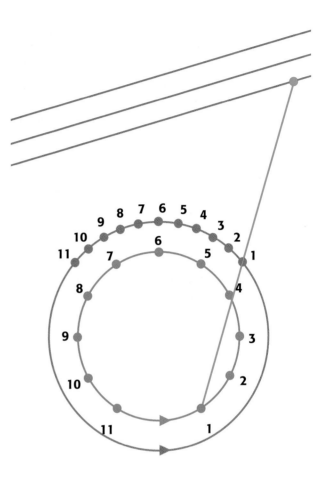

Analyze the Results

1 What do the green lines connecting points along Earth's orbit and Mars's orbit represent?

2 What does the red line connecting the dots along the diagonal lines look like? How can you explain this?

Draw Conclusions

3 What does this demonstration show about the motion of Mars?

4 Why do planets appear to move back and forth across the sky?

5 Were the Greeks justified in calling the planets *wanderers*? Explain.

Model-Making Lab

Eclipses

As the Earth and the moon revolve around the sun, they both cast shadows into space. An eclipse occurs when one planetary body passes through the shadow of another. You can demonstrate how an eclipse occurs by using clay models of planetary bodies.

MATERIALS

- clay, modeling
- flashlight, small
- paper, notebook (1 sheet)
- ruler, metric

Procedure

1. Make two balls out of the modeling clay. One ball should have a diameter of about 4 cm and will represent the Earth. The other should have a diameter of about 1 cm and will represent the moon.

2. Place the two balls about 15 cm apart on the sheet of paper. (You may want to prop the smaller ball up on folded paper or on clay so that the centers of the two balls are at the same level.)

3. Hold the flashlight approximately 15 cm away from the large ball. The flashlight and the two balls should be in a straight line. Keep the flashlight at about the same level as the clay. When the whole class is ready, your teacher will turn off the lights.

4. Turn on your flashlight. Shine the light on the larger ball, and sketch your model. Include the beam of light in your drawing.

5. Move the flashlight to the opposite side of the paper. The flashlight should now be approximately 15 cm away from the smaller clay ball. Repeat step 4.

Analyze the Results

1. What does the flashlight in your model represent?

2. As viewed from Earth, what event did your model represent in step 4?

3. As viewed from the moon, what event did your model represent in step 4?

4. As viewed from Earth, what event did your model represent in step 5?

5. As viewed from the moon, what event did your model represent in step 5?

6. According to your model, how often would solar and lunar eclipses occur? Is this accurate? Explain.

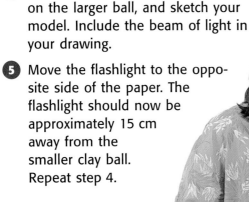

Skills Practice Lab

Phases of the Moon

It's easy to see when the moon is full. But you may have wondered exactly what happens when the moon appears as a crescent or when you cannot see the moon at all. Does the Earth cast its shadow on the moon? In this activity, you will discover how and why the moon appears as it does in each phase.

MATERIALS

- ball, plastic-foam
- globe, world
- light source

SAFETY

Procedure

1. Place your globe near the light source. Be sure that the north pole is tilted toward the light. Rotate the globe so that your state faces the light.

2. Using the ball as your model of the moon, move the moon between the Earth (the globe) and the sun (the light). The side of the moon that faces the Earth will be in darkness. Write your observations of this new-moon phase.

3. Continue to move the moon in its orbit around the Earth. When part of the moon is illuminated by the light, as viewed from Earth, the moon is in the crescent phase. Record your observations.

4. If you have time, you may draw your own moon-phase diagram.

Analyze the Results

1. About 2 weeks after the new moon appears, the entire moon is visible in the sky. Move the ball to show this event.

2. What other phases can you add to your diagram? For example, when does the quarter moon appear?

3. Explain why the moon sometimes appears as a crescent to viewers on Earth.

Model-Making Lab

Reach for the Stars

Have you ever thought about living and working in space? Well, in order for you to do so, you would have to learn to cope with the new environment and surroundings. At the same time that astronauts are adjusting to the topsy-turvy conditions of space travel, they are also dealing with special tools used to repair and build space stations. In this activity, you will get the chance to model one tool that might help astronauts work in space.

MATERIALS

- ball, plastic-foam
- box, cardboard
- hole punch
- paper brads (2)
- paper clips, jumbo (2)
- ruler, metric
- scissors
- wire, metal

SAFETY

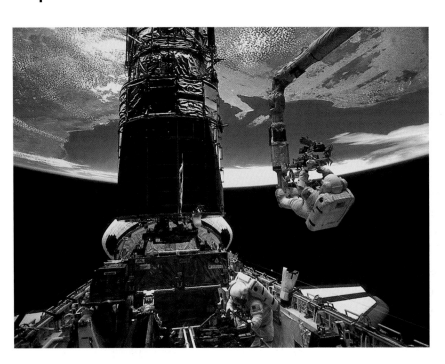

Ask a Question

❶ How can I build a piece of equipment that models how astronauts work in space?

Form a Hypothesis

❷ Write a possible answer for the question above. Describe a possible tool that would help astronauts work in space.

Test the Hypothesis

❸ Cut three strips from the cardboard box. Each strip should be about 5 cm wide. The strips should be at least 20 cm long but not longer than 40 cm.

4 Punch holes near the center of each end of the three cardboard strips. The holes should be about 3 cm from the end of each strip.

5 Lay the strips end to end along your table. Slide the second strip toward the first strip so that a hole in the first strip lines up with a hole in the second strip. Slip a paper brad through the holes, and bend its ends out to attach the cardboard strips.

6 Use another brad to attach the third cardboard strip to the free end of the second strip. Now, you have your mechanical arm. The paper brads create joints where the cardboard strips meet.

7 Straighten the wire, and slide it through the hole in one end of your mechanical arm. Bend about 3 cm of the wire in a 90° angle so that it will not slide back out of the hole.

8 Now, try to move the arm by holding the free ends of the cardboard and wire. The arm should bend and straighten at the joints. If it is difficult to move your mechanical arm, adjust the design. Consider loosening the brads, for example.

9 Your mechanical arm now needs a hand. Otherwise, it won't be able to pick things up! Straighten one paper clip, and slide it through the hole where you attached the wire in step 7. Bend one end of the paper clip to form a loop around the cardboard and the other end to form a hook. You will use this hook to pick things up.

10 Bend a second paper clip into a U shape. Stick the straight end of this paper clip into the foam ball. Leave the ball on your desk.

11 Move your mechanical arm so that you can lift the foam ball. The paper-clip hook on the mechanical arm will have to catch the paper clip on the ball.

Analyze the Results

1 Did you have any trouble moving the mechanical arm in step 8? What adjustments did you make?

2 Did you have trouble picking up the foam ball? What might have made picking up the ball easier?

Draw Conclusions

3 What improvements could you make to your mechanical arm that might make it easier to use?

4 How would a tool like this one help astronauts work in space?

Applying Your Data

Adjust the design for your mechanical arm. Can you find a way to lift objects other than the foam ball? For example, can you lift heavier objects or objects that do not have a loop attached? How?

Research the tools that astronauts use on space stations and on the space shuttle. How do their tools help them work in the special conditions of space?

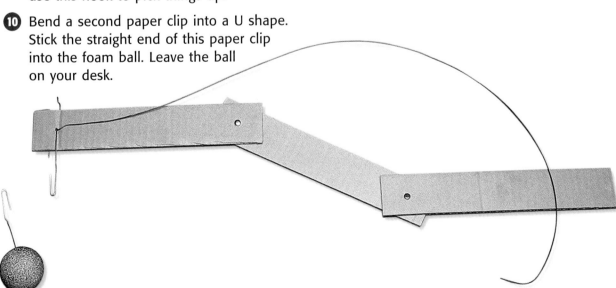

✓ Reading Check Answers

Chapter 1 Studying Space
Section 1
Page 5: Copernicus believed in a sun-centered universe.

Page 6: Newton's law of gravity helped explain why the planets orbit the sun and moons orbit planets.

Section 2
Page 8: The objective lens collects light and forms an image at the back of the telescope. The eyepiece magnifies the image produced by the objective lens.

Page 10: Air pollution, water vapor, and light pollution distort the images produced by optical telescopes.

Page 13: because the atmosphere blocks most X-ray radiation from space

Section 3
Page 15: Different constellations are visible in the Northern and Southern Hemispheres because different portions of the sky are visible from the Northern and Southern hemispheres.

Page 17: The apparent movement of the sun and stars is caused by the Earth's rotation on its axis.

Page 18: 9.46 trillion kilometers

Page 20: One might conclude that all of the galaxies are traveling toward the Earth and that the universe is contracting.

Chapter 2 Stars, Galaxies, and the Universe
Section 1
Page 32: Rigel is hotter than Betelgeuse because blue stars are hotter than red stars.

Page 34: A star's absorption spectrum indicates some of the elements that are in the star's atmosphere.

Page 36: Apparent magnitude is the brightness of a light or star.

Page 37: A light-year is the distance that light travels in 1 year.

Page 38: The actual motion of stars is hard to see because the stars are so distant.

Section 2
Page 41: A red giant star is a star that expands and cools once it uses all of its hydrogen. As the center of a star continues to shrink a red giant star can become a red supergiant star.

Page 45: A black hole is an object that is so massive that even light cannot escape its gravity. A black hole can be detected when it gives off X rays.

Section 3
Page 46: Spiral galaxies have a bulge at the center and spiral arms. The arms of spiral galaxies are made up of gas, dust, and new stars.

Page 48: A globular cluster is a tight group of up to 1 million stars that looks like a ball. An open cluster is a group of closely grouped stars that are usually located along the spiral disk of a galaxy.

Page 49: Quasars are starlike sources of light that are extremely far away. Some scientists think that quasars may be the core of young galaxies that are in the process of forming.

Section 4
Page 51: Cosmic background radiation is radiation that is left over from the big bang. After the big bang, cosmic background radiation was distributed everywhere and filled all of space.

Page 52: One way to calculate the age of the universe is to measure the distance from Earth to various galaxies.

Page 53: If gravity stops the expansion of the universe, the universe might collapse. If the expansion of the universe continues forever, stars will age and die and the universe will eventually become cold and dark.

Chapter 3 Formation of the Solar System
Section 1
Page 65: The solar nebula is the cloud of gas and dust that formed our solar system.

Page 67: Jupiter, Saturn, Uranus, and Neptune

Section 2
Page 69: Energy from gravity is not enough to power the sun, because if all of the sun's gravitational energy were released, the sun would last for only 45 million years.

Page 71: The nuclei of hydrogen atoms repel each other because they are positively charged and like charges repel each other.

Page 72: Sunspots are cooler, dark spots on the sun. Sunspots occur because when activity slows down in the convective zone, areas of the photosphere become cooler.

Section 3
Page 74: During Earth's early formation, planetesimals collided with the Earth. The energy of their motion heated the planet.

Page 76: Scientists think that the Earth's first atmosphere was a steamy mixture of carbon dioxide and water vapor.

Page 78: When photosynthetic organisms appeared on Earth, they released oxygen into the Earth's atmosphere. Over several million years, more and more oxygen was added to the atmosphere, which helped form Earth's current atmosphere.

Section 4

Page 81: Kepler's third law of motion states that planets that are farther away from the sun take longer to orbit the sun.

Page 82: Newton's law of universal gravitation states that the force of gravity depends on the product of the masses of the objects divided by the square of the distance between the objects.

Chapter 4   A Family of Planets

Section 1

Page 95: Light travels about 300,000 km/s.

Page 97: Jupiter, Saturn, Uranus, Neptune, and Pluto are in the outer solar system.

Section 2

Page 99: Radar technology was used to map the surface of Venus.

Page 100: Earth Science Enterprise is a NASA program that uses satellites to study Earth's atmosphere, land, oceans, life, and ice. This program will help scientists understand how humans affect the environment and how different parts of the global system interact.

Page 102: Mars' crust is chemically different from Earth's crust, so the Martian crust does not move. As a result, volcanoes build up in the same spots on Mars.

Section 3

Page 105: Saturn's rings are made of icy particles ranging in size from a few centimeters to several meters wide.

Page 107: Neptune's interior releases energy to its outer layers, which creates belts of clouds in Neptune's atmosphere.

Section 4

Page 111: The moon formed from a piece of Earth's mantle, which broke off during a collision between Earth and a large object.

Page 113: During a solar eclipse, the moon blocks out the sun and casts a shadow on Earth.

Page 114: We don't see solar and lunar eclipses every month because the moon's orbit around Earth is tilted.

Page 115: Because Titan's atmosphere is similar to the atmosphere on Earth before life evolved, scientists can study Titan's atmosphere to learn how life began.

Page 116: Pluto is eclipsed by Charon every 120 years.

Section 5

Page 119: Comets come from the Oort cloud and the Kuiper belt.

Page 121: The major types of meteorites are stony, metallic, and stony-iron meteorites.

Page 122: Large objects strike Earth every few thousand years.

Chapter 5   Exploring Space

Section 1

Page 134: Tsiolkovsky helped develop rocket theory. Goddard developed the first rockets.

Page 136: Rockets carry oxygen so that their fuel can be burned.

Section 2

Page 139: Answers may vary. LEO is much closer to the Earth than GEO.

Page 141: Information from one location is transmitted to a communications satellite. The satellite then sends the information to another location on Earth.

Page 143: Satellites in the EOS program are designed to work together so that many different types of data can be integrated.

Section 3

Page 145: The Magellan mission showed that, in many ways, the surface of Venus is similar to the surface of Earth.

Page 146: The Mars Pathfinder mission found evidence that water once flowed across the surface of Mars.

Page 148: The mission of the Stardust probe is to gather samples from a comet's tail and return them to Earth.

Section 4

Page 151: the orbiter, the liquid-fuel tank, and the solid-fuel booster rockets

Page 153: The Russians are supplying a service module, docking modules, life-support and research modules, and transportation to and from the station. The Americans are providing lab modules, the supporting frame, solar panels, living quarters, and a biomedical laboratory.

Page 155: Space-age spinoffs are technologies that were developed for the space program but are now used in everyday life.

Study Skills

FoldNote Instructions

Have you ever tried to study for a test or quiz but didn't know where to start? Or have you read a chapter and found that you can remember only a few ideas? Well, FoldNotes are a fun and exciting way to help you learn and remember the ideas you encounter as you learn science!

FoldNotes are tools that you can use to organize concepts. By focusing on a few main concepts, FoldNotes help you learn and remember how the concepts fit together. They can help you see the "big picture." Below you will find instructions for building 10 different FoldNotes.

Pyramid

1. Place a sheet of paper in front of you. Fold the lower left-hand corner of the paper diagonally to the opposite edge of the paper.

2. Cut off the tab of paper created by the fold (at the top).

3. Open the paper so that it is a square. Fold the lower right-hand corner of the paper diagonally to the opposite corner to form a triangle.

4. Open the paper. The creases of the two folds will have created an X.

5. Using scissors, cut along one of the creases. Start from any corner, and stop at the center point to create two flaps. Use tape or glue to attach one of the flaps on top of the other flap.

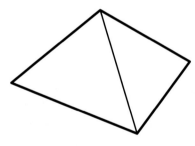

Double Door

1. Fold a sheet of paper in half from the top to the bottom. Then, unfold the paper.

2. Fold the top and bottom edges of the paper to the crease.

Booklet

1. Fold a sheet of paper in half from left to right. Then, unfold the paper.

2. Fold the sheet of paper in half again from the top to the bottom. Then, unfold the paper.

3. Refold the sheet of paper in half from left to right.

4. Fold the top and bottom edges to the center crease.

5. Completely unfold the paper.

6. Refold the paper from top to bottom.

7. Using scissors, cut a slit along the center crease of the sheet from the folded edge to the creases made in step 4. Do not cut the entire sheet in half.

8. Fold the sheet of paper in half from left to right. While holding the bottom and top edges of the paper, push the bottom and top edges together so that the center collapses at the center slit. Fold the four flaps to form a four-page book.

Layered Book

1. Lay one sheet of paper on top of another sheet. Slide the top sheet up so that 2 cm of the bottom sheet is showing.

2. Hold the two sheets together, fold down the top of the two sheets so that you see four 2 cm tabs along the bottom.

3. Using a stapler, staple the top of the FoldNote.

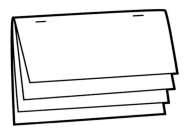

Key-Term Fold

1. Fold a sheet of lined notebook paper in half from left to right.

2. Using scissors, cut along every third line from the right edge of the paper to the center fold to make tabs.

Four-Corner Fold

1. Fold a sheet of paper in half from left to right. Then, unfold the paper.

2. Fold each side of the paper to the crease in the center of the paper.

3. Fold the paper in half from the top to the bottom. Then, unfold the paper.

4. Using scissors, cut the top flap creases made in step 3 to form four flaps.

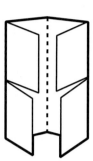

Three-Panel Flip Chart

1. Fold a piece of paper in half from the top to the bottom.

2. Fold the paper in thirds from side to side. Then, unfold the paper so that you can see the three sections.

3. From the top of the paper, cut along each of the vertical fold lines to the fold in the middle of the paper. You will now have three flaps.

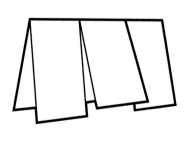

Table Fold

1. Fold a piece of paper in half from the top to the bottom. Then, fold the paper in half again.

2. Fold the paper in thirds from side to side.

3. Unfold the paper completely. Carefully trace the fold lines by using a pen or pencil.

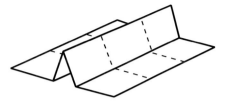

Two-Panel Flip Chart

1. Fold a piece of paper in half from the top to the bottom.

2. Fold the paper in half from side to side. Then, unfold the paper so that you can see the two sections.

3. From the top of the paper, cut along the vertical fold line to the fold in the middle of the paper. You will now have two flaps.

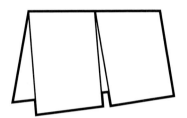

Tri-Fold

1. Fold a piece a paper in thirds from the top to the bottom.

2. Unfold the paper so that you can see the three sections. Then, turn the paper sideways so that the three sections form vertical columns.

3. Trace the fold lines by using a pen or pencil. Label the columns "Know," "Want," and "Learn."

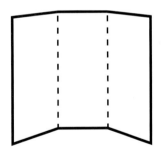

Appendix

Graphic Organizer Instructions

 Have you ever wished that you could "draw out" the many concepts you learn in your science class? Sometimes, being able to *see* how concepts are related really helps you remember what you've learned. Graphic Organizers do just that! They give you a way to draw or map out concepts.

All you need to make a Graphic Organizer is a piece of paper and a pencil. Below you will find instructions for four different Graphic Organizers designed to help you organize the concepts you'll learn in this book.

Spider Map

1. Draw a diagram like the one shown. In the circle, write the main topic.

2. From the circle, draw legs to represent different categories of the main topic. You can have as many categories as you want.

3. From the category legs, draw horizontal lines. As you read the chapter, write details about each category on the horizontal lines.

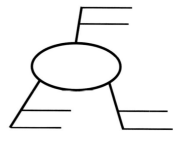

Comparison Table

1. Draw a chart like the one shown. Your chart can have as many columns and rows as you want.

2. In the top row, write the topics that you want to compare.

3. In the left column, write characteristics of the topics that you want to compare. As you read the chapter, fill in the characteristics for each topic in the appropriate boxes.

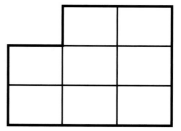

Appendix

Chain-of-Events-Chart

1. Draw a box. In the box, write the first step of a process or the first event of a timeline.

2. Under the box, draw another box, and use an arrow to connect the two boxes. In the second box, write the next step of the process or the next event in the timeline.

3. Continue adding boxes until the process or timeline is finished.

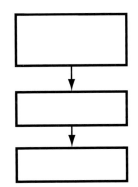

Concept Map

1. Draw a circle in the center of a piece of paper. Write the main idea of the chapter in the center of the circle.

2. From the circle, draw other circles. In those circles, write characteristics of the main idea. Draw arrows from the center circle to the circles that contain the characteristics.

3. From each circle that contains a characteristic, draw other circles. In those circles, write specific details about the characteristic. Draw arrows from each circle that contains a characteristic to the circles that contain specific details. You may draw as many circles as you want.

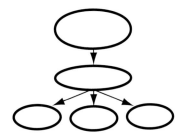

SI Measurement

The International System of Units, or SI, is the standard system of measurement used by many scientists. Using the same standards of measurement makes it easier for scientists to communicate with one another.

SI works by combining prefixes and base units. Each base unit can be used with different prefixes to define smaller and larger quantities. The table below lists common SI prefixes.

SI Prefixes

Prefix	Symbol	Factor	Example
kilo-	k	1,000	kilogram, 1 kg = 1,000 g
hecto-	h	100	hectoliter, 1 hL = 100 L
deka-	da	10	dekameter, 1 dam = 10 m
		1	meter, liter, gram
deci-	d	0.1	decigram, 1 dg = 0.1 g
centi-	c	0.01	centimeter, 1 cm = 0.01 m
milli-	m	0.001	milliliter, 1 mL = 0.001 L
micro-	μ	0.000 001	micrometer, 1 μm = 0.000 001 m

SI Conversion Table

SI units	From SI to English	From English to SI
Length		
kilometer (km) = 1,000 m	1 km = 0.621 mi	1 mi = 1.609 km
meter (m) = 100 cm	1 m = 3.281 ft	1 ft = 0.305 m
centimeter (cm) = 0.01 m	1 cm = 0.394 in.	1 in. = 2.540 cm
millimeter (mm) = 0.001 m	1 mm = 0.039 in.	
micrometer (μm) = 0.000 001 m		
nanometer (nm) = 0.000 000 001 m		
Area		
square kilometer (km^2) = 100 hectares	$1 \text{ km}^2 = 0.386 \text{ mi}^2$	$1 \text{ mi}^2 = 2.590 \text{ km}^2$
hectare (ha) = 10,000 m^2	1 ha = 2.471 acres	1 acre = 0.405 ha
square meter (m^2) = 10,000 cm^2	$1 \text{ m}^2 = 10.764 \text{ ft}^2$	$1 \text{ ft}^2 = 0.093 \text{ m}^2$
square centimeter (cm^2) = 100 mm^2	$1 \text{ cm}^2 = 0.155 \text{ in.}^2$	$1 \text{ in.}^2 = 6.452 \text{ cm}^2$
Volume		
liter (L) = 1,000 mL = 1 dm^3	1 L = 1.057 fl qt	1 fl qt = 0.946 L
milliliter (mL) = 0.001 L = 1 cm^3	1 mL = 0.034 fl oz	1 fl oz = 29.574 mL
microliter (μL) = 0.000 001 L		
Mass		
kilogram (kg) = 1,000 g	1 kg = 2.205 lb	1 lb = 0.454 kg
gram (g) = 1,000 mg	1 g = 0.035 oz	1 oz = 28.350 g
milligram (mg) = 0.001 g		
microgram (μg) = 0.000 001 g		

Temperature Scales

Temperature can be expressed by using three different scales: Fahrenheit, Celsius, and Kelvin. The SI unit for temperature is the kelvin (K).

Although 0 K is much colder than 0°C, a change of 1 K is equal to a change of 1°C.

Three Temperature Scales

	Fahrenheit	Celsius	Kelvin
Water boils	212°	100°	373
Body temperature	98.6°	37°	310
Room temperature	68°	20°	293
Water freezes	32°	0°	273

Temperature Conversions Table

To convert	Use this equation:	Example
Celsius to Fahrenheit °C → °F	$°F = \left(\dfrac{9}{5} \times °C\right) + 32$	Convert 45°C to °F. $°F = \left(\dfrac{9}{5} \times 45°C\right) + 32 = 113°F$
Fahrenheit to Celsius °F → °C	$°C = \dfrac{5}{9} \times (°F - 32)$	Convert 68°F to °C. $°C = \dfrac{5}{9} \times (68°F - 32) = 20°C$
Celsius to Kelvin °C → K	$K = °C + 273$	Convert 45°C to K. $K = 45°C + 273 = 318\ K$
Kelvin to Celsius K → °C	$°C = K - 273$	Convert 32 K to °C. $°C = 32K - 273 = -241°C$

Measuring Skills

Using a Graduated Cylinder

When using a graduated cylinder to measure volume, keep the following procedures in mind:

1 Place the cylinder on a flat, level surface before measuring liquid.

2 Move your head so that your eye is level with the surface of the liquid.

3 Read the mark closest to the liquid level. On glass graduated cylinders, read the mark closest to the center of the curve in the liquid's surface.

Using a Meterstick or Metric Ruler

When using a meterstick or metric ruler to measure length, keep the following procedures in mind:

1 Place the ruler firmly against the object that you are measuring.

2 Align one edge of the object exactly with the 0 end of the ruler.

3 Look at the other edge of the object to see which of the marks on the ruler is closest to that edge. (Note: Each small slash between the centimeters represents a millimeter, which is one-tenth of a centimeter.)

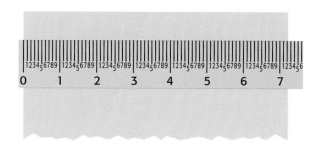

Using a Triple-Beam Balance

When using a triple-beam balance to measure mass, keep the following procedures in mind:

1 Make sure the balance is on a level surface.

2 Place all of the countermasses at 0. Adjust the balancing knob until the pointer rests at 0.

3 Place the object you wish to measure on the pan. **Caution:** Do not place hot objects or chemicals directly on the balance pan.

4 Move the largest countermass along the beam to the right until it is at the last notch that does not tip the balance. Follow the same procedure with the next-largest countermass. Then, move the smallest countermass until the pointer rests at 0.

5 Add the readings from the three beams together to determine the mass of the object.

6 When determining the mass of crystals or powders, first find the mass of a piece of filter paper. Then, add the crystals or powder to the paper, and remeasure. The actual mass of the crystals or powder is the total mass minus the mass of the paper. When finding the mass of liquids, first find the mass of the empty container. Then, find the combined mass of the liquid and container. The mass of the liquid is the total mass minus the mass of the container.

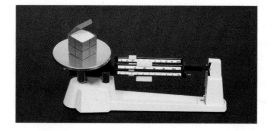

Scientific Methods

The ways in which scientists answer questions and solve problems are called **scientific methods.** The same steps are often used by scientists as they look for answers. However, there is more than one way to use these steps. Scientists may use all of the steps or just some of the steps during an investigation. They may even repeat some of the steps. The goal of using scientific methods is to come up with reliable answers and solutions.

Six Steps of Scientific Methods

 Good questions come from careful **observations.** You make observations by using your senses to gather information. Sometimes, you may use instruments, such as microscopes and telescopes, to extend the range of your senses. As you observe the natural world, you will discover that you have many more questions than answers. These questions drive investigations.

Questions beginning with *what, why, how,* and *when* are important in focusing an investigation. Here is an example of a question that could lead to an investigation.

Question: How does acid rain affect plant growth?

 After you ask a question, you need to form a **hypothesis.** A hypothesis is a clear statement of what you expect the answer to your question to be. Your hypothesis will represent your best "educated guess" based on what you have observed and what you already know. A good hypothesis is testable. Otherwise, the investigation can go no further. Here is a hypothesis based on the question, "How does acid rain affect plant growth?"

Hypothesis: Acid rain slows plant growth.

The hypothesis can lead to predictions. A prediction is what you think the outcome of your experiment or data collection will be. Predictions are usually stated in an if-then format. Here is a sample prediction for the hypothesis that acid rain slows plant growth.

Prediction: If a plant is watered with only acid rain (which has a pH of 4), then the plant will grow at half its normal rate.

 After you have formed a hypothesis and made a prediction, your hypothesis should be tested. One way to test a hypothesis is with a controlled experiment. A **controlled experiment** tests only one factor at a time. In an experiment to test the effect of acid rain on plant growth, the **control group** would be watered with normal rain water. The **experimental group** would be watered with acid rain. All of the plants should receive the same amount of sunlight and water each day. The air temperature should be the same for all groups. However, the acidity of the water will be a variable. In fact, any factor that is different from one group to another is a **variable.** If your hypothesis is correct, then the acidity of the water and plant growth are *dependant variables.* The amount a plant grows is dependent on the acidity of the water. However, the amount of water each plant receives and the amount of sunlight each plant receives are *independent variables.* Either of these factors could change without affecting the other factor.

Sometimes, the nature of an investigation makes a controlled experiment impossible. For example, the Earth's core is surrounded by thousands of meters of rock. Under such circumstances, a hypothesis may be tested by making detailed observations.

 After you have completed your experiments, made your observations, and collected your data, you must analyze all the information you have gathered. Tables and graphs are often used in this step to organize the data.

Appendix

5 Draw Conclusions

After analyzing your data, you can determine if your results support your hypothesis. If your hypothesis is supported, you (or others) might want to repeat the observations or experiments to verify your results. If your hypothesis is not supported by the data, you may have to check your procedure for errors. You may even have to reject your hypothesis and make a new one. If you cannot draw a conclusion from your results, you may have to try the investigation again or carry out further observations or experiments.

6 Communicate Results

After any scientific investigation, you should report your results. By preparing a written or oral report, you let others know what you have learned. They may repeat your investigation to see if they get the same results. Your report may even lead to another question and then to another investigation.

Scientific Methods in Action

Scientific methods contain loops in which several steps may be repeated over and over again. In some cases, certain steps are unnecessary. Thus, there is not a "straight line" of steps. For example, sometimes scientists find that testing one hypothesis raises new questions and new hypotheses to be tested. And sometimes, testing the hypothesis leads directly to a conclusion. Furthermore, the steps in scientific methods are not always used in the same order. Follow the steps in the diagram, and see how many different directions scientific methods can take you.

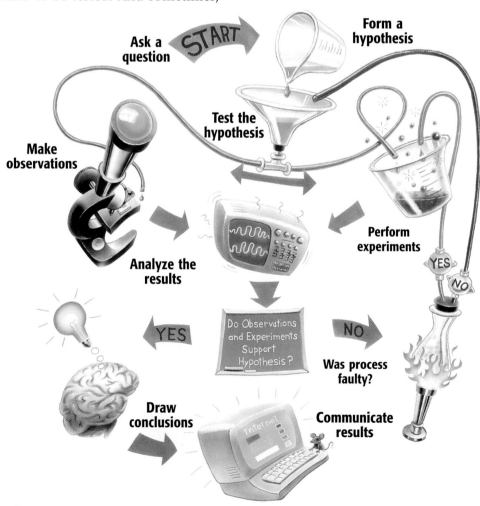

Making Charts and Graphs

Pie Charts

A pie chart shows how each group of data relates to all of the data. Each part of the circle forming the chart represents a category of the data. The entire circle represents all of the data. For example, a biologist studying a hardwood forest in Wisconsin found that there were five different types of trees. The data table at right summarizes the biologist's findings.

Wisconsin Hardwood Trees	
Type of tree	Number found
Oak	600
Maple	750
Beech	300
Birch	1,200
Hickory	150
Total	3,000

How to Make a Pie Chart

1 To make a pie chart of these data, first find the percentage of each type of tree. Divide the number of trees of each type by the total number of trees, and multiply by 100.

$$\frac{600 \text{ oak}}{3,000 \text{ trees}} \times 100 = 20\%$$

$$\frac{750 \text{ maple}}{3,000 \text{ trees}} \times 100 = 25\%$$

$$\frac{300 \text{ beech}}{3,000 \text{ trees}} \times 100 = 10\%$$

$$\frac{1,200 \text{ birch}}{3,000 \text{ trees}} \times 100 = 40\%$$

$$\frac{150 \text{ hickory}}{3,000 \text{ trees}} \times 100 = 5\%$$

2 Now, determine the size of the wedges that make up the pie chart. Multiply each percentage by 360°. Remember that a circle contains 360°.

$20\% \times 360° = 72°$ $25\% \times 360° = 90°$

$10\% \times 360° = 36°$ $40\% \times 360° = 144°$

$5\% \times 360° = 18°$

3 Check that the sum of the percentages is 100 and the sum of the degrees is 360.

$20\% + 25\% + 10\% + 40\% + 5\% = 100\%$

$72° + 90° + 36° + 144° + 18° = 360°$

4 Use a compass to draw a circle and mark the center of the circle.

5 Then, use a protractor to draw angles of 72°, 90°, 36°, 144°, and 18° in the circle.

6 Finally, label each part of the chart, and choose an appropriate title.

A Community of Wisconsin Hardwood Trees

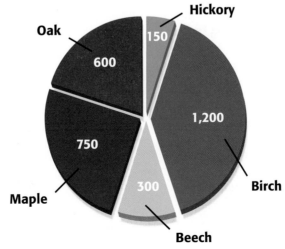

Line Graphs

Line graphs are most often used to demonstrate continuous change. For example, Mr. Smith's students analyzed the population records for their hometown, Appleton, between 1900 and 2000. Examine the data at right.

Because the year and the population change, they are the *variables*. The population is determined by, or dependent on, the year. Therefore, the population is called the **dependent variable,** and the year is called the **independent variable.** Each set of data is called a **data pair.** To prepare a line graph, you must first organize data pairs into a table like the one at right.

Population of Appleton, 1900–2000	
Year	Population
1900	1,800
1920	2,500
1940	3,200
1960	3,900
1980	4,600
2000	5,300

How to Make a Line Graph

1 Place the independent variable along the horizontal (*x*) axis. Place the dependent variable along the vertical (*y*) axis.

2 Label the *x*-axis "Year" and the *y*-axis "Population." Look at your largest and smallest values for the population. For the *y*-axis, determine a scale that will provide enough space to show these values. You must use the same scale for the entire length of the axis. Next, find an appropriate scale for the *x*-axis.

3 Choose reasonable starting points for each axis.

4 Plot the data pairs as accurately as possible.

5 Choose a title that accurately represents the data.

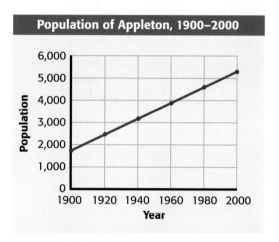

Population of Appleton, 1900–2000

How to Determine Slope

Slope is the ratio of the change in the *y*-value to the change in the *x*-value, or "rise over run."

1 Choose two points on the line graph. For example, the population of Appleton in 2000 was 5,300 people. Therefore, you can define point *a* as (2000, 5,300). In 1900, the population was 1,800 people. You can define point *b* as (1900, 1,800).

2 Find the change in the *y*-value. (*y* at point *a*) − (*y* at point *b*) = 5,300 people − 1,800 people = 3,500 people

3 Find the change in the *x*-value. (*x* at point *a*) − (*x* at point *b*) = 2000 − 1900 = 100 years

4 Calculate the slope of the graph by dividing the change in *y* by the change in *x*.

$$slope = \frac{change\ in\ y}{change\ in\ x}$$

$$slope = \frac{3,500\ people}{100\ years}$$

$$slope = 35\ people\ per\ year$$

In this example, the population in Appleton increased by a fixed amount each year. The graph of these data is a straight line. Therefore, the relationship is **linear.** When the graph of a set of data is not a straight line, the relationship is **nonlinear.**

Appendix

Using Algebra to Determine Slope

The equation in step 4 may also be arranged to be

$$y = kx$$

where y represents the change in the y-value, k represents the slope, and x represents the change in the x-value.

$$slope = \frac{change\ in\ y}{change\ in\ x}$$

$$k = \frac{y}{x}$$

$$k \times x = \frac{y \times x}{x}$$

$$kx = y$$

Bar Graphs

Bar graphs are used to demonstrate change that is not continuous. These graphs can be used to indicate trends when the data cover a long period of time. A meteorologist gathered the precipitation data shown here for Hartford, Connecticut, for April 1–15, 1996, and used a bar graph to represent the data.

Precipitation in Hartford, Connecticut April 1–15, 1996			
Date	Precipitation (cm)	Date	Precipitation (cm)
April 1	0.5	April 9	0.25
April 2	1.25	April 10	0.0
April 3	0.0	April 11	1.0
April 4	0.0	April 12	0.0
April 5	0.0	April 13	0.25
April 6	0.0	April 14	0.0
April 7	0.0	April 15	6.50
April 8	1.75		

How to Make a Bar Graph

1 Use an appropriate scale and a reasonable starting point for each axis.

2 Label the axes, and plot the data.

3 Choose a title that accurately represents the data.

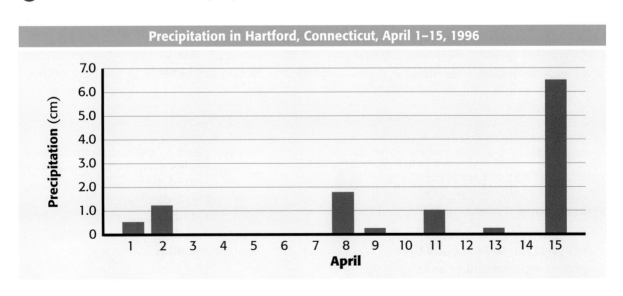

Math Refresher

Science requires an understanding of many math concepts. The following pages will help you review some important math skills.

Averages

An **average,** or **mean,** simplifies a set of numbers into a single number that *approximates* the value of the set.

Example: Find the average of the following set of numbers: 5, 4, 7, and 8.

Step 1: Find the sum.
$$5 + 4 + 7 + 8 = 24$$

Step 2: Divide the sum by the number of numbers in your set. Because there are four numbers in this example, divide the sum by 4.
$$\frac{24}{4} = 6$$

The average, or mean, is **6.**

Ratios

A **ratio** is a comparison between numbers, and it is usually written as a fraction.

Example: Find the ratio of thermometers to students if you have 36 thermometers and 48 students in your class.

Step 1: Make the ratio.
$$\frac{36 \text{ thermometers}}{48 \text{ students}}$$

Step 2: Reduce the fraction to its simplest form.
$$\frac{36}{48} = \frac{36 \div 12}{48 \div 12} = \frac{3}{4}$$

The ratio of thermometers to students is **3 to 4,** or $\frac{3}{4}$. The ratio may also be written in the form 3:4.

Proportions

A **proportion** is an equation that states that two ratios are equal.
$$\frac{3}{1} = \frac{12}{4}$$

To solve a proportion, first multiply across the equal sign. This is called *cross-multiplication.* If you know three of the quantities in a proportion, you can use cross-multiplication to find the fourth.

Example: Imagine that you are making a scale model of the solar system for your science project. The diameter of Jupiter is 11.2 times the diameter of the Earth. If you are using a plastic-foam ball that has a diameter of 2 cm to represent the Earth, what must the diameter of the ball representing Jupiter be?
$$\frac{11.2}{1} = \frac{x}{2 \text{ cm}}$$

Step 1: Cross-multiply.
$$\frac{11.2}{1} \times \frac{x}{2}$$
$$11.2 \times 2 = x \times 1$$

Step 2: Multiply.
$$22.4 = x \times 1$$

Step 3: Isolate the variable by dividing both sides by 1.
$$x = \frac{22.4}{1}$$
$$x = 22.4 \text{ cm}$$

You will need to use a ball that has a diameter of **22.4** cm to represent Jupiter.

Percentages

A **percentage** is a ratio of a given number to 100.

> **Example:** What is 85% of 40?

Step 1: Rewrite the percentage by moving the decimal point two places to the left.

$$0.85$$

Step 2: Multiply the decimal by the number that you are calculating the percentage of.

$$0.85 \times 40 = 34$$

85% of 40 is **34.**

Decimals

To **add** or **subtract decimals,** line up the digits vertically so that the decimal points line up. Then, add or subtract the columns from right to left. Carry or borrow numbers as necessary.

> **Example:** Add the following numbers: 3.1415 and 2.96.

Step 1: Line up the digits vertically so that the decimal points line up.

$$\begin{array}{r} 3.1415 \\ + 2.96 \\ \hline \end{array}$$

Step 2: Add the columns from right to left, and carry when necessary.

$$\begin{array}{r} {}^{1\ \ 1} \\ 3.1415 \\ + 2.96 \\ \hline 6.1015 \end{array}$$

The sum is **6.1015.**

Fractions

Numbers tell you how many; **fractions** tell you *how much of a whole.*

> **Example:** Your class has 24 plants. Your teacher instructs you to put 5 plants in a shady spot. What fraction of the plants in your class will you put in a shady spot?

Step 1: In the denominator, write the total number of parts in the whole.

$$\frac{?}{24}$$

Step 2: In the numerator, write the number of parts of the whole that are being considered.

$$\frac{5}{24}$$

So, $\frac{5}{24}$ of the plants will be in the shade.

Reducing Fractions

It is usually best to express a fraction in its simplest form. Expressing a fraction in its simplest form is called *reducing* a fraction.

> **Example:** Reduce the fraction $\frac{30}{45}$ to its simplest form.

Step 1: Find the largest whole number that will divide evenly into both the numerator and denominator. This number is called the *greatest common factor* (GCF).

Factors of the numerator 30:
1, 2, 3, 5, 6, 10, **15,** 30

Factors of the denominator 45:
1, 3, 5, 9, **15,** 45

Step 2: Divide both the numerator and the denominator by the GCF, which in this case is 15.

$$\frac{30}{45} = \frac{30 \div 15}{45 \div 15} = \frac{2}{3}$$

Thus, $\frac{30}{45}$ reduced to its simplest form is $\frac{2}{3}$.

Appendix

Adding and Subtracting Fractions

To **add** or **subtract fractions** that have the **same denominator,** simply add or subtract the numerators.

Examples:

$$\frac{3}{5} + \frac{1}{5} = ? \text{ and } \frac{3}{4} - \frac{1}{4} = ?$$

Step 1: Add or subtract the numerators.

$$\frac{3}{5} + \frac{1}{5} = \frac{4}{} \text{ and } \frac{3}{4} - \frac{1}{4} = \frac{2}{}$$

Step 2: Write the sum or difference over the denominator.

$$\frac{3}{5} + \frac{1}{5} = \frac{4}{5} \text{ and } \frac{3}{4} - \frac{1}{4} = \frac{2}{4}$$

Step 3: If necessary, reduce the fraction to its simplest form.

$\frac{4}{5}$ cannot be reduced, and $\frac{2}{4} = \frac{1}{2}$.

To **add** or **subtract fractions** that have **different denominators,** first find the least common denominator (LCD).

Examples:

$$\frac{1}{2} + \frac{1}{6} = ? \text{ and } \frac{3}{4} - \frac{2}{3} = ?$$

Step 1: Write the equivalent fractions that have a common denominator.

$$\frac{3}{6} + \frac{1}{6} = ? \text{ and } \frac{9}{12} - \frac{8}{12} = ?$$

Step 2: Add or subtract the fractions.

$$\frac{3}{6} + \frac{1}{6} = \frac{4}{6} \text{ and } \frac{9}{12} - \frac{8}{12} = \frac{1}{12}$$

Step 3: If necessary, reduce the fraction to its simplest form.

The fraction $\frac{4}{6} = \frac{2}{3}$, and $\frac{1}{12}$ cannot be reduced.

Multiplying Fractions

To **multiply fractions,** multiply the numerators and the denominators together, and then reduce the fraction to its simplest form.

Example:

$$\frac{5}{9} \times \frac{7}{10} = ?$$

Step 1: Multiply the numerators and denominators.

$$\frac{5}{9} \times \frac{7}{10} = \frac{5 \times 7}{9 \times 10} = \frac{35}{90}$$

Step 2: Reduce the fraction.

$$\frac{35}{90} = \frac{35 \div 5}{90 \div 5} = \frac{7}{18}$$

Dividing Fractions

To **divide fractions,** first rewrite the divisor (the number you divide by) upside down. This number is called the *reciprocal* of the divisor. Then multiply and reduce if necessary.

Example:

$$\frac{5}{8} \div \frac{3}{2} = ?$$

Step 1: Rewrite the divisor as its reciprocal.

$$\frac{3}{2} \rightarrow \frac{2}{3}$$

Step 2: Multiply the fractions.

$$\frac{5}{8} \times \frac{2}{3} = \frac{5 \times 2}{8 \times 3} = \frac{10}{24}$$

Step 3: Reduce the fraction.

$$\frac{10}{24} = \frac{10 \div 2}{24 \div 2} = \frac{5}{12}$$

Scientific Notation

Scientific notation is a short way of representing very large and very small numbers without writing all of the place-holding zeros.

Example: Write 653,000,000 in scientific notation.

Step 1: Write the number without the place-holding zeros.

653

Step 2: Place the decimal point after the first digit.

6.53

Step 3: Find the exponent by counting the number of places that you moved the decimal point.

6.53000000

The decimal point was moved eight places to the left. Therefore, the exponent of 10 is positive 8. If you had moved the decimal point to the right, the exponent would be negative.

Step 4: Write the number in scientific notation.

6.53×10^8

Area

Area is the number of square units needed to cover the surface of an object.

Formulas:

$area\ of\ a\ square = side \times side$
$area\ of\ a\ rectangle = length \times width$
$area\ of\ a\ triangle = \frac{1}{2} \times base \times height$

Examples: Find the areas.

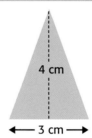

Triangle

$area = \frac{1}{2} \times base \times height$
$area = \frac{1}{2} \times 3\ cm \times 4\ cm$
$area = \mathbf{6\ cm^2}$

4 cm

3 cm

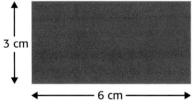

Rectangle

$area = length \times width$
$area = 6\ cm \times 3\ cm$
$area = \mathbf{18\ cm^2}$

3 cm

6 cm

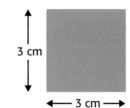

Square

$area = side \times side$
$area = 3\ cm \times 3\ cm$
$area = \mathbf{9\ cm^2}$

3 cm

3 cm

Volume

Volume is the amount of space that something occupies.

Formulas:

$volume\ of\ a\ cube =$
$side \times side \times side$

$volume\ of\ a\ prism =$
$area\ of\ base \times height$

Examples:

Find the volume of the solids.

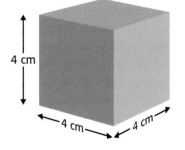

Cube

$volume = side \times side \times side$
$volume = 4\ cm \times 4\ cm \times 4\ cm$
$volume = \mathbf{64\ cm^3}$

4 cm

4 cm   4 cm

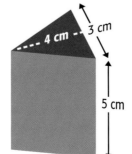

4 cm   3 cm

5 cm

Prism

$volume = area\ of\ base \times height$
$volume = (area\ of\ triangle) \times height$
$volume = (\frac{1}{2} \times 3\ cm \times 4\ cm) \times 5\ cm$
$volume = 6\ cm^2 \times 5\ cm$
$volume = \mathbf{30\ cm^3}$

Physical Science Refresher

Atoms and Elements

Every object in the universe is made up of particles of some kind of matter. **Matter** is anything that takes up space and has mass. All matter is made up of elements. An **element** is a substance that cannot be separated into simpler components by ordinary chemical means. This is because each element consists of only one kind of atom. An **atom** is the smallest unit of an element that has all of the properties of that element.

Atomic Structure

Atoms are made up of small particles called subatomic particles. The three major types of subatomic particles are **electrons, protons,** and **neutrons.** Electrons have a negative electric charge, protons have a positive charge, and neutrons have no electric charge. The protons and neutrons are packed close to one another to form the **nucleus.** The protons give the nucleus a positive charge. Electrons are most likely to be found in regions around the nucleus called **electron clouds.** The negatively charged electrons are attracted to the positively charged nucleus. An atom may have several energy levels in which electrons are located.

Atomic Number

To help in the identification of elements, scientists have assigned an **atomic number** to each kind of atom. The atomic number is the number of protons in the atom. Atoms with the same number of protons are all the same kind of element. In an uncharged, or electrically neutral, atom there are an equal number of protons and electrons. Therefore, the atomic number equals the number of electrons in an uncharged atom. The number of neutrons, however, can vary for a given element. Atoms of the same element that have different numbers of neutrons are called **isotopes.**

Periodic Table of the Elements

In the periodic table, the elements are arranged from left to right in order of increasing atomic number. Each element in the table is in a separate box. An uncharged atom of each element has one more electron and one more proton than an uncharged atom of the element to its left. Each horizontal row of the table is called a **period.** Changes in chemical properties of elements across a period correspond to changes in the electron arrangements of their atoms. Each vertical column of the table, known as a **group,** lists elements with similar properties. The elements in a group have similar chemical properties because their atoms have the same number of electrons in their outer energy level. For example, the elements helium, neon, argon, krypton, xenon, and radon all have similar properties and are known as the noble gases.

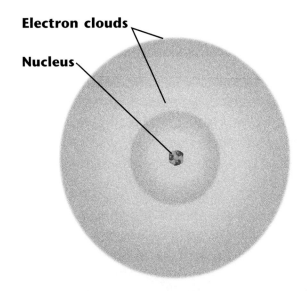

Electron clouds

Nucleus

Molecules and Compounds

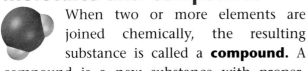

When two or more elements are joined chemically, the resulting substance is called a **compound.** A compound is a new substance with properties different from those of the elements that compose it. For example, water, H_2O, is a compound formed when hydrogen (H) and oxygen (O) combine. The smallest complete unit of a compound that has the properties of that compound is called a **molecule.** A chemical formula indicates the elements in a compound. It also indicates the relative number of atoms of each element present. The chemical formula for water is H_2O, which indicates that each water molecule consists of two atoms of hydrogen and one atom of oxygen. The subscript number after the symbol for an element indicates how many atoms of that element are in a single molecule of the compound.

Acids, Bases, and pH

An ion is an atom or group of atoms that has an electric charge because it has lost or gained one or more electrons. When an acid, such as hydrochloric acid, HCl, is mixed with water, it separates into ions. An **acid** is a compound that produces hydrogen ions, H+, in water. The hydrogen ions then combine with a water molecule to form a hydronium ion, H_3O^+. A **base,** on the other hand, is a substance that produces hydroxide ions, OH^-, in water.

To determine whether a solution is acidic or basic, scientists use pH. The **pH** is a measure of the hydronium ion concentration in a solution. The pH scale ranges from 0 to 14. The middle point, pH = 7, is neutral, neither acidic nor basic. Acids have a pH less than 7; bases have a pH greater than 7. The lower the number is, the more acidic the solution. The higher the number is, the more basic the solution.

Chemical Equations

A chemical reaction occurs when a chemical change takes place. (In a chemical change, new substances with new properties are formed.) A chemical equation is a useful way of describing a chemical reaction by means of chemical formulas. The equation indicates what substances react and what the products are. For example, when carbon and oxygen combine, they can form carbon dioxide. The equation for the reaction is as follows: $C + O_2 \rightarrow CO_2$.

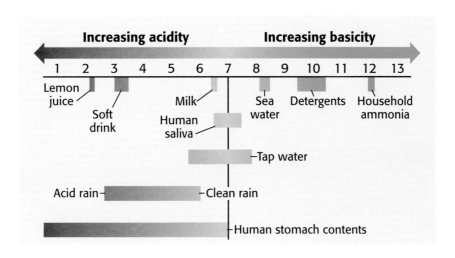

Sky Maps

Spring

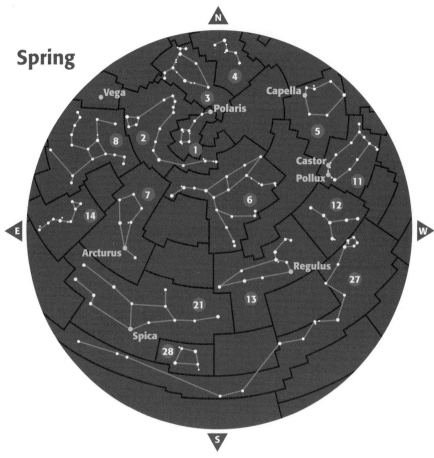

Summer

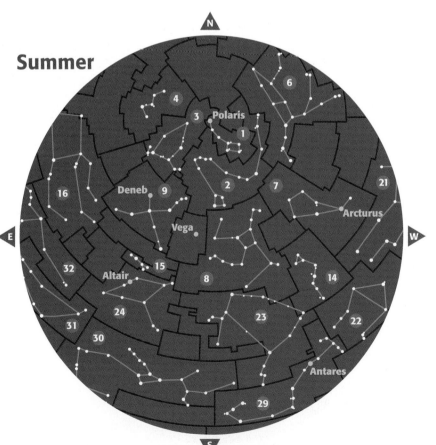

Constellations

1 Ursa Minor
2 Draco
3 Cepheus
4 Cassiopeia
5 Auriga
6 Ursa Major
7 Bootes
8 Hercules
9 Cygnus
10 Perseus
11 Gemini
12 Cancer
13 Leo
14 Serpens
15 Sagitta
16 Pegasus
17 Pisces

Autumn

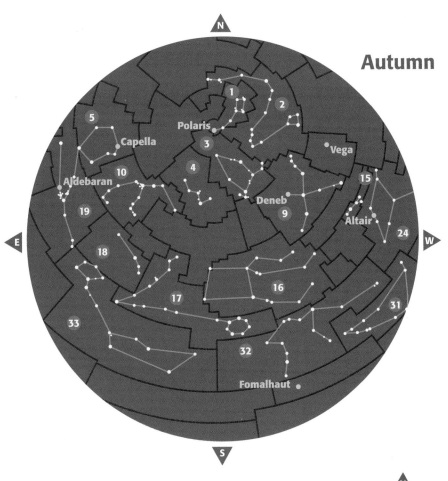

Winter

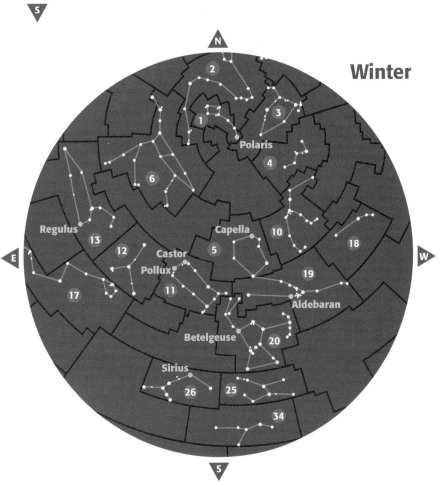

Constellations

18 Aries
19 Taurus
20 Orion
21 Virgo
22 Libra
23 Ophiuchus
24 Aquila
25 Lepus
26 Canis Major
27 Hydra
28 Corvus
29 Scorpius
30 Sagittarius
31 Capricornus
32 Aquarius
33 Cetus
34 Columba

Glossary

Glossary

A

absolute magnitude the brightness that a star would have at a distance of 32.6 light-years from Earth (36)

altitude the angle between an object in the sky and the horizon (16)

apparent magnitude the brightness of a star as seen from the Earth (36)

artificial satellite any human-made object placed in orbit around a body in space (138)

asteroid a small, rocky object that orbits the sun, usually in a band between the orbits of Mars and Jupiter (120)

asteroid belt the region of the solar system that is between the orbits of Mars and Jupiter and in which most asteroids orbit (120)

astronomical unit the average distance between the Earth and the sun; approximately 150 million kilometers (symbol, AU) (95)

astronomy the study of the universe (4)

B

big bang theory the theory that states that the universe began with a tremendous explosion about 13.7 billion years ago (51)

black hole an object so massive and dense that even light cannot escape its gravity (45)

C

comet a small body of ice, rock, and cosmic dust that follows an elliptical orbit around the sun and that gives off gas and dust in the form of a tail as it passes close to the sun (118)

constellation a region of the sky that contains a recognizable star pattern and that is used to describe the location of objects in space (14)

core the central part of the Earth below the mantle (75)

cosmology the study of the origin, properties, processes, and evolution of the universe (50)

crust the thin and solid outermost layer of the Earth above the mantle (75)

D

day the time required for Earth to rotate once on its axis (4)

E

eclipse an event in which the shadow of one celestial body falls on another (113)

electromagnetic spectrum all of the frequencies or wavelengths of electromagnetic radiation (11)

G

galaxy a collection of stars, dust, and gas bound together by gravity (46)

gas giant a planet that has a deep, massive atmosphere, such as Jupiter, Saturn, Uranus, or Neptune (104)

geostationary orbit an orbit that is about 36,000 km above the Earth's surface and in which a satellite is above a fixed spot on the equator (139)

globular cluster a tight group of stars that looks like a ball and contains up to 1 million stars (48)

H

horizon the line where the sky and the Earth appear to meet (16)

H-R diagram **H**ertzsprung-**R**ussell diagram, a graph that shows the relationship between a star's surface temperature and absolute magnitude (42)

L

light-year the distance that light travels in one year; about 9.46 trillion kilometers (18, 37)

low earth orbit an orbit that is less than 1,500 km above the Earth's surface (139)

M

main sequence the location on the H-R diagram where most stars lie; it has a diagonal pattern from the lower right (low temperature and luminosity) to the upper left (high temperature and luminosity) (43)

mantle the layer of rock between the Earth's crust and core (75)

meteor a bright streak of light that results when a meteoroid burns up in the Earth's atmosphere (121)

meteorite a meteoroid that reaches the Earth's surface without burning up completely (121)

meteoroid a relatively small, rocky body that travels through space (121)

month a division of the year that is based on the orbit of the moon around the Earth (4)

N

NASA the National Aeronautics and Space Administration (135)

nebula a large cloud of gas and dust in interstellar space; a region in space where stars are born or where stars explode at the end of their lives (48, 64)

neutron star a star that has collapsed under gravity to the point that the electrons and protons have smashed together to form neutrons (44)

nuclear fusion the combination of the nuclei of small atoms to form a larger nucleus; releases energy (70)

O

open cluster a group of stars that are close together relative to surrounding stars (48)

orbit the path that a body follows as it travels around another body in space (80)

P

parallax an apparent shift in the position of an object when viewed from different locations (37)

phase the change in the sunlit area of one celestial body as seen from another celestial body (112)

prograde rotation the counterclockwise spin of a planet or moon as seen from above the planet's North Pole; rotation in the same direction as the sun's rotation (99)

pulsar a rapidly spinning neutron star that emits rapid pulses of radio and optical energy (44)

Q

quasar a very luminous, starlike object that generates energy at a high rate; quasars are thought to be the most distant objects in the universe (49)

R

red giant a large, reddish star late in its life cycle (41)

reflecting telescope a telescope that uses a curved mirror to gather and focus light from distant objects (9)

refracting telescope a telescope that uses a set of lenses to gather and focus light from distant objects (9)

retrograde rotation the clockwise spin of a planet or moon as seen from above the planet's North Pole (99)

revolution the motion of a body that travels around another body in space; one complete trip along an orbit (80)

rocket a machine that uses escaping gas from burning fuel to move (134)

rotation the spin of a body on its axis (80)

S

satellite a natural or artificial body that revolves around a planet (110)

solar nebula the cloud of gas and dust that formed our solar system (65)

space probe an uncrewed vehicle that carries scientific instruments into space to collect scientific data (144)

space shuttle a reusable space vehicle that takes off like a rocket and lands like an airplane (151)

space station a long-term orbiting platform from which other vehicles can be launched or scientific research can be carried out (152)

spectrum the band of colors produced when white light passes through a prism (33)

sunspot a dark area of the photosphere of the sun that is cooler than the surrounding areas and that has a strong magnetic field (72)

supernova a gigantic explosion in which a massive star collapses and throws its outer layers into space (44)

T

telescope an instrument that collects electromagnetic radiation from the sky and concentrates it for better observation (8)

terrestrial planet one of the highly dense planets nearest to the sun; Mercury, Venus, Mars, and Earth (98)

thrust the pushing or pulling force exerted by the engine of an aircraft or rocket (136)

W

white dwarf a small, hot, dim star that is the left-over center of an old star (41)

Y

year the time required for the Earth to orbit once around the sun (4)

Z

zenith the point in the sky directly above an observer on Earth (16)

Glossary

Spanish Glossary

A

absolute magnitude/magnitud absoluta el brillo que una estrella tendría a una distancia de 32.6 años luz de la Tierra (36)

altitude/altitud el ángulo que se forma entre un objeto en el cielo y el horizonte (16)

apparent magnitude/magnitud aparente el brillo de una estrella como se percibe desde la Tierra (36)

artificial satellite/satélite artificial cualquier objeto hecho por los seres humanos y colocado en órbita alrededor de un cuerpo en el espacio (138)

asteroid/asteroide un objeto pequeño y rocoso que se encuentra e n órbita alrededor del Sol, normalmente en una banda entre las órbitas de Marte y Júpiter (120)

asteroid belt/cinturón de asteroides la región del Sistema Solar que está entre las órbitas de Marte y Júpiter, en la que la mayoría de los asteroides se encuentran en órbita (120)

astronomical unit/unidad astronómica la distancia promedio entre la Tierra y el Sol; aproximadamente 150 millones de kilómetros (símbolo: UA) (95)

astronomy/astronomía el estudio del universo (4)

B

big bang theory/teoría del Big Bang la teoría que establece que el universo comenzó con una tremenda explosión hace aproximadamente 13.7 mil millones de años (51)

black hole/hoyo negro un objeto tan masivo y denso que ni siquiera la luz puede salir de su campo gravitacional (45)

C

comet/cometa un cuerpo pequeño formado por hielo, roca y polvo cósmico que sigue una órbita elíptica alrededor del Sol y que libera gas y polvo, los cuales forman una cola al pasar cerca del Sol (118)

constellation/constelación una región del cielo que contiene un patrón reconocible de estrellas y que se utiliza para describir la ubicación de los objetos en el espacio (14)

core/núcleo la parte central de la Tierra, debajo del manto (75)

cosmology/cosmología el estudio del origen, propiedades, procesos y evolución del universo (50)

crust/corteza la capa externa, delgada y sólida de la Tierra, que se encuentra sobre el manto (75)

D

day/día el tiempo que se requiere para que la Tierra rote una vez sobre su eje (4)

E

eclipse/eclipse un suceso en el que la sombra de un cuerpo celeste cubre otro cuerpo celeste (113)

electromagnetic spectrum/espectro electromagnético todas las frecuencias o longitudes de onda de la radiación electromagnética (11)

G

galaxy/galaxia un conjunto de estrellas, polvo y gas unidos por la gravedad (46)

gas giant/gigante gaseoso un planeta con una atmósfera masiva y profunda, como por ejemplo, Júpiter, Saturno, Urano o Neptuno (104)

geostationary orbit/órbita geoestacionaria una órbita que está a aproximadamente 36,000 km de la superficie terrestre, en la que un satélite permanece sobre un punto fijo en el ecuador (139)

globular cluster/cúmulo globular un grupo compacto de estrellas que parece una bola y contiene hasta un millón de estrellas (48)

H

horizon/horizonte la línea donde parece que el cielo y la Tierra se unen (16)

H-R diagram/diagrama H-R diagrama de Hertzsprung-Russell; una gráfica que muestra la relación entre la temperatura de la superficie de una estrella y su magnitud absoluta (42)

L

light-year/año luz la distancia que viaja la luz en un año; aproximadamente 9.46 trillones de kilómetros (18, 37)

low earth orbit/órbita terrestre baja una órbita ubicada a menos de 13,5000 km sobre la superficie terrestre (139)

M

main sequence/secuencia principal la ubicación en el diagrama H-R donde se encuentran la mayoría de las estrellas; tiene un patrón diagonal de la parte inferior derecha (baja temperatura y luminosidad) a la parte superior izquierda (alta temperatura y luminosidad) (43)

mantle/manto la capa de roca que se encuentra entre la corteza terrestre y el núcleo (75)

meteor/meteoro un rayo de luz brillante que se produce cuando un meteoroide se quema en la atmósfera de la Tierra (121)

meteorite/meteorito un meteoroide que llega a la superficie de la Tierra sin quemarse por completo (121)

meteoroid/meteoroide un cuerpo rocoso relativamente pequeño que viaja en el espacio (121)

month/mes una división del año que se basa en la órbita de la Luna alrededor de la Tierra (4)

N

NASA/NASA la Administración Nacional de Aeronáutica y del Espacio (135)

nebula/nebulosa una nube grande de gas y polvo en el espacio interestelar; una región en el espacio donde las estrellas nacen o donde explotan al final de su vida (48, 64)

neutron star/estrella de neutrones una estrella que se ha colapsado debido a la gravedad hasta el punto en que los electrones y protones han chocado unos contra otros para formar neutrones (44)

nuclear fusion/fusión nuclear combinación de los núcleos de átomos pequeños para formar un núcleo más grande; libera energía (70)

O

open cluster/conglomerado abierto un grupo de estrellas que se encuentran juntas respecto a las estrellas que las rodean (48)

orbit/órbita la trayectoria que sigue un cuerpo al desplazarse alrededor de otro cuerpo en el espacio (80)

P

parallax/paralaje un cambio aparente en la posición de un objeto cuando se ve desde lugares distintos (37)

phase/fase el cambio en el área iluminada de un cuerpo celeste según se ve desde otro cuerpo celeste (112)

prograde rotation/rotación progresiva el giro en contra de las manecillas del reloj de un planeta o de una luna según lo vería un observador ubicado encima del Polo Norte del planeta; rotación en la misma dirección que la rotación del Sol (99)

pulsar/pulsar una estrella de neutrones que gira rápidamente y emite pulsaciones rápidas de energía radioeléctrica y óptica (44)

Q

quasar/cuasar un objeto muy luminoso, parecido a una estrella, que genera energía a una gran velocidad; se piensa que los cuásares son los objetos más distantes del universo (49)

R

red giant/gigante roja una estrella grande de color rojizo que se encuentra en una etapa avanzada de su vida (41)

reflecting telescope/telescopio reflector un telescopio que utiliza un espejo curvo para captar y enfocar la luz de objetos lejanos (9)

refracting telescope/telescopio refractante un telescopio que utiliza un conjunto de lentes para captar y enfocar la luz de objetos lejanos (9)

retrograde rotation/rotación retrógrada el giro en el sentido de las manecillas del reloj de un planeta o de una luna según lo vería un observador ubicado encima del Polo Norte del planeta (99)

revolution/revolución el movimiento de un cuerpo que viaja alrededor de otro cuerpo en el espacio; un viaje completo a lo largo de una órbita (80)

rocket/cohete un aparato que para moverse utiliza el gas de escape que se origina a partir de la combustión (134)

rotation/rotación el giro de un cuerpo alrededor de su eje (80)

S

satellite/satélite un cuerpo natural o artificial que gira alrededor de un planeta (110)

solar nebula/nebulosa solar la nube de gas y polvo que formó nuestro Sistema Solar (65)

space probe/sonda espacial un vehículo no tripulado que lleva instrumentos científicos al espacio con el fin de recopilar información científica (144)

space shuttle/transbordador espacial un vehículo espacial reutilizable que despega como un cohete y aterriza como un avión (151)

space station/estación espacial una plataforma orbital de largo plazo desde la cual pueden lanzarse otros vehículos o en la que pueden realizarse investigaciones científicas (152)

spectrum/espectro la banda de colores que se produce cuando la luz blanca pasa a través de un prisma (33)

sunspot/mancha solar un área oscura en la fotosfera del Sol que es más fría que las áreas que la rodean y que tiene un campo magnético fuerte (72)

supernova/supernova una explosión gigantesca en la que una estrella masiva se colapsa y lanza sus capas externas hacia el espacio (44)

T

telescope/telescopio un instrumento que capta la radiación electromagnética del cielo y la concentra para mejorar la observación (8)

terrestrial planet/planeta terrestre uno de los planetas muy densos que se encuentran más cerca del Sol; Mercurio, Venus, Marte y la Tierra (98)

thrust/empuje la fuerza de empuje o arrastre ejercida por el motor de un avión o cohete (136)

W

white dwarf/enana blanca una estrella pequeña, caliente y tenue que es el centro sobrante de una estrella vieja (41)

Y

year/año el tiempo que se requiere para que la Tierra le dé la vuelta al Sol una vez (4)

Z

zenith/cenit el punto del cielo situado directamente sobre un observador en la Tierra (16)

Index

Index **205**

Index

Index

Index

temperature (*continued*)
  labs on, 54–55
  in nebulas, 65
  star classification by, 34, **35**
  units of, 183
Terra I, 143
terrestrial planets, 96, **96**, 98, **98**
  Earth, 100, **100** (*see also* Earth)
  Mars, **94**, 101–103, **101, 102,
    103**
  Mercury, 80, **94**, 98, **98**
  Venus, **94**, 99, **99**, 145, **145**
Tethys, **105**
thermal energy, 51, 74
thermometers, **183**
third law of motion, Newton's, 136
three-panel flip chart instructions
    (FoldNote), 178, **178**
thrust, 136, **136**
thunderstorms, 141
Titan, 115, **115**, 148
Torino Scale, 123
triangulation, **140**
tri-fold instructions (FoldNote),
    179, **179**
triple-beam balances, 184
Triton, 116, **116**
Tsiolkovsky, Konstantin, 134
Twin Rover mission, 103
two-panel flip chart instructions
    (FoldNote), 179, **179**
Tycho Brahe, 6, **6**, 80
Tyson, Neil DeGrasse, 29

U

ultraviolet (UV) radiation, 13, 77–78
units
  astronomical, 95, **95**
  conversion table, **182, 183**
  of length, **182**
  of mass, **182**
  prefixes for, 182, **182**
  of temperature, 183
  of volume, **182**
universal gravitation, Newton's law
    of, 82–83, **82, 83**
universe
  age of, 52
  ancient models of, 5–6, **5, 6**
  expansion of, 20, 50–53
  formation of, 50–53, **50–51**
  size and scale of, 18, **18, 19**
  structure of, 52, **52**
Uranus
  axis of rotation of, 106, **106**

discovery of, 96
  moons of, 116, **116**
  relative size of, **94**
  statistics on, **106**
Ursa Major constellation, 15, **15**
UV (ultraviolet) radiation, 13, 77–78

V

variables, 186
Venera 9, 145, **145**
Venus, **94**, 99, **99**, 145, **145**
vernal equinox, **17**
Verne, Jules, 134
Very Large Array (VLA), 12
Vesta, 120, **120**
Viking missions, 101, 146, **146**
visible light, 11, **11**
VLA (Very Large Array), 12
volcanoes
  gas release from, 77, **77**
  ice, 116
  on Mars, 102
  on Venus, 99, **99**
volume, **182**, 193
von Braun, Wernher, 135
Voyager missions
  to Jupiter, 104, 147
  to Neptune, 107, **107, 116**
  to the outer solar system, 147,
    147
  to Saturn, 105, **105**
  to Uranus, **106, 116**
V-2 rockets, 135, **135**

W

waning moon, 112, **112**
water
  boiling point of, **102**, 183
  from comets, 77
  on Europa, 115
  freezing point of, 183
  on Mars, 101–102, **101**, 162
  rockets, 156–157
water rockets, 156–157
Watt-Evans, Lawrence, 28
waxing moon, 112, **112**
weather forecasting, 141
weather satellites, 141
weightlessness, 152, **152**
Weinbaum, Stanley, 130
wetland ecosystems, **142**

white dwarf stars, 40–41, **40, 41,
    42,** 91
"Why I Left Harry's All-Night
    Hamburgers," 28
Wilson, Robert, **51**
wind, solar, 119

X

X-ray telescopes, **12**, 13, **13**, 91
X-21 space planes, 152, **152**

Y

years, 4, **4,** 80

Z

zenith, 16, **16**

Credits

Abbreviations used: (t) top, (c) center, (b) bottom, (l) left, (r) right, (bkgd) background

PHOTOGRAPHY

Front Cover Larry Landolfi/Photo Researchers, Inc.

Skills Practice Lab Teens Sam Dudgeon/HRW

Connection to Astrology Corbis Images; **Connection to Biology** David M. Phillips/Visuals Unlimited; **Connection to Chemistry** Digital Image copyright © 2005 PhotoDisc; **Connection to Environment** Digital Image copyright © 2005 PhotoDisc; **Connection to Geology** Letraset Phototone; **Connection to Language Arts** Digital Image copyright © 2005 PhotoDisc; **Connection to Meteorology** Digital Image copyright © 2005 PhotoDisc; **Connection to Oceanography** © ICONOTEC; **Connection to Physics** Digital Image copyright © 2005 PhotoDisc

Table of Contents iv (bl), Peter Van Steen/HRW; iv (b), Bill & Sally Fletcher/Tom Stack & Associates; v (t), NASA/Peter Arnold, Inc.; vi–vii, Victoria Smith/HRW; x (bl), Sam Dudgeon/HRW; xi (tl), John Langford/HRW; xi (b), Sam Dudgeon/HRW; xii (tl), Victoria Smith/HRW; xii (bl), Stephanie Morris/HRW; xii (br), Sam Dudgeon/HRW; xiii (tl), Patti Murray/Animals, Animals; xiii (tr), Jana Birchum/HRW; xiii (b), Peter Van Steen/HRW

Chapter One 2–3, Roger Ressmeyer/CORBIS; 4, David L. Brown/Tom Stack & Associates; 6, The Bridgeman Art Library; 7, Roger Ressmeyer/Corbis; 8 (bl), Peter Van Steen/HRW; 8 (r), Fred Espenek; 10 (tl), Simon Fraser/Science Photo Library/Photo Researchers, Inc.; 10 (b), NASA; 10 (inset), Roger Ressmeyer/Corbis; 11 (radio), Sam Dudgeon/HRW; 11 (microwave) Sam Dudgeon/HRW; 11 (keyboard), Chuck O'Rear/Woodfin Camp & Associates, Inc.; 11 (sunburn), HRW; 11 (x–ray), David M. Dennis/Tom Stack & Associates; 11 (head), Michael Scott/Getty Images/Stone; 11 (tea), Tony McConnell/SPL/Photo Researchers, Inc.; 12 (gamma), NASA; 12 (radio), NASA; 12 (x–ray), NASA; 12 (infrared), NASA; 13, MSFC/NASA; 16, Peter Van Steen/HRW; 16 (bkgd), Frank Zullo/Photo Researchers, Inc.; 19 (tl), Jim Cummings/Getty Images/Taxi; 19 (tc), Mike Yamashita/Woodfin Camp/Picture Quest; 19 (tr), NASA; 19 (cr), Nozomi MSI Team/ISAS; 19 (bc), Jerry Lodriguss/Photo Researchers, Inc.; 19 (br), Tony & Daphne Hallas/Science Photo Library/Photo Researchers, Inc.; 20 (b), Jane C. Charlton, Penn State/HST/ESA/NASA; 20 (tc), NCAR/Tom Stack & Associates; 22, Peter Van Steen/HRW; 23, Peter Van Steen/HRW; 24 (t), MSFC/NASA; 24 (tea),Tony McConnell/SPL/Photo Researchers, Inc.; 28 (t), Craig Matthew and Robert Simmon/NASA/GSFC/DMSP; 29 (t), American Museum of Natural History; 29 (bl), Richard Berenholtz/CORBIS

Chapter Two 30–31, NASA; 582 (bl), Phil Degginger/Color-Pic, Inc.; 32 (br), John Sanford/Astrostock; 33, Sam Dudgeon/HRW; 35, Roger Ressmeyer/CORBIS; 36, Andre Gallant/Getty Images/The Image Bank; 40, V. Bujarrabal (OAN, Spain), WFPC2, HST, ESA/ NASA ; 41, Royal Observatory, Edinburgh/SPL/Photo Researchers, Inc.; 44 (br), Dr. Christopher Burrows, ESA/STScI/NASA; 44, blt nglo–Australian Telescope Board; 44 (bl), Anglo–Australian Telescope Board; 45, V. Bujarrabal (OAN, Spain), WFPC2, HST, ESA/ NASA ; 46, Bill & Sally Fletcher/Tom Stack & Associates; 47 (br), Dennis Di Cicco/Peter Arnold, Inc.; 47 (bl), David Malin/Anglo–Australian Observatory; 48 (bl), I M House/Getty Images/Stone; 48 (br), Bill &Sally Fletcher/Tom Stack & Associates; 48 (bc), Jerry Lodriguss/Photo Researchers, Inc; 49, NASA/CXC/Smithsonian Astrophysical Observatory; 54, Sam Dudgeon/HRW; 55, John Sanford/Photo Researchers, Inc.; 60 (bl), NASA; 60 (tr), Jon Morse (University of Colorado)/NASA; 61 (r), The Open University; 61 (bkgd), Dutlev Van Ravenswaay/SPL/Photo Researchers, Inc.

Chapter Three 62–63, Anglo–Australian Observatory/Royal Obs. Edinburgh; 64, David Malin/Anglo–Australian Observatory/Royal Observatory, Edinburgh; 72, NASA/Mark Marten/Photo Researchers, Inc.; 73, NASA/TSADO/Tom Stack & Associates; 74, Earth Imaging/Getty Images/Stone; 77, SuperStock; 78 (l), Breck P. Kent/Animals Animals/Earth Scenes; 78 (r), John Reader/Science Photo Library/Photo Researchers, Inc; 80 (bc), Scott Van Osdol/HRW; 84, Sam Dudgeon/HRW; 636, Earth Imaging/Getty Images/Stone; 90 (b), NSO/NASA; 90 (tr), Jon Lomberg/Science Photo Library/Photo Researchers, Inc.; 90 (inset), David A. Hardy/Science Photo Library/Photo Researchers, Inc.; 91 (r), NASA/CXC/SAO/AIP/Niels Bohr Library; 91 (l), Corbis Sygma

Chapter Four 92–93, NASA/CORBIS; 94 (Mercury), NASA; 694 (Venus), NASA/Peter Arnold, Inc; 94 (Earth), Paul Morrell/Getty Images/Stone; 94 (Mars), USGS/TSADO/Tom Stack & Associates; 94 (Jupiter), Reta Beebe (New Mexico State University)/NASA; 98, NASA/Mark S. Robinson; 99, NASA; 100 (b), NASA; 100 (tl), Frans Lanting/Minden Pictures; 101, World Perspective/Getty Images/Stone; 101 (b), 102 (b), 102 (inset), NASA; 103, ESA; 104, NASA/Peter Arnold, Inc.; 105 (t), 105 (br), 105 (Saturn), 105 (Uranus), 105, (Neptune), 105 (Pluto), 106 (t), 107, 108 (t), 110, NASA; 112 (moons), John Bova/Photo Researchers, Inc.; 113, Fred Espenek; 114 (tl), Jerry Lodriguss/Photo Researchers, Inc.; 115 (b), NASA; 116 (t), USGS/Science Photo Library/Photo Researchers, Inc.; 116 (b), World Perspective/Getty Images/Stone; 117 (t), NASA; 118, Bill & Sally Fletcher/Tom Stack & Associates; 121 (bc), Breck P. Kent/Animals Animals/Earth Scenes; 121 (bl), E.R. Degginger/Bruce Coleman Inc.; 121 (br), Ken Nichols/Institute of Meteorites/University of New Mexico; 121 (t), Dennis Wilson/Science Photo Library/Photo Researchers, Inc.; 122, NASA; 123, Ken Nichols/Institute of Meteorites/University of New Mexico; 126, NASA; 127, ESA; 127 (b), NASA; 130 (tr), Richard Murrin; 131 (t), NASA; 131 (bl), Mehau Kulyk/Science Photo Library/Photo Researchers, Inc.

Chapter Five 132, Smithsonian Institution/Lockhead Corportation/Courtesy of Ft. Worth Museum of Science and History; 134, NASA; 135 (tr), Hulton Archive/Getty Images; 138 (bl), Brian Parker/Tom Stack & Associates; 138 (br), Sam Dudgeon/HRW; 140, Aerial Images, Inc. and SOVINFORMSPUTNIK; 141, NASA Marshall/National Space Science and Technology Center; 142 (bl, br), USGS; 144 (bkgd), Jim Ballard/Getty Images/Stone; 145 (bl), JPL/TSADO/Tom Stack & Associates; 145 (bkgd), Jim Ballard/Getty Images/Stone; 146 (bkgd), Jim Ballard/Getty Images/Stone; 146 (b), NASA/JPL/Malin Space Station Systems; 147 (bkgd), Jim Ballard/Getty Images/Stone; 149, JPL/NASA; 150 (bl, br), Bettmann/CORBIS; 151 (t), NASA; 151 (br), Corbis Images; 152 (plane), NASA; 152 (bkgd), Telegraph Colour Library/Getty Images/Taxi; 153, NASA; 154 (b), JPL/NASA; 162 (bl), NASA; 162 (tr), Photo courtesy Robert Zubrin, Mars Society; 163 (tr, b), NASA

Lab Book/Appendix 164, Victoria Smith/HRW; 165, Peter Van Steen/HRW; 166, 167, 168, 170, 171, Sam Dudgeon/HRW; 172, NASA/Getty Images/Stone; 173, Sam Dudgeon/HRW